PETROCHEMICAL FANTASIES

STUDIES IN COMICS AND CARTOONS
Charles Hatfield and Rebecca Wanzo, Series Editors

PETROCHEMICAL FANTASIES

The Art and Energy of American Comics

Daniel Worden

THE OHIO STATE UNIVERSITY PRESS
COLUMBUS

Library of Congress Cataloging-in-Publication Data
Names: Worden, Daniel, 1978– author.
Title: Petrochemical fantasies : the art and energy of American comics / Daniel Worden.
Other titles: Studies in comics and cartoons.
Description: Columbus : The Ohio State University Press, [2024] | Series: Studies in comics and cartoons | Includes bibliographical references and index. | Summary: "Surveys the work of acclaimed comics artists such as Nell Brinkley, George Herriman, Jack Kirby, Winsor McCay, and R. F. Outcault and recovers little-known works such as the 1930s Standard Oil Comics to tell the story of how comics emerged alongside fossil fuels in the US"—Provided by publisher.
Identifiers: LCCN 2024013887 | ISBN 9780814215708 (hardback) | ISBN 081421570X (hardback) | ISBN 9780814283660 (ebook) | ISBN 0814283667 (ebook)
Subjects: LCSH: Brinkley, Nell, 1886–1944—Criticism and interpretation. | Herriman, George, 1880–1944—Criticism and interpretation. | Kirby, Jack—Criticism and interpretation. | McCay, Winsor—Criticism and interpretation. | Outcault, Richard Felton, 1863–1928—Criticism and interpretation. | Comic books, strips, etc.—United States—History and criticism. | Fossil fuels—Environmental aspects—United States. | Fossil fuels—Social aspects—United States. | Petroleum chemicals—Environmental aspects—United States. | Petroleum industry and trade in literature. | Climatic changes—History.
Classification: LCC PN6714 .W66 2024 | DDC 741.5/973—dc23/eng/20240521
LC record available at https://lccn.loc.gov/2024013887

Other identifiers: ISBN 9780814259184 (paperback) | ISBN 0814259189 (paperback)

Cover design by Susan Zucker
Text composition by Juliet Williams
Type set in Palatino Linotype

∞ The paper used in this publication meets the minimum requirements of the American National Standard for Information Sciences—Permanence of Paper for Printed Library Materials. ANSI Z39.48-1992.

CONTENTS

ILLUSTRATIONS

COLOR PLATES

FIGURES

ACKNOWLEDGMENTS

I grew up in Houston, where the oil and gas industry is omnipresent. My dad worked in that industry for decades, eventually retiring after years in the refinery business. Fossil fuels underlie not just my own upbringing but also the air-conditioned and automobile-dependent culture I was raised in. During my lifetime, climate change has made the weather more extreme in Texas, and I struggle with the simple fact that my family's own history in the fossil fuel industry has contributed to the heightened intensity of storms, the increased cancer rates, and the searing heat now routine in the places where I grew up. This book is an essay toward understanding this world that I came from, the carbon-intensive United States that makes so many promises about prosperity while burning the past and choking the future.

This book is also about comics, an art form that has changed my life, broadened my worldview, and connected me with people around the world. One of the first comic books I remember from my childhood was a giveaway from the *Dallas Times Herald* newspaper titled *The Uncanny X-Men at the State Fair of Texas* (1983). Like many of the comics that I discuss in this book, *The Uncanny X-Men at the State Fair of Texas* is a work of petrochemical fantasy, and I was drawn to the energetic powers, mutated bodies, and multivalent social allegory in its pages. Superheroes felt fantastical but proximate. I read more, and I was fascinated with how comic book universes had their own mythologies and histories. Comics and their worlds quickly replaced the Bible study and Cub Scout meetings that I had previously attended. Comics opened up new worlds for me, and in this book I explore how comics contributed to the broader construction of modern American culture. Just as comics provided images and stories for the fossil fuel era, so too can the comics medium visualize climate change and alternative energy cultures. It is clear now that the time and space of fossil fuels must end, and I think that comics can provide ways of thinking about time and space that differ from the pace of American fossil fuel culture.

I received a lot of support while working on this book. The Billy Ireland Cartoon Library and Museum at The Ohio State University was crucial to my research. Thanks as well to the New York Historical Society, the New York Public Library, the Brighton Memorial Library in the Monroe County Library System of New York, the Cary Graphic Arts Collection at RIT, and the Wallace Library at RIT. Work on this book was supported by a Lucy Shelton Caswell Research Award from the Billy Ireland Cartoon Library and Museum, a FEAD Grant from the RIT College of Art and Design, a Miller Fellowship from the RIT College of Liberal Arts, and research funds from the RIT College of Art and Design's Dean's Office. At The Ohio State University Press, Ana Maria Jimenez-Moreno has been a wonderful editor. This book would not have been possible without her suggestions and advice. Many thanks to the Studies in Comics and Cartoons series editors and the anonymous readers of this manuscript, who made this book better. Special thanks to Elizabeth Zaleski at The Ohio State University Press for ushering this book into print, and to Shannon Li for creating the book's index.

I am also grateful for the conversations that shaped this book. Many thanks to José Alaniz, Frances Chang Andreu, David M. Ball, Ross Barrett, Laura J. Beard, Bart Beaty, Brent Ryan Bellamy, Alex Beringer, Jenny Bingham-Blenk, Evan Bobrow, Sarah Brouillette, Claudia Bucciferro, Caitlin Cass, Ricia Anne Chansky, Hillary Chute, Lori Cole, Bridget Collins, Stephen Cooper, Siobhan Convery, Clayton Cowles, Benoît Crucifix, Robert Crumb, Jackie Davis, Pat Davis, Thomas S. Davis, Melissa Dean, Sharae Deckard, Jeff Diamanti, Steven Galbraith, Margaret Galvan, Jared Gardner, Marty Golia, Charles Hatfield, Trent Hergenrader, Amelia Hugill-Fontanel, Caren Irr, Stephen Jacobs, Eva-Lynn Jagoe, Bob Johnson, Brian Johnson, Frederik Byrn Køhlert, Adam Kubert, Tracy Kubert, Martha Kuhlman, Tom Lake, Stephanie LeMenager, Jacob W. Lewis, Susan Liberator, Don Lombardo, Erik Loyer, Graeme Macdonald, Caitlin McGurk, Rachel Miller, Leah Misemer, Jonanthan Najarian, Wayne Nellis (and everyone at Wonderland Comics in Rochester, New York!), Franny Nudelman, Nancy Pedri, Jason Poole,

John Porcellino, Barbara Postema, Jenny Robb, Joe Sacco, Jeremy Sachran, Matthew Schneider-Meyerson, Jonathan Schroeder, Jesse W. Schwartz, Tate Shaw, Chip Sheffield, Nancy Silberkleit, Mark Simpson, Marc Singer, Joseph Slaughter, Nick Sousanis, Jordan Alexander Stein, Janet Stewart, Imre Szeman, Sarah Thompson, Marc Tomko, Carol Tyler, Noah Van Sciver, Rebekah Walker, Rebecca Wanzo, Laura Watts, Franzie Weldgen, Bart Welling, Jennifer Wenzel, Claire Westall, Qiana Whitted, Kriota Willberg, Alesha Williams, Benjamin Woo, Gene Luen Yang, Caitlin Yarsky, Alex T. Young, and many more. I have also learned a lot from my family, and especially my parents, Brenda and Dan Worden. Thanks for understanding. Infinite thanks to the students in my comics studies courses at RIT. I look forward to each class.

Earlier versions of some material in this book appeared in edited volumes. Many thanks to the editors of these books, each of whom helped me to refine this work. Sections of chapters 3 and 4 appeared as "Speed Lines: Futurism and Superheroes" in *Comics and Modernism: History, Form, and Culture,* edited by Jonathan Najarian (UP of Mississippi, 2024). Sections of chapter 4 also appeared as "Plastic Man and Other Petrochemical Fantasies" in *Life in Plastic: Artistic Responses to Petromodernity,* edited by Caren Irr (U of Minnesota P, 2021). An earlier version of chapter 5 appeared as "Apocalyptic Everyday: Climate Change in Contemporary Comics" in *The Routledge Companion to Literature and the Environment,* edited by Treasa De Loughry, Sharae Deckard, Kerstin Oloff, and Claire Westall (Routledge, 2024).

This book is for Cat and Clementine.

INTRODUCTION

The Energy of Comics

The history of American comics is fundamentally intertwined with fossil fuels. Coal, gas, and oil powered the development of the modern comics medium, quite literally. Comics emerged from the industrial printing press, thrived on the newsstand, and boasted characters who could "run faster than an express train" (Siegel and Shuster, "Superman" 8). Coal burned, gas combusted, and engines churned to produce and distribute print comics. Funded in part by corporate partnerships with the sprawling fossil fuel industry, comics documented the transition to fossil fuels as adventure, comedy, romance, and tragedy, and comics creators developed iconic characters like Superman who embody the superhuman properties of fossil fuel energy. Furthermore, comics artists adopted visual styles that conveyed the actions and speeds made possible in everyday life by fossil fuel energy. Early comics characters like R. F. Outcault's Buster Brown, speeding along in a new automobile in 1903, and contemporary superheroes like Marvel Comics' Cosmic Ghost Rider, traveling outer space on a motorcycle in 2018, achieve velocities that are drawn to be fantastical yet mundane, chaotic yet controllable. The transition to coal and oil in the nineteenth and twentieth centuries is reflected in these comics characters, whose powers and life spans increased in proportion with fossil fuel consumption in the United States.

The energetic associations that comics conglomerate stem from the medium's historical ties to industrialism, and as Ramzi Fawaz has explained, the superheroes that emerged in American comics in the 1930s and 1940s "mimicked the capacities of industrial technologies" (6). In *All-American Comics* #16, for example, railroad engineer Alan Scott finds a magical lantern that "glows with energy!" (Finger and Dellon 4). In this superhero origin story, Scott harnesses "the light of the Green Lantern" with a metal ring (Finger and Dellon 8). Tellingly, the 1940 Green Lantern's only weakness is a preindustrial material. He exclaims, "Curious . . . Lead bullets and steel knives don't get me . . . but wood does! Guess I'm only immune to metals!" (Finger and Dellon 7; ellipses in original). This synthesis of story with industrialization makes comics a site of imaginative possibility in modern American culture, creating what Fawaz theorizes as "popular fantasy," "expressions of fantasy that suture together current social and political realities with impossible happenings" (28). As Bart Beaty notes in a groundbreaking essay on superheroes and energy, "scholars seeking to understand the popularization of energy discourses and aesthetics will be well-served by turning to the vast collection of superhero comic books that have circulated for almost eight decades," for those comics are a repository of the popular fantasies that have shaped US energy culture (337). Related to this insight, critic Mark Bould's concept of the "anthropocene unconscious" refers to the presence of climate change in culture, even in stories that are not explicitly about climate change. Examples of the "Anthropocene unconscious," like the comics characters Swamp Thing, Groot, and Man-Thing, possess a "nonhuman aliveness" that Bould links to the climate crisis (110).[1] The comics that Bould discusses make the "Anthropocene unconscious" visible, and in the comics that I analyze in this book, fossil fuels are likewise present on the page, though not often the center of the story. By connecting the "popular fantasies" theorized by Fawaz with the "anthropocene unconscious" that Bould locates in popular media, this book analyzes how comics represent the widespread adoption of fossil fuels in the nineteenth- and twentieth-century US, participate in the normalization of fossil fuel consumption, and imagine a future beyond fossil fuels today.

As scholars in the field of the energy humanities have argued, fossil fuels shaped modern American culture in formative ways from the nineteenth century to the present.[2] In the field of comics studies, scholars have

1. Bould also discusses Warren Ellis and Jason Howard's *Trees* (2014–20) as a further demonstration of radical difference, surmising that the lesson of Ellis and Howard's comics series is that "whatever the trees have to say, it is not for human ears" (Bould 112).

2. For a wide range of scholarly work on fossil fuel culture, see Barrett and Worden, *Oil Culture*; Boyer and Szeman, *Energy Humanities*; Szeman et al., *Fueling Culture*; S. Wilson et al., *Petrocultures*.

established how American comics participated in the creation, production, and ubiquity of mass cultural forms from the captioned cartoon to the billion-dollar blockbuster film with its global network of licensed products and experiences.[3] At turns a part of mass media as well as a distinctive art medium, comics offer ways of understanding how fossil fuels have intertwined with American cultural ideals, norms, and stories. Accordingly in this book, I explain how comics transformed fossil fuels into culture, distilling petrochemical fantasies from the new industries, materials, powers, sciences, and spectacles of fossil fuel capitalism as they unfolded from the nineteenth century to the present.

This book is about the myriad connections between comics and fossil fuels in the United States and how petrochemical fantasies emerged from the historical conjunction of comics and fossil fuel development throughout the medium's and the industry's histories. While comics have historically championed fossil fuels, comics creators today often craft stories in which fossil fuels no longer connote progress but instead evidence the continuation of a deadly status quo or a coming apocalypse. Comics have both consolidated American fossil fuel culture into a series of genre tropes and also produced sites of critique where alternatives to fossil fuel capitalism and its extractivist, free market ideology develop. The artistic styles that proliferate in American comics come from fossil fuel culture, and whether comics naturalize or criticize fossil capitalism, the medium is inflected by fossil fuels in everything from speed lines to four-color industrial printing.[4] Many comics studies scholars use the concept of energy to describe comics, a critical shorthand that gestures to the ties to fossil fuel energy explored

3. For a range of methods and approaches in comics studies, see Fawaz et al.'s *Keywords* and Hatfield and Beaty's *Comics Studies.* Nineteenth- and twentieth-century American comics history is covered in many works of comics studies scholarship, including Dauber; Gabilliet; Gardner, *Projections*; Kidman; and Smolderen.

4. As a modern media form, comics represent modernity in complex and numerous ways, many of which are bound to fossil fuels. Scholars have typically focused on cultural issues in mid-twentieth-century American comics, such as the aesthetics of popular types like superheroes (Bukatman's *Matters of Gravity*), representations of modern war (Chute's *Disaster Drawn*), the gender politics of mainstream American comics (Gabilliet's *Of Comics and Men*), the medium's seriality and relationship to film (Gardner's *Projections*), its role in commodity and consumer culture (Gordon's *Comic Strips*), its status as a modernist art form (Najarian's *Comics and Modernism*), its use of industrial imagery (Regalado's *Bending Steel*), its role in turn-of-the-century mass culture (Roeder's *Wide Awake*), its imbrication in the history of race and racism in the US (Whitted's *Desegregating Comics*), and its role as a mouthpiece for midcentury social norms (Wright's *Comic Book Nation*). The above list is merely a sample of the extraordinary work in comics studies today, and the current work extends this ongoing analysis of American comics history to energy.

in this book. In his study of comics artist Jack Kirby, for example, Charles Hatfield analyzes the artist's iconic "graphic energy," evident in everything from the "stylized violence" of his superheroes to the "distinctive design sense" evident in Kirby's technofuturist vistas (*Hand of Fire* 73). In his study of Winsor McCay's comic strip *Little Nemo in Slumberland* (1905–27) and the aesthetics of animation, Scott Bukatman claims that "comics and cartoons are bastions of plasmatic and animistic energies," and while Bukatman associates these energies with children and "'primitive' beliefs" (13), McCay's representations of "uncontainable energy" also connote fossil fuel power's explosive, modern possibilities (*Poetics* 22). Invoking energy as a metaphor for the continued relevance of comics as a cultural form, Hillary Chute and Marianne DeKoven describe how contemporary comics exhibit the "undimmed power of the hand-drawn image" in twenty-first-century global culture (194). Building on these energy metaphors in comics studies, this book's concept of "petrochemical fantasies" refers to the ideological constructions—the narrative tropes, character types, actions, settings, objects, and visual styles—that authorized fossil-fueled lifestyles in the twentieth- and twenty-first-century United States, petrochemical fantasies that are particularly apparent in American comics.

Coal, natural gas, and petroleum transformed American society, and as contemporary energy histories have documented, the fossil fuel industry did not so much make American society more democratic and efficient, as it consolidated cultural, economic, and political power in fossil fuel corporations while undermining the collectivist efforts of organized labor.[5] Comics were sometimes sponsored directly by the fossil fuel industry, yet comics artists also used critical and satirical modes to represent the struggles over energy that defined the twentieth century. In a handful of contemporary works, comics studies scholars have analyzed how climate change registers in comics, such as in Ryan Poll's book-length study of how DC's *Aquaman* series from the years 2011 to 2014 "develops multiple, critical allegories that help make visible how, in the Anthropocene, the Global Ocean has become a site of unceasing colonial-capitalist onslaught causing slow and systemic death in all Oceanic regions" (33).[6] The comics medium emerged from the

5. See Daggett, *Birth of Energy*; Malm, *Fossil Capital*; Mitchell, *Carbon Democracy*.

6. Comics studies scholarship about climate change has typically focused on modern and contemporary comics. For readings of contemporary comics and their relationships to climate change and environmentalism, see Brianna Anderson; Clint Jones; Philip Smith; and Squier. The most comprehensive account of comics and environmentalism to date is Dobrin's edited volume *Eco-Comix,* which largely addresses modern and contemporary comics from the 1980s to the present, with some context from the 1960s and 1970s. In the current work, I extend this history of comics and climate change to encompass the broader history of US comics.

transition to fossil fuels, and today comics can help artists and readers represent climate change and enact alternatives. Environmental humanities scholar Stephanie LeMenager uses Marc Herbst's minicomic *Fashion 2012* as an example of how contemporary "artists and environmentalists both face the challenge of powering down to create smaller-scale, post-oil economies with imagination and courage" ("Aesthetics" 59). In support of this, I develop the concept of "petrochemical fantasies" in this book to identify representations of fossil fuels and thus clarify how energy ideologies work in the history of US comics.

In the field of energy humanities, scholars examine how energy systems function within culture. In keeping with this project, this book focuses on comics in the United States, a nation distinctive for its rapid adoption and outsized consumption of fossil fuels since the late nineteenth century. As Imre Szeman and Dominic Boyer claim, "The use and abuse of energy have had a significant impact—perhaps *the* most significant impact—on the shape in which we find the planet today. This is especially the case when it comes to the use of fossil fuels—first coal, and then oil and natural gas" (1). The effects of fossil fuels are not limited merely to ecology or the environment, as they argue:

> energy is absolutely necessary for modern societies. To be modern is to depend on the capacities and abilities generated by energy. Without the forms of energy to which we've had access and which we've come to take for granted, we would never have been modern. We are citizens and subjects of fossil fuels through and through, whether we know it or not. (Szeman and Boyer 1)

From railroads and fertilizer to the interstate highway system and household plastics, fossil fuels have shaped everyday life and economic structures in the United States. As Heidi C. M. Scott explains, "culture's material fuel source opens a landscape of possibility for the kinds of ideas, ambitions, and progress in which that culture can engage. . . . A broad arc of infrastructure, social relations, values, and environmental impacts characterizes different fuel cultures through time" (9).[7] Fossil fuels have shaped concepts as abstract and seemingly universal as the "economy," along with more obvious ideals like "efficiency" and "automation." As David E. Nye wrote in a formative study of American energy's social history, energy systems "create the structures that underlie personal expectations and assumptions about

7. Other scholarly work on American energy and culture includes Huber, *Lifeblood*; Johnson, *Carbon Nation*; LeMenager, *Living Oil*.

what is normal and possible. These structures appear natural because they have been there since the beginning of an individual's historical consciousness" (7). While energy transitions might not be overt in many comics, the transition to fossil fuels nonetheless underpins the experiences, powers, and speeds made visible in comics. For many Americans in the twentieth century, comic books and other cheap print materials were a ubiquitous element of what Nye describes as an energy culture's "sustaining environment," facilitated through the industrialized printing press (7). Comics are products of fossil fuel culture, and as such, comics carry along both formal and thematic representations of fossil fuel's power and the social norms governing it.

In his study of newspaper editor Joseph Pulitzer, historian George Juergens describes how industrialization made high-circulation print objects like newspapers and their Sunday comics supplements possible: "the phrase 'mass circulation daily' is meaningless without high-speed presses to turn out hundreds of thousands of copies of a newspaper within hours" (49). Juergens goes on to enumerate the "mechanical wonders of the nineteenth century" that facilitated the production of newspapers like Pulitzer's *New York World*:

> in such inventions as the telephone and typewriter; in press folders that could cut, paste, fold, count, and deliver twenty-four page papers at the speed they were printed; in the Hoe Company's web feed quadruple press, capable of printing 24,000 sixteen-page papers per hour; in Ottmar Mergenthaler's Linotype machine, which relieved printers of the costly and tedious process of setting type by hand; and not least, in improved techniques of illustration, from woodcuts to zincographs to halftone photo-engraving. (49)

The industrial printing press is central to the history of American comics. It is the apparatus through which comics can be produced as inexpensive serial periodicals for a mass readership.[8] In developing an account of the comics medium's distinct cultural functions, comics studies scholars have documented how serial comics create social worlds and identities, and also how comics are formed by the different local, national, and global networks through which they circulate.[9] In the US, these features of comics culture

8. For cultural histories of American comics that emphasize print culture, see Gabilliet, *Of Comics and Men*; Gardner, *Projections*; Woo and Stoll.

9. Scholarly accounts of seriality, world-building, and local, national, and global contexts in comics include Fawaz; Kelp-Stebbins; Woo and Stoll. These studies do not engage with energy or the environment but are notably instructive for thinking about comics as social and cultural objects.

were facilitated by the burning of massive amounts of fossil fuels. This book analyzes how comics represented this transition to fossil fuels from the late nineteenth century to the present, a transition that shaped the comics medium itself. Comics played a key role in normalizing and idealizing fossil fuels in the United States, and today, comics can play a role in undoing fossil fuel ideologies.

Outcault's Industrialism

Fossil fuels shaped comics art, just as they shaped American culture more broadly, and this is evident in one of the major artists in late nineteenth-century newspaper comics. Before he created the Yellow Kid and Buster Brown in American newspapers in the late 1890s and early 1900s, Richard F. Outcault published technical illustrations of power plants and railroads for *Electrical World* magazine, a proponent of new, largely coal-powered electricity technology. When Outcault began creating newspaper comics for both Pulitzer's *New York World* and William Randolph Hearst's *New York Journal* in the 1890s, the artist had already been documenting the transition to fossil fuels in more practical and serious modes. As the fossil fuel industry develops at the turn of the twentieth century, so do American comics.

The young Outcault got his start with Thomas Edison. The famed inventor employed the young artist to paint the Edison Laboratories electricity exhibit for the 1888 Centennial Exposition of the Ohio Valley and Middle Atlantic States in Cincinnati. According to comics historian Robert C. Harvey, Outcault "more than passed muster, and when Edison subsequently hired him to do mechanical drawings as well as illustrations, Richard moved to Edison's headquarters at West Orange, New Jersey. Edison named him the official artist for the company's traveling exhibit and sent him to France for the Paris Exposition of 1889–90, where Richard supervised the installation of the Edison exhibits." Outcault then became an illustrator for *Electrical World* magazine, providing both technical drawings of new electrical machinery as well as illustrations of the places and people associated with electricity, from large illuminated interior spaces like churches to the inventors who propagated the new technology. An *Electrical World* illustration that predicts the comic strip format with which Outcault would become associated by the end of the nineteenth century, "The Electrical Inventor and the Capitalist" contains three image and text juxtapositions, detailing a reversal and then reconciliation between "invention" and "capital" (figure 0.1). In the three-panel comic, the figure representing "invention" chases "capital," a well-dressed man in a top hat. In the second illustration, framed by a

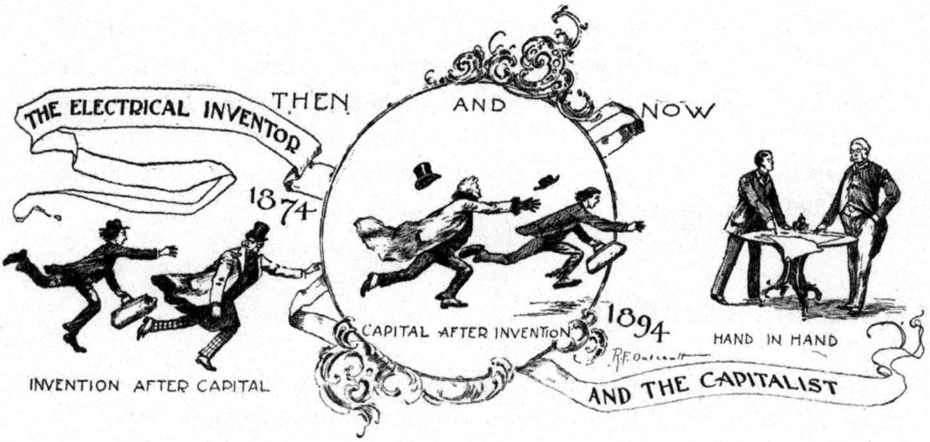

FIGURE 0.1. R. F. Outcault, "The Electrical Inventor and the Capitalist." *Electrical World,* March 3, 1894, p. 271.

decorative panel border, "capital" chases "invention," whose hand and bag reach beyond the panel border and toward the third illustration, of invention and capital "hand in hand," standing and talking over a table of documents. This tripartite cartoon is a comedy, a madcap chase that ends well with a marriage between new technology and capital investment.

Outcault's "The Electrical Inventor and the Capitalist" exemplifies the narratives of genius, equality, inevitability, necessity, progress, and resolution that have long been associated with modern energy. Technological innovation and free market capitalism ultimately converge, thus leading society to the future, or so the story goes. As Cara Daggett has explained, there is a "dominant narrative, or myth, about how humans have changed fuel systems over time" ("Energy and Domination" 645). In this energy myth, Daggett continues, "humans as a species desire ever more energy, and a series of technological innovations have provided it. Any attendant exploitation and injustice are mostly understood as externalities: ungainly appendages to the human drive for fuel that can be repaired by further technological innovation" (645). Outcault's vision of progress in "The Electrical Inventor and the Capitalist" visualizes this logic, which tethers the increasing use of fossil fuels to a naturalized vision of capitalist progress. Pursuing and using more and more energy becomes a natural cycle, a fundamental dialectic of society.

Even after leaving *Electrical World* magazine to work as a cartoonist in the booming New York newspaper industry, Outcault and his comics remained grounded in modern energy. First at the *New York World* in 1895 and then at the *New York Journal* until 1898, Outcault famously created a comic strip named *Hogan's Alley* that featured his iconic "Yellow Kid." On October 25, 1896, the *New York Journal* ran a story presenting "the first pictures ever telegraphed," including "the Journal's famous Yellow Kid" (figure 0.2). The other telegraphed images were portraits of Democratic presidential and vice presidential candidates William Jennings Bryan and Arthur Sewall, inventor Thomas Edison, a landscape, and a picture of three dancing female figures. In the Yellow Kid drawing, the tiny dots that reproduce linework through the telegraph are visible, an early example of how mechanical facets of image reproduction like benday dots are formally integral to the comics image, rather than an indication of the image's degradation through reproduction. The *Journal* naturalizes the fully mechanical drawing process and describes the picture-telegraph's mark-making needles as "building down the line as patiently as the coral insect builds a reef." This natural process is, of course, fully mechanical, and as Christina Meyer concludes in her analysis of this episode, the *Journal*'s coverage of the electrical transmission celebrates "the velocity with which the Yellow Kid 'traveled' and the geographic distance he was able to traverse" (22).

FIGURE 0.2. The Yellow Kid from "Here Are the First Pictures Ever Telegraphed." *New York Journal*, October 25, 1896, p. 31.

To the *Journal*, these telegraphed pictures "represent another really important triumph of man over the unruly antics of that subtle fluid electricity." The newspaper also acknowledges the technical limitations of Edison and Patrick Kenny's picture telegraph:

> [Edison] found that his present instrument would carry a picture satisfactorily from New York to Chicago only. Even over a line of that length the outlines of the drawing appeared on the receiving paper in a slightly blurred condition . . . it should be distinctly understood that the present outer limit by no means means that greater distances cannot be traversed in the immediate future, when larger, more powerful and more perfect machines shall have been built.

As Meyer notes, the telegraphic transmission of the Yellow Kid was both a technological accomplishment and a marker of the Yellow Kid's unique aesthetic principles: "the emblematic form of the Yellow Kid comic figure—that is, both his shape and the words he speaks—can be easily encoded and decoded through electric transmission devices . . . copies of the Yellow Kid can be reproduced quickly and distributed widely" (22). Traveling through the telegraph, the Yellow Kid's adventures gather an explosive simultaneity, proliferating through wires and printing presses across vast geographic distances. Inventor Kenny predicted in 1896 that "before the end of another year the Journal will be able to send wire pictures of occurrences in Chicago or St. Louis as readily as it now sends written descriptions of them. These pictures will be received in New York within less than five minutes after the finished drawing has been placed in the instrument at the other end" ("Here"). The Yellow Kid was a figure so schematically iconic that he was easily recognized even when crudely rendered by a machine. Comics are at once fully mechanical yet also completely natural, an industrial extension of the artist's hand.

The industrial printing presses that put the Yellow Kid in newspapers, and the telegraph machines that transmitted his image within minutes across great distances, largely relied on coal as a fuel, and these technologies were also dependent on newly coal-intensive industries such as copper and iron mining. The adoption of and transition to electricity was swift in the United States during this time. According to historian Timothy J. LeCain, "between 1880 and 1914, the use of electricity in manufacturing went from essentially zero to almost nine million horsepower of installed equipment" (28). Correspondingly, coal consumption in the United States rose sharply from 1870 to 1920, followed by an even sharper rise in petroleum consumption in the later twentieth century (color plate 0.1).[10] This increased consumption of coal fueled early newspaper comics. Meyer describes the "modern transportation infrastructure" and the "sped up, synchronized, and expanded" presses of the 1890s US as "the engines of the Yellow Kid" (25). Meyer accounts for how fossil-fueled industrial systems "generated" the Yellow Kid, and this energy metaphor fits well as a descriptor of American comics in general (25). The form, production, and dissemination of the comics medium in the late nineteenth and early twentieth centuries is a product of the transition to fossil fuels and the exponential increases in energy consumption that fossil fuel technologies accomplished. The Yellow Kid's connection to fossil fuels was so evident that the character quickly became a spokesperson for

10. For further data, see "Energy Consumption."

coal. The *Coal Trade Journal* reported in its December 9, 1896, issue that "an enterprising Washington firm recently put upon the street two live 'Yellow Kids,' dressed in the highest of Hogan's Alley fashion, with yellow fez and gloves. The dresses bore the customary poor spelling, but announced the fact that the firm were the greatest coal dealers in the city" ("With the Retailers"). The Yellow Kid was an unlicensed mascot for coal.

The Yellow Kid's association with coal and the telegraph was not the sum total of this early comics character's connections to fossil fuels. In Outcault's 1897 cartoon "The Yellow Kid Treats the Crowd to a Horseless Carriage Ride," the speed of fossil fuel transportation scatters figures across the newspaper page and across "Uneasy Street," where the Yellow Kid drives in his early automobile (color plate 0.2). Horses panic, the automobile runs over pedestrians, yet the Yellow Kid's companions mostly appear to be enjoying their road trip, with the exception of the racist figure in the automobile's cab, who looks appropriately shocked. This commingling of mayhem, mischief, violence, glee, shock, racist objectification, and wonder is a hallmark of the Yellow Kid comics, and the explosive interruption of boring everyday life is one of humor comics' major tropes. This madcap explosiveness emanates from fossil fuels, which make simultaneity, superhuman speed, and inhuman forces available in everyday life. In just a few years, the Yellow Kid introduced the telegraph, sold coal, and raced through the city in a wildly dangerous automobile. Social conventions are overturned, as the transition to fossil fuel energy registers in the Yellow Kid as progress and anarchy, comedy and tragedy. In the cartoon, Outcault positions the Yellow Kid directly above the automobile's only Black passenger, and the two figures' matching expressions connote simultaneous joy and fear. This doubling of figures makes visible what scholar Rebecca Wanzo has described as the racial logic of American comics: "White excessive types function as citizen ideals, but black subjects are their shadows" (17). The horseless carriage ride is a vehicle for the expression of both enthusiasm and trepidation about fossil fuel power, and the cartoon uses racist tropes to establish the modernity of the automobile as a doubled sensation of excitement and shock.

The Yellow Kid's "horseless carriage ride" telegraphs the cultural emergence of the automobile as an everyday mode of transportation. His smock commends the new technology with a pun, "Gee dis beats the carpet, wich is hard to beat." The Yellow Kid also embodies a populist urge to make fossil-fueled recreation and travel available to everyone. The automobile's flag compares the mayhem favorably to "a professional game of feetball between Yale an Princeton only dis ain't so rough." Yet despite this comparison to elite athletics, the cartoon nonetheless makes visible the harm and violence wrought by the automobile on living beings. Through the image, it is clearly better to be inside of the speeding automobile than in its path of terror. In the Yellow Kid's explosive antics, Outcault represents the incredible power and proximity of fossil fuels amid America's transition to fossil fuels. In an ominous tone appropriate to the scale of the climate crisis, historian Dipesh Chakrabarty noted in a 2009 essay about climate change that "humans now wield a geological force" (30). In early newspaper comics, the Yellow Kid and his companions play on the fringes of that "geological force," visualizing its dangerous, disorienting, and exciting potential.

Representations of fossil fuel power were ubiquitous in turn-of-the-century US comics art, not just at the level of content but also in their formal structure. In his study of early comics, Thierry Smolderen describes gag comic strips like Rudolph Dirks's *Katzenjammer Kids* (1897–1913) and its German predecessor, Wilhelm Busch's *Max and Moritz* (1865), as "clearly the self-propelled products of the modern industrial age," locating in the fast-paced action of the comic strip the seemingly "self-propelled" force provided increasingly by the combustion of fossil fuels in dynamos and locomotives (113). The seriality of newspaper comics likewise imbued comics with a mechanical regularity accomplished through the adoption of fossil fuels, which displace seasonal and natural time with the regulated time of industrial capitalism. Despite the Yellow Kid's tremendous popularity, and perhaps due to the demands placed on an artist by the industrialized newspaper industry's daily demand for new content, Outcault moved on from the character rather quickly. In an 1898 essay published in the *New York World* titled "How the Yellow Kid Was Born," Outcault complained about his character's ubiquity:

> Now, it is more than six years since my pen first traced the outlines of Micky Dugan [the Yellow Kid] on the paper. I look back on that fateful day and it is hard to realize that not a sun has set since then that has not seen at least one more representation of the Yellow Kid produced. In that time I suppose I have myself made twenty thousand Yellow Kids, and when the million buttons, the innumerable toys and cigarette boxes and labels and what not are taken into consideration, some idea can be gleaned of how tired I am of him.

Exhausted by the proliferation of Yellow Kids, Outcault felt trapped by his own creation: "But the Yellow Kid will not separate himself from me, try as I may to make him, and I have given up my whole life to him" ("How the

Yellow Kid"). Outcault's reluctant production of more Yellow Kids also led him to return to his roots in electricity exhibitions, with a more cynical take than was ever evident in his illustrations and comics for the industry-boosting *Electrical World* magazine. In a May 21, 1899, cartoon titled "Kelly's Kids Have a Shocking Time at the Electrical Show," children and adults look at electric lights, get blown over by electric fans, shock each other, and even try out an X-ray (color plate 0.3). Thomas Edison smokes an electric cigarette, and Nikola Tesla drinks a "lightning [cocktail] made from high alternating currents." While Outcault's earlier *Electrical World* comic presents electricity as American progress, his newspaper comics rendition of electricity highlights exploitation and pain rather than clarity and comfort. Outcault's electricity exhibit is crowded with advertisements, and most of "Kelly's Kids" are being shocked, their hair standing on end. Electricity is frightening, an idea reinforced by the grinning, skeletal child in X-ray, a wide-eyed kid ogling him in shock from the side. An adult couple laughs in a spotlight (it is labeled the "Mazet Committee Search Light" after a committee that investigated corruption in New York), but next to them is a telegraph that humorously warns readers of electricity's danger: "Electricity is shocking, but if you want to be really shocked go to see some of the shows in New York theatres and music halls. They will give you a greater shock and there's no danger—not even to the manager of the show." This warning is reinforced by other signs, like "A live wire is better than a dead hero" and an advertisement for the "Electric Furniture Co.," "Electric chairs a specialty—you can go to sleep in them and never wake up."

Outcault's earlier work for Edison associated electricity with American progress, and five years later in "Kelly's Kids Have a Shocking Time at the Electrical Show," the artist depicts it as a dangerous novelty for gullible consumers. Outcault's kids are all willing participants in the electrical show, happily paying to be shocked, blown over, X-rayed, and illuminated by a spotlight. As Fred Nadis notes in his study of electricity exhibitions during this time, electricity "was compatible with progressive desires for a more efficient and scientific culture. And yet it was a mysterious power as great as any known to nature" (53). Part of electricity's mysterious power was its distance from a fuel source, as electricity traveled from distant power stations to homes and thus was not proximate like household furnaces. Tesla and Westinghouse's Niagara Falls power plant demonstrated the viability of hydroelectric power in 1895, yet Edison's earlier, coal-fired Pearl Street Station provided the model for much more energy production in the United States. An illustrated article in the August 26, 1882, issue of *Scientific American* magazine included a detailed drawing of Pearl Street Station's boiler room and stoke hole, explaining the coal-dependent infrastructure of Edison's electrical plant in technical terms: "Beginning with the basement, the area in front, underneath the sidewalk, is used for the reception of coal and the discharging of ashes from the boiler furnaces" ("Edison"). This underlying fossil fuel infrastructure became widespread. As Barbara Freese notes, "coal consumption doubled every decade between 1850 and 1890. In the late 1890s, the United States became the world leader in coal production, finally bypassing Britain" (137). Outcault's comics take place during this transition to coal, an uneven and violent process turned into dark comedy on the newspaper comics page. From Outcault and his fellow turn-of-the-twentieth-century newspaper cartoonists to contemporary creators of book-length comics about climate change, comics artists have illustrated the new space and time of fossil fuel culture, using stylistic conventions like caricature and motion lines to convey its scale and speed.

Comics, Modernity, and Modernism

Comics are a major part of modernity and modernism, and this has been established by a number of comics studies scholars. In the introduction to his edited volume *Comics and Modernism,* for example, Jonathan Najarian explains how scholarship in the area of new modernist studies on periodicals and print culture complements work in comics studies. Since "the divisions between high and low forms of art were never as strong as conventional accounts of modernism made them seem," he argues, scholars in recent years have begun to establish accounts of "how modernism was disseminated in the newspapers, accepted into the world of magazine illustration, and finally memorialized in the space of the comics page" (5, 9). Like animation, film, and photography, comics were a new medium at the turn of the twentieth century, and descriptions of distinctively modern experiences in the nineteenth and early twentieth centuries often invoke the structure of comics. For example, to use the railroad as an indication of modernity's overturning of time and space, Paul Verlaine's verse in *La Bonne Chanson* (1870) about railway travel likens the train carriage's window to a moving picture:

> The scene behind the carriage window-panes
> Goes flitting past in furious flight; whole plains
> With streams and harvest-fields and trees and blue
> Are swallowed by the whirlpool, whereinto

The telegraph's slim pillars topple o'er,
Whose wires look strangely like a music-score. (22)[11]

Verlaine's verse was published when comics were an experimental form common in nineteenth-century illustrated magazines, a component of the new mass culture developing through industrialized production.[12] In his excellent study of railroads and modern culture, Wolfgang Schivelbusch compares Verlaine's verse with nineteenth-century visual panoramas (40). The poet's view from the train carriage consists of moving images (the swirling landscape visible through the windowpanes), separated by black panel borders (the telegraph poles), and read in temporal sequence (the strange "music score" composed by the train's speed). Not quite music, not quite painting, Verlaine's steam-powered landscape requires a new form and a new mode of reading.

The influence of the railroad extended beyond poetry as well. For instance, scholar Michael Denning emphasizes in his study of late nineteenth-century American dime novels that "the culture of the railroad is deeply inscribed in the dime novel, whether as the technical force that makes mass distribution possible, as the mode of transportation that encourages reading, or the subject of innumerable novels themselves" (40). Ultimately an extension of the popular genres codified by dime novels, comics similarly carry material and symbolic traces of the railroad in their production, consumption, and aesthetics. Film scholar Tom Gunning has described how "the appearance of comics in the nineteenth and twentieth century also partakes of a modern fascination with visual motion whether virtual or real," and fossil fuels provided the energy for much of this modern motion (37).

The association of comics with modern, fossil-fuel-powered movement continued in the twentieth century. For example, critic Gilbert Seldes's 1924 book *The Seven Lively Arts* praises comic strips alongside slapstick comedy, jazz, and vaudeville theater. Seldes devotes a chapter to his particular favorite comic, George Herriman's *Krazy Kat,* and the chapter's title itself, "The Krazy Kat Who Walks by Himself," invokes the new automating energy sources available in the early twentieth century (231). Herriman's iconic comic strip features the ambiguously gendered Krazy Kat and their love interest, Ignatz the Mouse, who typically hurls a brick at Krazy Kat in response. Herriman's *Krazy Kat* has long been celebrated by critics as a prime example of comics' connection to modernism. In his 1990 book *Comics*

11. This stanza is quoted in Schivelbusch 40.

12. For a discussion of early comics in American illustrated magazines, see Beringer. The early history of comics is explored in Smolderen.

as Culture, for example, M. Thomas Inge devotes a chapter to "Krazy Kat as American Dada Art," finding "much that is lighthearted and gay in Krazy's world, yet underlying the action is a deep-rooted sense of determinism and Naturalistic despair, not unlike the worldview of Theodore Dreiser or the more extreme Dadaists" (52). This aesthetic despair stems, in part, from the comic strip's repetitive structure over decades, a regularity that mimics the mechanical workings of industrial machinery. This regularity is only accomplished and normalized by the abundant, cheap, and reliable fossil fuels that replaced animals, water, and wind as energy sources in the nineteenth and early twentieth centuries.

The ideological connection between comics action and energy culture is made even more evident by Seldes's choice of a *Krazy Kat* Sunday comic strip to illustrate his analysis of Herriman's "freedom of movement; in his large pictures and small, the scene changes at will—it is actually our one work in the expressionistic mode" (242; see figure 0.3). Seldes explicates the November 3, 1918, *Krazy Kat* comic strip as a series of destructive actions that are ironically justified as good and true at the comics' end:

> Ignatz orders Krazy to push a huge rock off its base, then to follow it downhill. Down they go, crashing through houses, uprooting trees, tearing tunnels through mountains, the bowlder first, Krazy so intently after that he nearly crashes into it when it stops. He toils painfully back uphill. "Did it gather any moss?" asks Ignatz. "No." "That's what I thought." "L'il fillossiffa," comments Krazy, "always he seeks the truth, and always he finds it." (243–44)

In his concluding paragraph, Seldes summarizes his view of Krazy Kat and, by extension, the imaginative possibilities of the comics medium: "The strange, unnerving, distorted trees, the language inhuman, un-animal, the events so logical, so wild, are all magic carpets and faery foam—all charged with unreality. Through them wanders Krazy, the most tender and the most foolish of creatures, a gentle monster of our new mythology" (245). Krazy Kat's "inhuman, un-animal" yet logical energy associates him with what modernists often called the "machine age."[13] Krazy Kat is an automaton who moves like an engine on the comics page, careening through the landscape in a more individualized, self-propelled mode than Verlaine's train passenger. Herriman's slanted world with seemingly impossible yet utterly logical rules evokes the transition to fossil fuels that reshaped time and

13. For readings of bodies, machines, and modernity, see Johnson, *Mineral Rites;* North.

FIGURE 0.3. George Herriman, *Krazy Kat,* November 3, 1918. Rpt. in Gilbert Seldes, *The Seven Lively Arts,* Harper and Brothers, 1924.

space in a few decades around the turn of the twentieth century. Comics studies scholars have emphasized the industrial energy that courses through Herriman's *Krazy Kat.* Paul Peppis associates Herriman's early Sunday comics with "a pyrotechnic and maximalist popular modernism, flamboyantly pushing against the conditions and constraints of his medium" (164), and Peter R. Sattler accounts for how "*Krazy Kat* is an *industrial* work and reflects its creator's adaptation to the material limitations and conditions of his field" (137). Daniel Stein even describes Herriman's work as a daily newspaper artist in terms of industrial production: "Like a conveyor belt, he was in continuous motion" (62). In light of these characterizations of the comic strip as a well-running modernist machine, it is clear that Herriman's *Krazy Kat* represents fossil-fueled culture, both in its narrative content and in its formal production. Krazy Kat and the boulder blow through town and country just as if they were zipping by in an automobile or railroad car, destroying small towns and wrecking the environment. This comic is an ironic representation of fossil fuel culture during its entrenchment, illustrating the manipulation of time and space as a hilarious and violent facet of everyday life.

Just as Paul Verlaine experienced comics in the window of a railroad car and Gilbert Seldes encountered fossil fuel automation in the "gentle monster" Krazy Kat, the theorist Walter Benjamin likened Charlie Chaplin to a figure from the comics page, in an unpublished work from 1935. Benjamin writes, "the innovation of Chaplin's gestures is that he dissects the expressive movements of human beings into a series of minute innervations. Each single movement he makes is composed of a succession of staccato bits of movement" (94). While Benjamin attributes Chaplin's "jerky sequence" of movements to the technology of cinema, the abrupt juxtaposition of "bits of movement" invokes comics form with its juxtaposition of sequential images. Before Chaplin's "jerky sequence," the Yellow Kid had been transmitted as a sequence of electrical pulses, powered by coal-burning dynamos. Like film, comics were a complicated artistic response to the transition to fossil fuels in the nineteenth and twentieth centuries. The wild motions, exaggerated actions, and serial repetition of comics visualize and thematize the rapid increase in fossil fuel energy use ongoing in the United States.

Comics and Carbon Emissions

This book is about how comics depict and comment on the increasing reliance and consumption of fossil fuels in the United States. Outcault's Yellow Kid and Herriman's Krazy Kat are just two examples of this connection between American comics and fossil fuels, an association that extends both backward into the early history of comics art and forward into our current moment of climate crisis. The carbon-intensive activities on the comics page are part of a much larger history of the extraction of natural resources and their combustion for energy, a process that since the 1800s has resulted in a dramatically warming climate that threatens millions of humans today.[14]

14. There is a lot of scholarship and popular writing about the causes of climate change and how to describe it. Proposed by scientists Paul J. Crutzen and Eugene F. Stoermer in their short article "The 'Anthropocene'" in *Global Change Newsletter*, "anthropocene" has become a widely used term to describe the period of geological time during which humans have been changing the earth's climate, largely through the use of fossil

The ideologies of fossil fuel capitalism are evident throughout American comics history, though the comics themselves vary widely between different historical moments, publishing formats, editorial mandates, and artistic intentions from the nineteenth century to the present. While the formats in which comics are printed change over the decades, at least one historical reality underlies the history of American comics. From Outcault's turn-of-the-century moment when coal was ascendant to the time of this writing, Americans have burned disproportionately massive amounts of fossil fuels, and comics reflect that. American comics have often celebrated, elaborated, and embellished fossil fuel culture, and thus the medium has been entangled in the outsized carbon emissions of the United States throughout its history.

I write this book during an ongoing climate crisis, and comics are relevant to this crisis because the medium both shaped fossil fuel culture and offers ways of making, reading, seeing, and belonging that pull away from the time and space of fossil fuel culture. Cultural change is urgently needed today, because scientific consensus has not been enough to shift American industry or government away from fossil fuels. The effects of burning fossil fuels and emitting massive amounts of carbon into the atmosphere were understood by scientists in the 1970s and 1980s, yet global carbon emissions have more than doubled since 1970.[15] Furthermore, fossil fuel extraction has only increased in recent years, despite growing awareness of climate change and its devastating effects. Citing an International Energy Agency (IEA) report from May 2019, theorist Andreas Malm summarizes the dismal reality of fossil fuel entrenchment and even growth amidst ongoing climate crisis: "nowhere on the horizon of ongoing capital accumulation could a transition from fossil fuels to renewable energy be sighted (despite the latter now being 'consistently cheaper,' as noted by the billionaire's rag *Forbes*)" (*How to Blow Up* 26). The Intergovernmental Panel on Climate Change's 2023 report identifies the same problem: "projected cumulative future CO2 emissions over the lifetime of existing and planned fossil fuel infrastructure, if historical operating patterns are maintained and without additional abatement, are approximately equal to the remaining carbon budget for limiting warming to 2°C" (IPCC 20).

---

fuels. The term "anthropocene" has been criticized widely for its universalizing sense of humanity, especially since major historical and even contemporary carbon emissions on Earth have been located in Europe, especially Britain, and North America, especially the United States. For a collection of writings about how to historicize and conceptualize climate change, see Moore's *Anthropocene or Capitolocene?*, and for an excellent conceptual framework for the Anthropocene that centers capitalism, race, and difference, see Yusoff.

15. For accounts of climate change's emergence as a scientific consensus and the subsequent undermining of climate science by the fossil fuel industry in the United States, see Oreskes and Conway; Rich.

The continued entrenchment of fossil fuels in the face of climate change has been accompanied by an upsurge in the radical right, white nationalism, and fascism across the globe, and especially in the United States. Accordingly, as Malm argues, climate activism takes on a new urgency, as it is clear that "business as usual" in American capitalism has already killed millions and will kill many more through climate disasters. A transition away from fossil fuels can only be accomplished in the United States through a massive movement capable of shutting down fossil fuel infrastructure and ending carbon emissions, and this radical transition must happen culturally as well as technologically. Indeed, as many environmentalist and green energy advocates are quick to point out, renewable energy technologies have long been available, but cultural forces have kept them from being funded and supported to nearly the same degree as coal, oil, and gas companies in the United States.

Comics are a major part of American culture, and during the twenty-first-century surge in American oil production, comics became an even more visible component of American culture through transmedia adaptations of superhero stories by multinational corporations. Reading comics as expressions of fossil fuel culture reveals how deeply fantasy, genre, and narrative have been shaped by the sense of time and space achieved through the burning of fossil fuels. This book participates in the broader scholarly project underway in energy studies and the environmental humanities to understand art, culture, and society in the Anthropocene, speculatively dated to begin anywhere between the "discovery of fire" to the first nuclear bomb tests in the 1940s. Since the Anthropocene as a concept encompasses climate change and its origins in specific carbon-emitting cultures, I believe that anthropologist Anna Lowenhaupt Tsing is correct to declare that "the most convincing Anthropocene time line begins not with our species but rather with the advent of modern capitalism, which has directed long-distance destruction of landscapes and ecologies" (19).[16] By synthesizing the energy and environmental humanities with comics studies, this book explores how American comics have expressed fossil fuel culture and identifies artistic concepts, practices, strategies, and styles that offer alternatives to the historical entrenchment of fossil fuels in US culture. My hope is that comics, and the people who make and read comics, can contribute to a sustainable

16. In his study of DC's Aquaman, Ryan Poll also cites Tsing's definition of the Anthropocene. Poll's analysis of Aquaman focuses on how a comic book series represents "colonial capitalism," dramatizing the unevenness of climate change and its most violence effects through superhero allegory (27).

future and that this book can contribute to an environmentalist history of American comics.

The imbrication of comics with fossil fuels is clearly evident in the promotional comic books that Disney published with Exxon in the 1970s and 1980s.[17] A corporation so large and with so much territory that it has been described as a "private empire," the Exxon corporation "ranked year after year as one of the [United States'] very largest and most profitable corporations, always in the top five of the annual Fortune 500 lists" (Coll 19). The oil giant's collaboration with Disney represented Exxon as a major solution to the oil crises of the 1970s and as a good corporate citizen ready to adapt to the emerging scientific consensus around climate change. As Ariel Dorfman and Armand Mattelart argue in their classic work of cultural criticism *How to Read Donald Duck: Imperialist Ideology in the Disney Comic* (1971), Disney published comics around the globe that trumpeted American economic principles and values during the Cold War, and Disney stories of madcap adventures with trademark characters "deceive the reader, who is but another little wheel in the great grinding mill of consumption" (118). Similarly, Disney's Exxon comics also champion consumption. The first installment of the Disney and Exxon collaboration was 1976's *Mickey Mouse and Goofy Explore Energy,* a post-1973 oil crisis narrative in which Mickey and Goofy run out of gasoline while driving—they have been complaining about fuel costs and the "energy crunch"—and are then transported through the history of energy by a glowing nucleus named "Enny, the Spirit of Energy!" Enny departs with an Exxon-approved message about the need "to find and develop new sources of power!" These "new sources of power" include oil shale. Goofy holds a rock and asks, "Y'mean there's oil in this chunk of rock?" and Mickey replies, "Sure! All you have to do is find the right way to get it out!" In 2012 ExxonMobil Senior Vice President Jack P. Williams delivered a speech titled "Shale Gas: An American Success Story," celebrating the exponential growth in shale gas production, or fracking, in the United States. The Environment America Research and Policy Center estimated that fracking created 280 billion gallons of toxic wastewater in

17. The comic books that comprise the Disney-Exxon trilogy are: *Mickey Mouse and Goofy Explore Energy, Mickey Mouse and Goofy Explore Energy Conservation,* and *Mickey and Goofy Explore the Universe of Energy.* The pages of each comic book are unnumbered. Thirty copies of *Mickey Mouse and Goofy Explore Energy* were included as a part of Walt Disney's "Wide World of Energy Mulitmedia Kit" for teachers, which was distributed nationwide. A copy of this multimedia kit is in the Thomas Inge papers 1879–2001, Special Collections and Archives, James Branch Cabell Library, Virginia Commonwealth University.

2012 alone, which is evidence of a very different reality than ExxonMobil's corporate success story (Ridlington and Rumpler).[18]

Exxon's fossil fuel boosterism is continued in the follow-up comic book *Mickey Mouse and Goofy Explore Energy Conservation* in 1978. Enny the Spirit of Energy visits Mickey and Goofy again, and the trio explores how consumers can conserve energy, as well as how Exxon can supply abundant fossil fuels well into the future. Excited by the development of new oil reserves, Mickey exclaims, "We can increase oil and gas supplies by drilling in new places like offshore!" This injunction remained part of Exxon's corporate strategy even after the Valdez oil spill in 1989 and the company's merger with fellow oil corporation Mobil in 1999.[19] In 2021, still unflagged by climate change, ExxonMobil announced that it planned to resume oil drilling off the coast of Santa Barbara, California, following a six-year shutdown after an oil spill "that released 140,000 gallons of oil into a biodiverse stretch of the Pacific coast" (Robertson). Mickey and Goofy induct readers into Exxon's corporate ideology.

The 1985 comic book *Mickey and Goofy Explore the Universe of Energy* pulls the series out of the 1970s themes of oil crisis and energy conservation and into the fossil fuel abundance of the 1980s. On the interior cover, there is a word search that, when completed, leads the reader to "discover what America's single most important fuel for the rest of the 20th Century will be!" The answer is "PETROLEUM." At the story's beginning, Mickey and Goofy stand outside the entrance to Exxon's "Universe of Energy" exhibit at Disney's Epcot Center. They go through the exhibit, gawk at its signature animatronic dinosaurs, and again advocate for the continued use and development of fossil fuels. The character of "Enny the Spirit of Energy" does not appear as a spokesperson in this third installment of the Disney-Exxon trilogy, dispersed instead into the exhibit that Mickey and Goofy enjoy. Like Exxon, Mickey and Goofy are notably skeptical when it comes to renewable

18. In the Donald Duck story "Oil in Good Time," drawn by John Carey and published in *Donald Duck* no. 170 (Gold Key, April 1976), the inventor Gyro Gearloose announces that he has "invented a way to turn water into oil!" Unfortunately, though, his invention turns out to produce "one pint of oil from five hundred trillion gallons of water!" This story reflects the same fossil fuel ideology as the Disney-Exxon comic books and promotes business as usual. Environmental spoilage is portrayed as an inevitable and even humorous part of fossil fuel development, a necessity of American life. At the story's conclusion, Scrooge McDuck worries about his water bill and rushes off to get "King Farout of Khartoon" on the phone for access to cheaper oil.

19. For a superhero comic book that depicts a fictional version of the Exxon Valdez oil spill, see the "Coyote Tears" story in DC Comics' *Green Arrow*, vol. 2, nos. 29–30 (1990). For an analysis of "Coyote Tears," see Otto.

energy sources. The Reaganite Mickey advises Goofy to be cautious about renewables: "Someday more of us may be able to use solar energy, when it becomes more affordable!" (color plate 0.4). They walk off happily to "Exxon's Energy Exchange" in the final panel, and the comic book's back cover encourages readers to "stop by the Exxon service station near the entrance to the Magic Kingdom." Any aesthetic distance between comics and economics, cartoons and fossil fuels, collapses in this work. This is a work of fossil fuel ideology, articulating the perspective of a major corporate denier of climate change in a giveaway comic book. In *How to Read Donald Duck*, Dorfman and Mattelart remark that Disney comics present a world "in which a man can amass great wealth, without facing its producer and product: the worker. Objects are cleansed of guilt. It is a world of pure surplus without the slightest suspicion of the worker demanding the slightest reward" (88). Disney comics present an American fantasy of "wealth without wages, deodorant without sweat" (88). The Disney-Exxon comic books likewise present a world of abundant fossil fuels without carbon emissions. Exploitation and pollution are certainly not acknowledged as underlying conditions of Disney and Exxon's "Universe of Energy."

The Disney-Exxon trilogy of comic books are obvious examples of fossil fuel ideology in a popular medium, and they highlight how many features of comics can be traced back to fossil fuels. Indeed, reading a comics page requires an understanding of time and space as inherently flexible, a notion that becomes readily accessible through fossil-fueled technologies that collapse space and time with faster communication and transportation. The juxtaposed images of comics involve the reader in piecing together rapid shifts in time and space and in thinking of those fragments as a complete system of meaning. In that regard, comics help readers to think within fossil fuel culture. Each piece of everyday life in the United States today, from the ubiquity of automobile transportation and coal-fired electricity to abundant petrochemical plastics and synthetic fertilizers, is likewise a fragment of a larger system, rendered in comics like *Mickey and Goofy Explore the Universe of Energy* for the American public to enjoy as amusing and endearing narratives about boundless energy.

Today, Exxon's "Universe of Energy" pavilion at Walt Disney World's Epcot Center is home to the "Guardians of the Galaxy: Cosmic Rewind" roller coaster. On the coaster, riders pursue a glowing orb called the "Cosmic Generator," a fictional energy source of immense power. An understanding of energy that was once pedagogical with Mickey Mouse is now fantastical with Rocket Raccoon, a plot device that is both the cause and effect of superheroic action. In Marvel's 2022 *Guardians of the Galaxy: Cosmic Rewind* comic book tie-in, the Guardians fight through a horde of small alien creatures. The superhero Drax explains that the aliens are upset "that we're stealing their gems," to which his teammate Gamora replies, "We're not stealing them, Drax! We just need a power source to jump-start the ship, and our scanners suggest there's one here that could work" (Shinick). Intrepid energy seekers, the Guardians of the Galaxy power up their ship with the "Cosmic Generator," and though an adventure narrative, this story of energy exploration, extraction, and consumption repeats the lessons of Exxon's "Universe of Energy." The message remains the same: energy is scarce; energy should be secured; energy should be used in excess. Chase the "Cosmic Generator" to keep the galaxy safe, just as Mickey advocated for keeping the Earth safe by increasing domestic oil production through offshore drilling. The tropes of comic book energy remain in play and evident in genre conceits. American comics convey fossil fuel ideology, whether for education or entertainment.

The Disney-Exxon trilogy of comic books and the "Guardians of the Galaxy: Cosmic Rewind" amusement park ride and comic book enact petrochemical fantasies through their didactic talking animals, spirits, and superheroes. A cultural ideology analyzed in different contexts throughout this book, "petrochemical fantasies" are the clusters of conventions and tropes that naturalize and romanticize fossil fuel culture.[20] Emergent in the Yellow Kid's association with coal, automobiles, and electricity, and refined in Mickey Mouse's endorsement of Exxon's oil production targets, a petrochemical fantasy enacts the tremendous energy, speed, and flexibility available through fossil fuels as a quality in and of itself, freely at play in the world and without consequence for Earth's climate. A medium for petrochemical fantasies, comics visualize bodies, places, and actions that bear traces of their fossil-fueled origins yet often elide those material connotations through imaginative world-building. In so doing, comics have naturalized fossil fuels as well as transformed them into metaphors for human abilities. Comics have imagined worlds without limits from within a fossil fuel culture that advertised abundant, cheap, and harmless energy as an essential component to everyday life. Today, it is imperative to imagine new worlds that do not rely on fossil fuels or their values. Comics can help to make that possible. This is especially so because the comics medium can readily manipulate narrative space and time, elements of aesthetic and his-

20. As I argue throughout this book, petrochemical fantasies are some of the most significant ideologies in American comics, and I think of them as a subset of the "popular fantasies" that Fawaz has identified in American comic books (*New Mutants* 26–33). All fantasies are not necessarily petrochemical fantasies in American comics, yet like fossil fuels themselves, petrochemical fantasies saturate American culture.

torical experience that are today malformed by the cultural ubiquity of fossil fuels.

Petrochemical Fantasies is divided into five chapters that proceed chronologically and thematically through US comics history. Each chapter develops an account of both the literal connections between comics and the petroleum industry, and the metaphorical connections between comics and petrochemicals: fuels, plastics, fabrics, solvents, lubricants, and more. Chapter 1 charts the transition to steam power in nineteenth-century comics and cartoons, from an American printing of Swiss artist Rodolphe Töpffer's "picture story" *The Adventures of Obadiah Oldbuck* to lithographs and newspaper cartoons about new fossil fuel technologies and the corporations that profited from them. Chapter 2 details how newspaper comic strips articulated the values of automobility in the early twentieth century, initially as an unruly and explosive pastime and then as a facet of everyday domestic life. Chapter 3 retells the history of American comic books from the perspective of the early comics pamphlets *Standard Oil Comics* and *Gulf Funny Weekly,* two of the many sponsored comics that advertised and normalized fossil fuel consumption and automobility starting in the early 1930s. Chapter 4 extends this analysis of comic books and fossil fuels by investigating how superheroes like Plastic Man, the Fantastic Four, and Ms. Marvel embody the possibilities of petrochemicals and other modern energy sources. Chapter 5 surveys contemporary comics about climate change and fossil fuel capitalism, finding in the comics medium a mode of visualizing the past, present, and future of energy cultures. Nonfiction comics about sacrifice zones that have been depleted by fossil fuel extraction, science fiction comics about survival during an environmental catastrophe, and historical comics about alternative ecological and social structures all present possibilities for life moving forward. Lastly, the conclusion develops a brief account of how comics might help in contemporary climate struggles and the development of alternative energy cultures. Comics is an art form that has accompanied fossil fuels from their emergence to their dominance as energy sources. Comics are also one way that artists and readers can explore alternative conceptions of time and space that do not rely on intensive fossil fuel consumption. As so many comics have already dramatized, the world is at stake.

CHAPTER 1

Caricatures and Corporations

One of the earliest comics published in the United States, *The Adventures of Mr. Obadiah Oldbuck* is a story of desire and pursuit, and it moves quickly. Printed as an extra edition of the *Brother Jonathan* newsweekly, Oldbuck's 1842 adventure is a translation of Swiss artist Rodolphe Töpffer's *Les amours de Mr. Vieux-Bois,* completed in 1827 and first published in Geneva in 1837.[1] The picaresque romance's title character, Obadiah Oldbuck in English translation, pursues his beloved but is thwarted at every turn.[2] In the adventure's opening two panels, Oldbuck salutes a young woman whose back is turned away. The text caption reads, "Mr. Oldbuck's first sight of his lady love," and the second panel depicts Oldbuck's frustration that his beloved has left him behind (Töpffer, *Adventures* ii). The caption draws out the implication

1. Töpffer's comics are collected in Kunzle, *Rodolphe Töpffer,* and for a study of Töpffer's life and work, see Kunzle, *Father of the Comics Strip.* There are 1842 and 1844 editions of *The Adventures of Mr. Obadiah Oldbuck,* both published by Wilson and Company in New York.

2. The complete title of the 1842 American edition of Töpffer's *Les amours de Mr. Vieux-Bois* is *The Adventures of Mr. Obadiah Oldbuck: Wherein are duly set forth the crosses, chagrins, calamities, checks, chills, changes, and circumgirations by which his courtship was attended; Showing also the issue of his suit and his espousal to his ladye-love.* It was published as *Brother Jonathan Extra* no. 9, and it is available at the Beinecke Rare Book and Manuscript Library, https://collections.library.yale.edu/catalog/10171474.

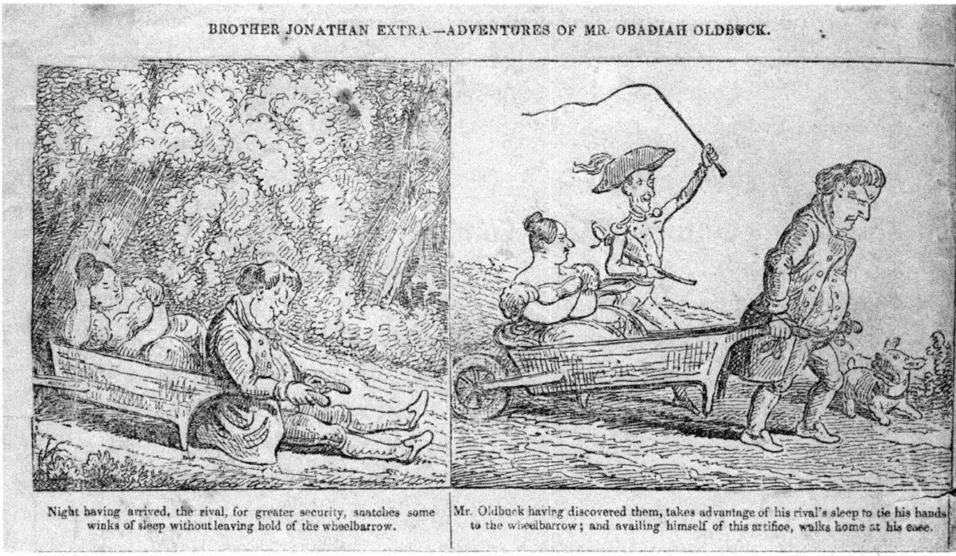

FIGURE 1.1. Rodolphe Töpffer, *The Adventures of Mr. Obadiah Oldbuck.* Wilson and Company, 1842, p. xl. Beinecke Rare Book and Manuscript Library.

that the beloved's ability to move has thwarted Oldbuck's romantic desires: "Mr. Oldbuck beholds her vanishing in the distance" (ii). Obadiah Oldbuck is a man in pursuit of a moving figure, and for the rest of his adventure, he must figure out how to catch up to her.

In illustrated panels and text captions, Töpffer's *The Adventures of Mr. Obadiah Oldbuck* cycles through a series of comedic scenarios: Oldbuck "seeks to conquer his tender passions by study," then "finding study ineffectual, tries music"; seated with a cello, Oldbuck "discovers all his efforts are in vain," until he "espies his lady-love"; he "rushes to the street, but she has vanished" once more (ii–iii). As the narrative continues, Oldbuck runs after his beloved with a roof beam tied to his neck from a failed suicide attempt and gets caught between two trees; Oldbuck buys a horse, but the horse throws him; a rival suitor woos Oldbuck's beloved away; meanwhile, Oldbuck is imprisoned for excessive dancing, joins a monastery, escapes while dressed as a lady, rehabilitates his sickly horse, and then at last woos his beloved, only to be abducted by monks and returned to the monastery; and so on.

After shenanigans with carriage, horse, mule, rowboat, and wheelbarrow, Oldbuck creeps up on his beloved and his rival suitor while they are asleep in the woods. The caption reads: "Mr. Oldbuck having discovered them, takes advantage of his rival's sleep to tie his hands to the wheelbarrow; and availing himself of this artifice, walks home at ease" (xl). In a wheelbarrow that now functions as a rickshaw, Oldbuck rides with his beloved at last (figure 1.1). Oldbuck and his beloved are married in the adventure's final panel, captioned as "happy denouement of the history of Mr. Oldbuck."

The Energy Culture of Early Comics

This early example of American comics does not seem to have anything to do with coal, oil, or carbon emissions, yet Töpffer's *The Adventures of Obadiah Oldbuck* appeared during the transition to coal power throughout Europe and the United States. Comics were structured from the beginning by the new speeds and technologies produced by industrialized energy systems. Töpffer's narratives involve intense movement through space and time, familiar to the picaresque romance and its symbolic journeys, yet these movements also reflect the major industrial energy sources before coal: horses, humans, and water. Oldbuck's adventure concludes when he turns his rival into an engine that carries Oldbuck and his beloved to marriage. The narrative is about speed and transportation, a road narrative before the automobile.

The forward momentum of Oldbuck's story thematizes Töpffer's own practice of comics-making. A professor at the University of Geneva who doodled for the enjoyment of his students, Töpffer developed a practice of caricature that is simplistic yet expressive, and his drawings are intentionally hasty. In his 1845 "Essay on Physiognomy," Töpffer defines his "picture stories" as "a series of sketches where accuracy is unimportant but, on the other hand, a clear, rapid expression of the essential idea is imperative" (5). Töpffer thinks of his picture stories as an art form defined more by time than space, and more by narrative than pictorial representation. The aesthetic values of his "picture stories" were quite different than those associated with more traditional forms of fine art in nineteenth-century Europe. Töpffer made his drawings fast, and that speed of execution coincides with and visually reinforces the fast pace of his narratives. Form and content both move fast in *The Adventures of Mr. Obadiah Oldbuck* and in Töpffer's other picture stories, and this chapter details how early comics were intertwined with modernity's energy and speed even in the fossil fuel transition's early decades.

Töpffer associated his artistic style with the speed of increasingly industrial printing presses in the early nineteenth century. Unlike the visual narratives of William Hogarth and other eighteenth-century artists who included lushly symbolic details in each image of a narrative sequence, Töpffer's picture stories emphasize action over visual symbolism, and the drawings look intentionally crude. In his use of caricature to narrate a comedy, Töpffer blurs the distinction between image and text, a distinction that reinforced classical aesthetic values during Töpffer's time. In his 1766 study *Laocoön,* for example, the German philosopher Gotthold Ephraim Lessing famously differentiates painting from poetry, and by extension the visual arts from the literary arts. Lessing argues that visual arts should strive for a discrete symbolism, while poetry should represent narrative action. In the preface to *Laocoön,* Lessing is critical of modernity's speed: "But we moderns have in many cases thought to surpass the ancients by transforming their pleasure-paths into highways, though at the risk of reducing the shorter and safer highways to such paths as lead through deserts" (viii–ix). In Lessing's metaphor, artworks that stray from classical aesthetics connote high-speed travel. Skeptical of modern motion, Lessing argues that visual art should solidify a sense of reality, not pose new possibilities: "invention and novelty in the subject are by no means what we chiefly require from the painter" (75).[3] Töpffer's style overturns this value system. Modern speed and wild invention are celebrated and popularized in works like *The Adventures of Obadiah Oldbuck* that proliferated on nineteenth-century printing presses. Historian Louis P. Masur describes this moment in US print culture: "Steam-driven and cylinder presses allowed the mass production of inexpensive newspapers and pamphlets. Starting in the 1830s, the penny press altered the nature of what constituted news itself as tens of thousands of readers gained access to papers that satisfied a desire for sensational, illustrated stories of crimes and accidents" (1420). Published during this period of accelerating mass production, *The Adventures of Obadiah Oldbuck* is an experiment in visual storytelling facilitated by the industrial printing press. The juxtaposition of image with text becomes technically possible in a mass medium during industrialization in the nineteenth and twentieth centuries, and comics emerge as a way to depict modernity through the speedy art of cartooning.[4]

With his fast-paced picture stories, Töpffer participated in the development of an art form on modernity's "highway," to use Lessing's metaphor. Early comics like Töpffer's are full of the symbolic meaning long associated with painting, and they are also structured by the "progressive action" that Lessing found admirable in poetry. Töpffer especially appreciated that moral

3. For a reading of *Laocoön* and image/text relations, see Mitchell, *Iconology.*

4. For an account of nineteenth-century comics and cartoons in American periodical, see Beringer. A range of approaches to comics in early periodical formats is evident in Brinker et al.

values could be transmitted through the fast-paced action of visual narratives, writing that the "picture-story, with its unique advantages of brevity and, consequently, of clarity, would be much more effective than the written story for two reasons: it would make a more lively appeal to more people, and second, the fact is that in every argument the man who goes straight to the point gets the better of one who rambles" ("Essay" 4). An educator himself, Töpffer thought that comics could instruct and inform readers in a culture where time is increasingly regimented by industry.

Töpffer's legible and lively caricatures hurrying through space invoke the classical tradition of "grotesques." Grotesques are fantastical figures, influentially described by Renaissance artist and writer Giorgio Vasari:

> The grotesque is a kind of free and humorous picture produced by the ancients for the decoration of vacant spaces in some position where only things placed high up are suitable. For this purpose they fashioned monsters deformed by a freak of nature or by the whim and fancy of the workers, who in these grotesque pictures make things outside of any rule, attaching to the finest thread a weight that it cannot support, to a horse legs of leaves, to a man the legs of a crane, and similar follies and nonsense without end. He whose imagination ran the most oddly, was held to be the most able. Afterwards the grotesques were reduced to rule and for friezes and compartments had a most admirable effect. Similar works in stucco were mingled with the painting. So generally was this usage adopted that in Rome and in every place where the Romans settled there is some vestige of it still preserved. And truly, when touched with gold and modelled in stucco such works are gay and delightful to behold. (246)

Impossible figures placed in the visual margins, Roman grotesques violate principles of classical form, and while these fanciful compositions might not be beautiful to Vasari, they nonetheless amuse and are "gay and delightful to behold." Töpffer's picture stories place the grotesque in the center of the composition rather than its margins, and this gives his figures a sense of complexity and even chaos. As Töpffer writes of his nonnaturalistic caricatures, "the most laughable physiognomies result usually from concocted, wholly arbitrary combinations of features, for not only do these offer a certain entertaining mysteriousness, but also they present in one face contrasts or mixtures of expression that are inherently funny" ("Essay" 25). Töpffer values his style of line drawing, boasting that it "can't be matched for jotting down, in running narrative, quick sketches that want only a sharp definition, images serving as links in a chain, often just as reminders or symbols"

(9). His drawings are occasional, determined by "the brevity authorized by the process of line drawing itself," and therefore each image is freed from the constraints of realism, shorthand as they are. As comics historian Thierry Smolderen notes, Töpffer "invented novel reasons for such extravagances" in his picture stories, predicting and establishing "the frenzied 'physics of the toons' in the twentieth century" (51). Moving grotesques from the far corners of formal compositions to the center of multiple illustrations, Töpffer draws figures that jump, race, and ride through sequential panels.

Töpffer's work relied on and was modeled after the temporal rhythms of the printing press, a technology that transformed rapidly in the nineteenth century. As he predicts in his "Essay on Physiognomy," newer, faster, and more direct printing technologies like autography, a variation of lithography used by Töpffer, would gradually improve to make the picture story a more refined art form, even while lithographic reproduction preserved the picture story's narrative speed and facilitated mass production:

> nothing can compare for speed, convenience, or economy to the technique of autography. No intermediary step of engraving is required; you don't have to draw the image in reverse so that when printed it will come out as intended, nor need you wait more than an hour for the transfer-drawing to become fixed on the stone and ready to print one or two thousand copies. We ourselves have always wanted to get quick results without much bother and have therefore employed the process only at its present, still quite crude stage of development, such as you see in bills and circulars. However, we have worked with it enough to be convinced of its unlimited possibilities, and someday it may yield results fully equal to a combination of etching, dry-point, and burin. (5–6)

Töpffer's picture stories were a new art form that used both the expressive linework of fine art and the narrative action of literature. They were also narratives that expressed the increasing speed of the printing press in the nineteenth century.

While modern in sensibility, Töpffer nonetheless drew a world powered by horses, humans, and water, in keeping with much of Europe and the United States in the earlier decades of the nineteenth century and before. Water was an abundant energy source in the United States for most of the nineteenth century, overtaken by steam power only in the century's later decades. As Andreas Malm explains, "Steam engines set foot on American soil at an early date, but were extremely slow in conquering the economy. Waterwheels provided the bulk of mechanical energy until after the Civil

War; in terms of total industrial horsepower, steam edged them out only in the census of 1870, with 52 percent as against 48 percent—a national shift occurring some four decades later than in Britain" (*Fossil Capital* 316). In a sequence from *The Adventures of Mr. Obadiah Oldbuck,* Oldbuck courts his beloved while his rival suitor is trapped in a waterwheel, spun around and dunked repeatedly in an extended sequence (figure 1.2). As comics historian David Kunzle notes, this waterwheel sequence moves time forward at a curious pace, "that of time running in two separate dimensions, one fast, the other slow" (*Father* 45). As the rival is dunked in a sequence that "cannot realistically last more than a few minutes at the most," Oldbuck escapes with his beloved for weeks, months, or even years (45). In juxtaposed panels, the suitor spins rapidly on the waterwheel, while Oldbuck and his beloved enjoy a "pastoral life" (Töpffer, *Adventures* xxix).

The panels of the suitor's repetitive dunking in the waterwheel and of Oldbuck's pastoral life juxtapose industry with leisure. Like the later steam engine, the waterwheel was a locus of energy, one of the chief power sources of early industrialization. The duration and intensity of the rival's spin on the waterwheel invokes the water energy regime of the nineteenth century, cheaper and more powerful than newer steam-powered alternatives in the early 1800s. In his history of steam power, Andreas Malm describes how water power was far more common than steam in the antebellum United States:

> In the subsistence economies of the early American settlements, water was the perfect source of mechanical energy: close at hand, free of charge. A population sprinkled in agricultural enclaves, only tenuously connected by trade across long distances arduous to traverse, corresponded well to the distribution of streams. In the 1840s . . . most American manufacturing still occurred within the fold of this rural frontier economy. In 1840, a mere 10.8 percent of the population could be classified as urban (living in towns with at least 2,500 inhabitants), falling to 10.7 percent in 1860. (*Fossil Capital* 319)

For American readers of *The Adventures of Obadiah Oldbuck,* the waterwheel would have been an industrial and technological norm, a fixture of energy culture. Notably, Oldbuck's madcap adventure features the waterwheel as a device that manipulates time on the comics page. The waterwheel delays the suitor indefinitely in *Obadiah Oldbuck,* giving Oldbuck hours and days in exchange for minutes in the water's energetic flow. As a dominant energy source, the waterwheel is both a mechanism in the material production of Töpffer's printed comics—his works were likely printed with water

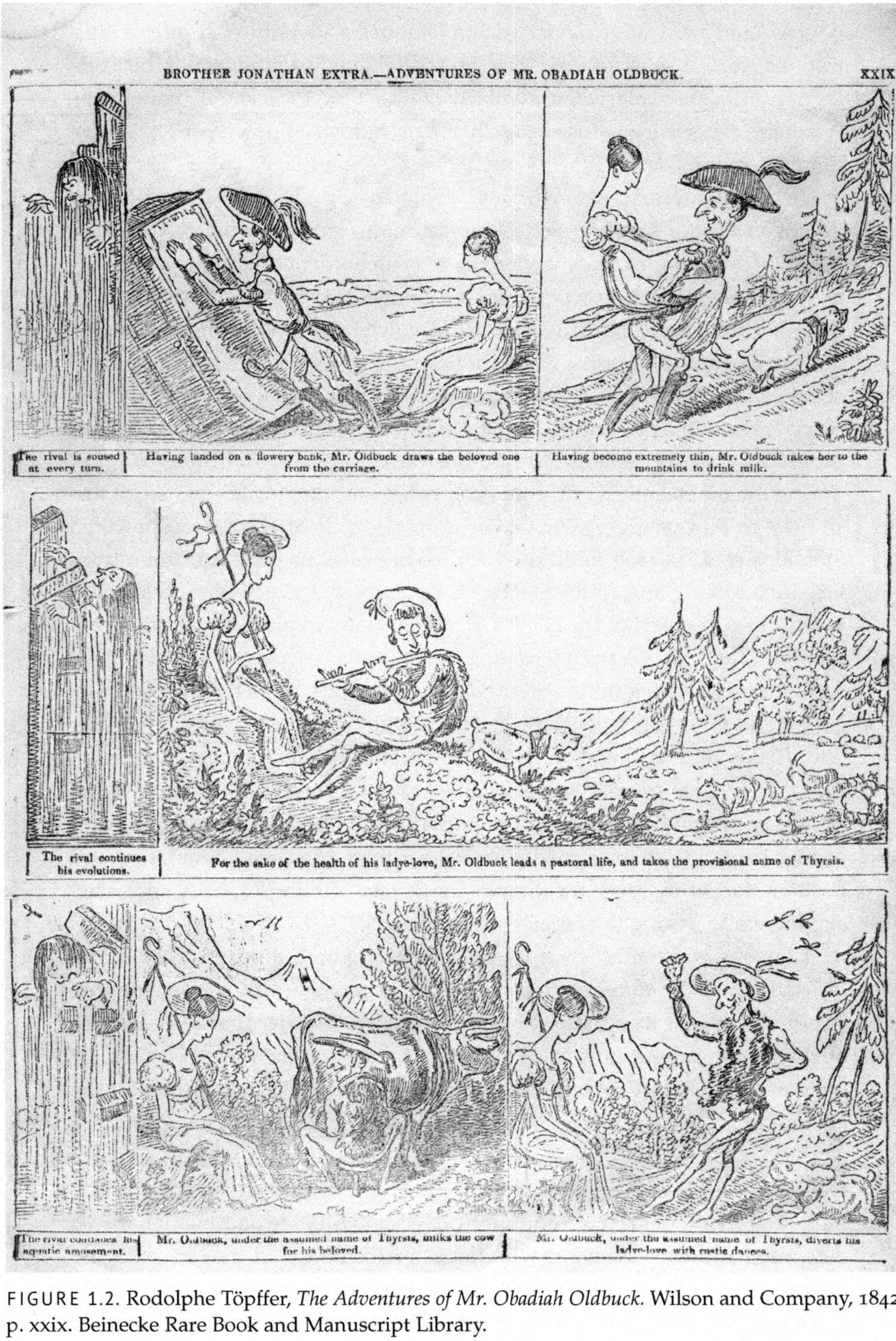

FIGURE 1.2. Rodolphe Töpffer, *The Adventures of Mr. Obadiah Oldbuck.* Wilson and Company, 1842, p. xxix. Beinecke Rare Book and Manuscript Library.

power—and a narrative device within Oldbuck's adventure. Töpffer's illustrations create a sense of time through spatial juxtaposition, and in his comics narrative, the waterwheel similarly creates time for leisurely enjoyment. Aesthetic experience is fused together with industrial power in *The Adventures of Obadiah Oldbuck.*

In an 1846 essay, the critic and professor Friedrich Theodor Vischer described Töpffer's picture stories as imagining a world beyond natural laws: "Gravity is no more, or suspended; there is no more necessity but what may be overcome; human powers know no limits. And human illusions magic us into a free, pure, comic world of their own" (189). The limitless human powers in Töpffer's comics emanate from the energetic flow of images and actions in his narratives, and his lengthy yet quickly drawn and printed stories were possible because of changes in printing technology. Töpffer's "free, pure, comic world" emerges from transformations to the printing industry during the nineteenth century that coincided with the increasing use of fossil fuels in Europe and America. For example, a cast-iron, human-powered Stanhope press in 1800 could produce 480 impressions per hour, and in 1814 Friedrich Koenig and Andreas Bauer's steam-powered cylinder press could produce 1,000 sheets of the *London Times* per hour, more than doubling production (Taunton). An 1818 Koenig steam-powered press could produce 2,400 impressions per hour, and by 1898 a Hoe rotary press at Pulitzer's *New York World* newspaper could print 20,000 eight-page color newspapers per hour (Baker and Brentano 8). Long emblematic of industrialization, turn-of-the-century large circulation newspaper comics extend from experiments in popular printing like Töpffer's *The Adventures of Obadiah Oldbuck,* and early comics helped to shape a media format for the widespread circulation and proliferation of petrochemical fantasies just as printing capacity increased exponentially during the nineteenth century.

Comics artists reflect the speed of modernity both through quick drawing styles and in representations of modern energy itself. It is notable that Töpffer's interest in representing speed emerges in the first few decades of the geological era now known as the Anthropocene. A term coined by meteorologist Paul Crutzen and biologist Eugene Stoermer to denote the geological era in which human activity changed the planet irrevocably, the Anthropocene "could be said to have started in the latter part of the eighteenth century, when analyses of air trapped in polar ice showed the beginning of growing global concentrations of carbon dioxide and methane. This date also happens to coincide with James Watt's design of the steam engine in 1784" (Crutzen, "Geology" 23). The concept of the Anthropocene is controversial, for it can isolate ecology and climate from the uneven economic, political, and social realities of carbon emissions and fossil fuel capitalism.[5] Yet the term has become a ubiquitous conceptual marker for climate change, its history, and most importantly, the future beyond fossil fuels.[6]

The perspective-shifting implications of climate change and the Anthropocene have provoked a lot of reflection on how to narrate the history of art, culture, and literature. Even the simple realization that energy has an effect on the world entails a complete rethinking of our aesthetic categories, premised as they often are on formal abstractions that cannot account for material conditions like carbon emissions. Fossil capitalism fundamentally shaped life, society, and state in the United States and the world, and culture similarly inflects and naturalizes energy systems. As Patricia Yaeger points out, energy systems are evident in cultural texts not only through direct representation but also "the touch-a-switch-and-it's-light magic of electrical power, the anxiety engendered by atomic residue, the odor of coal pollution, the viscous animality of whale oil, the technology of chopping wood: each resource instantiates a changing phenomenology that could recreate our ideas about the literary text's relation to its originating modes of production as quasi-objects" (Yaeger 309–10).[7] Early comics like Töpffer's picture stories are accordingly evidence of the transition to steam power, both through their artistic style—Töpffer's stories speed along, quickly produced and quickly understood—and as a subject of representation—Oldbuck and other Töpffer protagonists struggle to "catch up" as everyone and everything around them moves more quickly.

Illustrations of Steam Power

Other works much like Töpffer's *Adventures of Mr. Obadiah Oldbuck* were printed in the United States, such as *Journey to the Gold Diggins by Jeremiah Saddlebags* (1849) and *The Fortunes of Ferdinand Flipper* (1850). These stories similarly centered on traveling protagonists in comic narratives, movement-focused journeys that thematize the reorganization of time and space by industrial energy. More familiar to historians and scholars than early comics narratives, lithographic prints became a widespread form of visual culture in this period as well, and they represented the transition to fossil fuels

5. Work about and in critique of the Anthropocene includes Chakrabarty; Haraway; Moore, *Capitalism in the Web of Life*; Wiggin et al.

6. For an influential account of the Anthropocene, geology, culture, and politics, see Yusoff.

7. For a keywords volume on energy and culture, see Szeman et al., *Fueling Culture*.

directly. Historian Bryan LeBeau chronicles the economic and social conditions in which lithography developed, as "industrialization, urbanization, commercialization, and the development of a taste-conscious middle class with discretionary income, as well as technological developments, created a heightened demand for commercial printing, as well as art" (16). In the middle decades of the nineteenth century, he summarizes, lithographs "swept the nation. It has been called the 'Golden Age of American Engraving,' and Nathaniel Currier played a leading role in its development. By midcentury he could write confidently to distributors of his lithographic prints, 'Pictures are now a necessity'" (16). Currier's first widespread commercial success came from a steam engine disaster (*Awful Conflagration;* color plate 1.1). In 1840, while visiting the offices of the *New York Sun* newspaper, Currier heard about a terrible fire on the Long Island Sound steamship *Lexington.* As LeBeau chronicles, "Currier immediately set [artist] William K. Hewitt and [lithographer and photographer] Napoleon Sarony to work on a lithograph of the event, supplying them with fresh details as they became available from eyewitnesses. Within three days, the illustrated news extra hit the streets. It was an unprecedented feat" (12).

In Hewitt's drawing of the Lexington steamship, smoke and flames billow out from the ship's massive engine, and the steamship's wheel has smashed the only lifeboat. Survivors cling to debris in the foreground, and one corpse floats face-up, directly above the bold letters "Lexington" in the caption. The image of the steamship disaster was created quickly to capture an event in progress, and the rolling waves of Long Island Sound, the outstretched arms of survivors jumping ship, and the massive debris-filled flames all connote this sense of action and immediacy. The single image is drawn to represent not a singular moment but a span of time; it is a document of an event unfolding rather than a static image with a concrete symbolic value. The steamship explosion is both grotesque and realistic, a spatial representation of an inherently modern violence. In 1857 Nathaniel Currier partnered with James Merritt Ives to form Currier and Ives, and together they would publish a number of steamship disaster prints. Railroads were also frequent subject matter, though as LeBeau notes, "if prints picturing the power and might of steamboats were countered by several disaster prints, majestic railroad scenes were balanced by similarly threatening scenes only occasionally. There are no train wrecks" (300). Yet in the 1840s, Currier's prints are less celebratory than skeptical of the promises of fossil-fueled transportation.

In one 1848 Currier print titled *Blower, The King of the Road,* horse travel is visually contrasted with railroad travel (figure 1.3). In the print, the horse

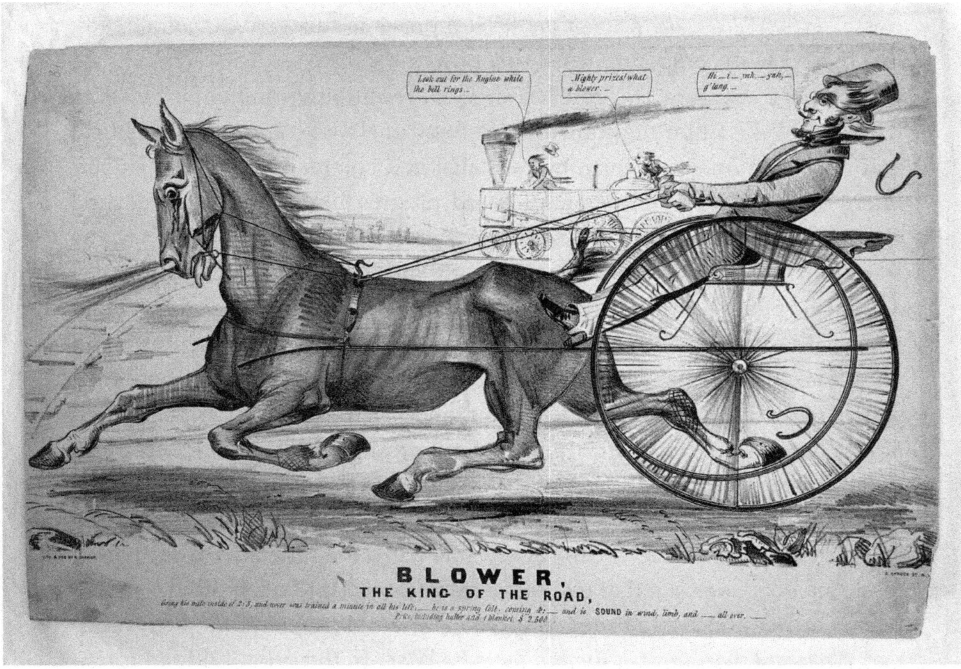

FIGURE 1.3. Nathaniel Currier, lithographer and publisher, *Blower, The King of the Road,* 1846. New York Historical Society Collection of Caricatures and Cartoons.

Blower speeds across railroad tracks, and like the locomotive in the image's background, the horse emits sound and steam. The caption extols the horse: "Going his mile inside of 2:5, and never was trained a minute in all his life: he is a spring Colt, coming 4: and is SOUND in wind, limb and all over. Price, including halter and 1 blanket $2,500." The high cost of Blower is an indication of the consumer and technological appeal of speed. At two and a half minutes per mile, Blower travels at the pace of a racehorse, about twenty-five miles an hour. At $2,500 in 1848, this horse and his gear were luxury, high-performance transportation. The image's juxtaposition of steam power with horsepower foregrounds the thrill of speeding along in a horse-drawn carriage, the driver smiling and smoking in the breeze. Blower the horse provides a more personal and even thrilling experience than the locomotive. By extension, horsepower is visually superior to steam in this image, even as they coexist in the mid-nineteenth-century American landscape. In their book *The Horse in the City,* Clay McShane and Joel Tarr document the horse's tremendous importance to nineteenth-century US energy and transportation systems: "the horse was indispensable as a living machine, to the point that we can label the nineteenth century as the golden age of the horse" (17). *Blower, the King of the Road* represents this golden age, already juxtaposed with competing fossil fuel power.

As historian Cara Daggett has argued, recent environmental histories have established that the transition to fossil fuels was an uneven political and economic process driven by capitalist and colonialist interests, far different than the inevitable march toward progress and efficiency that long characterized histories of modern energy: "an important catalyst for the transition was not the appearance of a technically superior fuel system [such as coal or petroleum], but the development of a new political technology that could organize and extract other humans' labor. Grain agriculture and fossil fuels proliferated because they were especially attractive to those pursuing hierarchy through extractive methods" ("Energy and Domination" 651). Currier's *Blower, The King of the Road* print positions horsepower and steam power in competition, and the steaming horse seems to win the day. Between the violent spectacle of the Lexington steamship disaster and the speed of Blower the horse, Currier's prints register a resistance to emergent fossil-fueled power, yet that resistance transformed into celebration by 1868, when Currier and Ives printed Frances Palmer's *Across the Continent,* subtitled *Westward the Course of Empire Takes Its Way.*[8] In the print, railroad tracks bisect the American landscape, and a locomotive steams ahead from a pioneer settlement in the foreground to an open Western landscape in the background, complete with a wagon train moving toward the horizon. Native Americans on horseback watch the train from the opposite side of the tracks, and the locomotive blows black and gray smoke into their path, a clear symbol meant to convey through carbon emissions the superiority of industrial capitalism. Historian Richard White describes the Currier and Ives print of Palmer's *Across the Continent* as "explicitly imperial, and it made the imperial mundane and modern" (496). The railroad and its coal-powered engine symbolize the American nation, a significant shift from the slow locomotive outpaced by Blower, the "king of the road," in 1848.

Published on the American centennial in 1876, the Currier and Ives print *The Progress of the Century* endorses fossil-fueled technologies emphatically and singularly (figure 1.4). LeBeau describes the print as "a collage of four important nineteenth-century inventions, American by implication: the 'lightning' steam press, the electric telegraph, the locomotive, and the steamship" (67). A seated figure at a telegraph taps out a message that quotes an 1830 speech by Massachusetts Senator Daniel Webster—"Liberty and Union Now and Forever"—which would by 1876 register as a slogan

8. Currier and Ives's print of Frances Palmer's *Across the Continent* (1868) is available online at the Library of Congress: https://www.loc.gov/item/90708413/.

FIGURE 1.4. Currier and Ives, *The Progress of the Century—The Lighting Steam Press. The Electric Telegraph. The Locomotive. The Steamboat,* 1876. Metropolitan Museum of Art.

for Reconstruction-era unity, and the telegraph operator is surrounded by industrial power, steam, and smoke. The smokestacks and giant steam wheels appear soft and nostalgic in the print, shaded with gray tones in the background. Steam power registers here as comfortable progress, and that progress is explicitly gendered and racially coded. Only white male figures appear in *The Progress of the Century.*

Currier and Ives's message of progress and "good will toward men" does not visibly extend, for example, to the figures in the popular "Darktown" print series that the lithographers also produced from the mid-1870s through the 1890s. In over one hundred prints that represented the fictional rural community of "Darktown," Currier and Ives presented racist caricatures of Black people in comic scenarios. In the Currier and Ives print titled *Off His Nut* (ca. 1886), a Black male bicycle rider clings to a steam locomotive, his eyes round with surprise.[9] The print's subtitle captions the racist

9. Currier and Ives's print *Off His Nut* (ca. 1886) is available online at the Library of Congress: https://www.loc.gov/item/2001700357/.

caricature with the exclamation, "Gracious massy, I'se struck de comet!" The caption's "comet" metaphor emphasizes the intense speed of the steam engine, and in the image, the Black male resident of "Darktown" clings to the locomotive's smokestack, displaced and humiliated for humor. Currier and Ives's *Off His Nut* print illustrates how fossil fuel power was configured not just as a mode of technological progress or an engine of economic efficiency but also as a technology of white supremacy and racist exploitation in late nineteenth-century America. Currier and Ives's "Darktown" prints depict Black Americans as a part of America's rural past, displaced and confounded by steam power. In an emancipated United States, fossil fuel "progress" benefited professional white men and their families, and racist caricatures made American fossil fuel power's marginalization of Black communities seem humorous and even natural. Currier and Ives imagined an American future that allocated energy for white men and their pursuit of efficient power, and in that imagined white America, fossil fuel power displaces Black Americans and Native Americans through technological progress and ingenuity. In a print like *The Progress of the Century,* it is clear that fossil-fueled progress was administered by white male Americans for the benefit of white male Americans. This type of progress was never universal, though it was projected as such in America's racist visual culture.

Currier and Ives's prints document the increasing power of fossil fuel technology in the late nineteenth-century United States as progress, and the transition from horsepower to fossil fuel power was likewise registered in magazine and newspaper illustrations. In the June 5, 1886, issue of *Harper's Weekly,* well-known cartoonist Thomas Nast illustrated the adoption of a standard railroad gauge as a moment of national unity, reconciling North and South through steam-powered trade.[10] As in Currier and Ives's *The Progress of the Century,* the late nineteenth-century railroad was represented as a national triumph, and one that explicitly produced a sense of a white, male national identity. Behind Nast's representation of the South as a white male in a suit stands a Black male figure wearing a work apron and holding a railroad tool. His face is not visible, invoking the masses of exploited Black laborers who have toiled in America. Comics studies scholar Rebecca Wanzo explains Nast's Reconstruction-era motif of Black bodies in supplication:

> That African Americans are still bowed down after emancipation in Nast's imagination is illustrative of the temporal resilience of black subjection as a

10. Nast's *Our Standard (Gauge) Adopted All Over the Union* (1886) is available online at the Library of Congress: https://www.loc.gov/item/90715543/.

> preferred image of African Americans in the nineteenth century. Such representations do not suggest that African Americans cannot move forward. On the contrary, the images proffer that even when African Americans move forward, their development is still somewhat arrested, and they are to some extent stuck in place. (80)

In an otherwise celebratory illustration of the railroad as a national and technological triumph, Nast's illustration of the railroad presents the ongoing exploitation of workers whose labor facilitates a sense of steam-powered modernity. The Black laborer is hidden behind the white railroad magnate, and this servile position is in striking contrast to not just the white figures but also the railroad locomotive itself, which steams forward with the word "Union" written on its chimney. Fossil-fueled power inaugurates a new era of white supremacy in Nast's drawing, under the banner of a "commercial union."

In his sentimental and symbolic cartoons, Nast also anthropomorphizes the railroad as a force in and of itself. Just a month after his celebration of the "last spike" in the standard gauge railroad, Nast's cartoon "The Senatorial Round-House" was published in the July 10, 1886, issue of *Harper's Weekly*.[11] In the cartoon, the Senate represents the "Rail-Road States of America," and five anthropomorphic locomotives blow exhaust while speechifying and frowning on the legislative floor. Personifying the railroad as a system, the cartoon gives intention, feeling, and ideological content to an industry, making an abstract system into a visual presence. Nast's steam-blowing locomotive senators prefigure metal-clad characters like Iron Man, expressions of fossil-fueled power as a new suit that enhances human abilities. Both celebratory and critical, Nast's depictions of the railroad both invoke the exploitative labor practices that undergird such a progressive technology, and also caricature the large fossil-fueled systems that reworked commerce, everyday life, and government after the Civil War.

Drawing the Fossil Fuel Transition

Printmakers like Currier and Ives and magazine cartoonists like Thomas Nast pictured the American railroad as a marker of national progress in the late nineteenth century. Railroad travel itself also encouraged the growth of

11. Nast's *The Senatorial Round-House* (1886) is available online at the United States Senate Collection: https://www.senate.gov/art-artifacts/historical-images/political-cartoons-caricatures/38_00094.htm.

newsstands and even cheaper periodicals by the turn of the twentieth century. Comics studies scholar Ian Gordon describes how the railroad shaped not just the content, but also the form of even Rodolphe Töpffer's early comics:

> The association between the bustling unfolding of economic modernity and the sort of regulation it required—trains, for instance, need organization, such as in timetables; indeed, it was the railroads that established the time zones in the United States—is what shaped the career of the pioneering comics artist. . . . Töpffer deliberately used sequential panels and diagrammatic explanations in order to tie the *form* of his satire to the very object of his ridicule: the sort of "generalized formatting" contained "in works on theatrical gestures, manuals on manners, and technical encyclopedias." This sort of reduction of difference to standardization was part and parcel of the coming age, as handmade artisanal craft gave way to industrial production. ("Comic Strips" 14–15)[12]

In England, *Ally Sloper's Half Holiday* (1884–1916) featured its recurring titular character in comics, and acknowledging railway danger, the penny paper advertised above its title: "This copy of Ally Sloper carries with it the advantages of a Railway Accident Life Policy for £150" (Gordon, "Comic Strips" 15–16). Likewise in American newspaper comics, rail travel is a sign of modern times that connotes danger as well as comfort. In newspaper cartoonist Frederick Burr Opper's 1912 "Diogenes Gets Free Ride on Railroad," for example, Diogenes claims to be "Judge Wogglesworth" and gets a free ticket on the New Haven Railroad (figure 1.5). He rides in comfort and comments to a porter that it "seems to me the train is running awfully fast." In the comic strip's third panel, Diogenes is violently thrown from the train when it collides with another in its "regular weekly smash-up." Opper's Diogenes is an explicitly Greek immigrant version of his popular Happy Hooligan character, who debuted in 1900. Opper's 1912 cartoon represents the railroad as a dangerous and corrupt enterprise, and in the strip's final panel, Diogenes, "aged philosopher, now out of hospital, swears vengeance on officials!" He waits outside of the New Haven Railroad office with a revolver and a club, ready to take revenge on the officials that he cheated in the comic strip's first panel. Diogenes's injuries are both explosively comic and real, fantastical in their representation on the page yet systematically prescient in

12. In this passage, Gordon translates and cites Thierry Smolderen's *Naissances de la bande desinée: De William Hogarth à Winsor McCay* (Impressions Nouvelles, 2009).

FIGURE 1.5. Frederick Burr Opper, "Diogenes Gets Free Ride on Railroad!" *The Commercial Appeal* [Memphis, TN], November 23, 1912, p. 6.

their connection to a highly profitable yet unsafe railroad system. Diogenes's thirst for revenge is justified—the train's "regular weekly smash-up" is an invocation of the real dangers of fossil-fueled travel—and comical: Diogenes did not even pay for his ticket, nor can he get to the railroad official, who is conveniently "gone to lunch" when Diogenes shows up. In its twinned racist immigrant caricature and populist critique of capitalism, Opper's Diogenes offers what scholar Jean Lee Cole describes as "comic solidarity" with the reader, a sense of shared identity created by newspapers and their comic strips in the early twentieth century: "The feeling of comic solidarity was just as important as labor unions, political parties, and churches in establishing group identity during an era of national transformation" (150). By 1912, as Opper's Diogenes makes evident, the railroad was both a threat to and a facet of everyday life in the United States.

Just as Opper used speed lines and dust clouds to produce a sense of fast action in the third panel of "Diogenes Gets Free Ride on Railroad," so did Töpffer draw exaggerated representations of speed decades prior. Töpffer's Obadiah Oldbuck speeds on horseback across the page in his *Adventures*, all four legs of the horse splayed out in the air. This visual convention is mocked by American artist A. B. Frost, in a cartoon from his 1888 book *Stuff and Nonsense* (figure 1.6). Titled *The Unprogressive One*, the cartoon compares Eadweard Muybridge's 1878 photographic study *The Horse in Motion* to an artist's painting of a horse, all four legs off the ground and fully extended as in Töpffer's own drawings of horsepower. Frost's cartoon has a hand-lettered poem at its center, captioning the image of the artist at his easel and above the drawn representation of Muybridge's photographic series. The poem reads:

> Said this artist "Now don't you suppose
> An intelligent man like me knows
> How a horse ought to go
> Yet you say I don't know
> And believe what a photograph shows." (Frost, *Stuff and Nonsense* 62)

Frost's juxtaposition of cartooning with photography mocks the unrealistic conventions of caricature, yet as comics historian Thierry Smolderen notes in his reading of this cartoon, "on the surface, the cartoon only points out the inadequacy of old models of artistic representation, but in a subtle way it also reinitiates, at the very place where Töpffer had left it fifty years earlier, the debate between image as *imitation* and image as *symbol*" (120). Frost's cartoon invokes the stark visual difference between a drawn image of a

FIGURE 1.6. A. B. Frost, *Stuff and Nonsense*. Charles Scribner's Sons, 1888, p. 62.

horse running, the figure elongated with all four legs extended in the air, and Muybridge's photographic sequence of a horse running, its legs curled inward while nonetheless moving forward. The "subtle" critique of photography in the cartoon is evident in the second horse in the sequence, facing the wrong direction and therefore undermining the realism of photographic documentation.

Frost's cartoon posits that a sequence of photographic images is just as subject to codes of representation, symbolism, and imaginative embellishment as a cartoon illustration. Dry-plate photography and comics are both modes of representing modern movement, and both are produced through increasingly industrial, fossil-fuel intensive processes from the late nineteenth century onward. Muybridge's *Horse in Motion* itself was commissioned by the president of the Southern Pacific Railroad, Leland Stanford, and as John Ott has demonstrated, "Stanford and his advocates publicly staged and disseminated these photographs in order to consolidate, promote, and naturalise the developments of industrial capitalism" (409). More than a mere figure study, "the stop-action photographs epitomised the inevitability and supremacy of the industrial, mechanised, and capitalised technologies in the saga of national progress. Many considered the strange images captured on glass almost sublime in their revelations of technotopian promise" (Ott 409). Frost's cartoon about Muybridge's *Horse in Motion* juxtaposes photography's technical precision with cartooning's expressive caricature. Photographs can detail movement in sequence, and cartoons convey movement in single images; therefore, as Frost demonstrates, comics are a synthetic form that connect symbolism with sequence, image with text, and narrative with modern movement.

Whether drawn or photographed, images have meaning irreducible to mere mimetic representation. By 1884, when Frost juxtaposed Töpffer's comics with Muybridge's photographic sequence, power was being consolidated by fossil fuel producers, transporters, and distributors in the United States. For example, the Standard Oil Trust was formed in 1882, just two years before Frost's *Stuff and Nonsense* was published. Fossil-fuel powered transportation was becoming more common, and with it new forms of visual narrative that denote modern experiences of speed. As Frost makes evident in his double-sided joke about "unprogressive" art, motion can be captured in both sequential images and in single cartoon illustrations. Both formal options—the single-image cartoon and sequential art—constitute the art medium of comics, capable of representing speed and motion during industrialization. Illustrated magazines like *La Caricature* (1830–43 and 1880–1904), *Punch*, or *The London Charivari* (1841–1992), *Judy*; or the *London Serio-Comic*

Journal (1867–1907), and in the United States, *Judge* (1881–1947), *Life* (1883–1936), and *Puck* (1876–1918) published a range of early cartoons and comics attuned to the themes of their contemporary moments.[13] Like photography, comics connoted modern progress and, by extension, fossil fuels.

By the early twentieth century, Frost's often nostalgic illustrations would register the development of car culture in the United States, which the artist depicted as an uneven and violent change. In Frost's 1904 *Book of Drawings,* a poem by Wallace Irwin is printed as a caption to Frost's *The Pleasures of Automobiling,* a drawing of an early automobile parked on a road, its driver and passengers gazing out at a river valley. Irwin's poem interprets Frost's idyllic image:

> This picture's instructive, if only to show
> That Automobile Fiends, wherever they go,
> Don't get *all* their fun at such practical jokes
> As frightening horses and murdering folks;
> For here they're discovered a moment or two
> Politely engaged in enjoying the view.[14]

The ironic juxtaposition of this humorous verse about murderous "Automobile Fiends" and Frost's lush drawing of a countryside road trip gives depth to Frost's otherwise unremarkably cliché illustration. *The Pleasures of Automobiling* image and its accompanying poem make it clear that Frost's tranquil vista captures a peaceful pause of just one "moment or two" in a spree of speed and violence undertaken by the "Automobile Fiends." Synthesizing image and text to create a sense of narrative time, Frost's image and Irwin's poem ironically document fossil fuel culture in the early twentieth-century United States as a systemic shift that produces new kinds of beauty while also creating new forms of separation and violence. On the one hand, Frost's illustration of *The Pleasures of Automobiling* represents just what its title purports: it testifies to the beauty of a leisure trip by automobile, a central selling point for consumer automobiles in the early decades of the twentieth century. Yet the juxtaposition of image and verse suggests other scenes that are quite different, as our idyllic automobile crew go about "frightening horses and murdering folks." The joke in all of this is that the automobile frees up its travelers to be both idyllic and violent, to see more natural beauty and to destroy it simultaneously.

---

13. For a study of *Life,* see Banta.

14. Frost's *A Book of Drawings* is available online at Hathi Trust: https://hdl.handle.net/2027/pst.000032334609.

The morbid humor of Frost's *Pleasures of Automobiling* persists across a range of different cartoons. In the illustrated humor magazine *Puck,* J. S. Pughe's "The Passing of the Horse" depicts a funeral procession for a weeping horse, an anthropomorphic energy source mourning its own obsolescence at the turn of the twentieth century (color plate 1.2). Driven to the Museum of Natural History in an early automobile, the horse is accompanied by a score of other animals on bicycles and autos. Pughe's "Passing of the Horse" was published as the centerfold cartoon in the February 22, 1899, issue of *Puck,* and its automobile and bicycle parade inaugurates the dominance of new transportation technologies.[15] Later that same year, in November 1899, the real-world Automobile Club of America held its first parade through Manhattan, filmed by Thomas Edison Incorporated.[16] As in Edison's automobile parade film, during which a horse-drawn carriage stops on the road while automobiles pass it by, *Puck*'s animal procession dramatizes the transition to fossil fuel transportation with a recognition of what has been displaced. The organic energy regime becomes historical in turn-of-the-century New York City; the horse belongs in a museum.

In a back-cover comic strip by J. S. Pughe from the April 13, 1904, issue of *Puck,* the passing of the horse is again reenacted for laughs.[17] A cowboy on horseback watches a car zoom by and tries to lasso the vehicle. The cowboy is pulled from his horse and spun wildly in the air; his lasso snaps, and he lands on the ground, looking off at the automobile as it vanishes on the horizon. Titled "Roped In" with the subtitle caption "How Lariat Lem Got It Good in the Bad Lands," Pughe's comic strip represents the speed achieved through the burning of fossil fuels as both unnatural—the horse doesn't stand a chance against the car here and doesn't even move—and as modern: the genre cowboy, already a ripe magazine convention by 1904 in the United States, is undone here by motorists who don't even notice the cowboy's existence. The automobile unseats the cowboy in the American landscape. These *Puck* cartoons about horses and automobiles express skepticism

15. *The Passing of the Horse* had already been predicted in an 1894 *New York Times* article of the same name, and the motif of the "passing of the horse" can be found in many turn-of-the-century publications, such as *Horseless Age* magazine (1895–1918). For discussions of the "passing of the horse" in US culture, see Bowman 632; McShane and Tarr 174.

16. William Daly Paley's 1900 film *Automobile Parade,* produced by Thomas Edison Inc., is available digitally at the Library of Congress, https://www.loc.gov/item/00694403/.

17. Pughe's "Roped In: How Lariat Lem Got It Good in the Bad Lands" (1904) from *Puck* is available digitally at Hathi Trust, https://hdl.handle.net/2027/mdp.39015030140159.

about the fossil fuel–powered technologies that were rapidly replacing traditional horse power in the late nineteenth and early twentieth centuries, yet they also register the seeming inevitability of the fossil fuel transition. The juxtaposition of new and old—a workhorse in an automobile on the way to his final resting place at the Museum of Natural History, or a cowboy whose cattle-roping skills simply cannot compete with a speeding car—turns the energy transition into a slapstick narrative of speed and loss.

This mode of representing early automobiles—as inherently modern icons of progress that liberate drivers from a reliance on literal horsepower and simultaneously as inherently dangerous contraptions that unleash chaos and violence on the public—was such a prominent theme that it was consolidated in *Puck's Monthly Magazine*'s May 1910 "Motoring Number," an issue that collected cartoons, comics, verse, and prose about automobiles. On the first page of "Motoring Number," an illustration of a man and woman driving in an automobile is accompanied by the poem "Romance." The satirical poem's final verse emphasizes the dark romantic allure of automobiles:

> Sudden death, in days of old or in the present,
> Were just as sweet by any other name.
> This style then that may be a bit more pleasant,
> But the undertaker gets there just the same.
> A motor-car for purposes of slaughter
> Is just as good as any ax or lance;
> So, considering the subject as we oughter,
> A motor life is reeking with romance. (B.L.T.)

In 1910 there were less than half a million cars registered in the United States.[18] With the increased production of automobile companies like Cadillac and Ford, the number of car registrations in the United States increased to over eight million by 1920. The "romance" of "motor life" became more common. *Puck*'s satirically critical view of automobiles ran counter to this popular romance, evident in William Randolph Hearst's *Motor Magazine*, founded in 1903 and still in publication today in a digital format. *Motor Magazine* celebrated automobile culture and documented it as a leisure and consumer pastime. A wealthy proponent of the individuality and mobility afforded by automobiles, Hearst took over *Puck* magazine in 1916, and after shifting the magazine away from social satire and to an arts and leisure

18. For statistics on automobile production and registrations from 1900–1927, see "State Motor"; *Statistical Abstract*.

perspective, *Puck* published its final issue in 1918, as automobile ownership continued to climb steeply in the United States. *Puck* documented the uneven transition to fossil fuels, and like in *The Passing of the Horse,* the magazine expired as automobiles arrived on the American scene.

Puck's cartoons and comics celebrated and critiqued the transition to fossil fuels in the late nineteenth- and early twentieth-century United States, and that included cartoons and comics about the major corporations that extracted, refined, and distributed fossil fuels. One such cartoon by Udo Keppler appeared in *Puck* magazine in 1904. Titled "Next!," the cartoon depicts Standard Oil as an octopus, wrapping itself around the steel industry and United States government buildings.[19] The monstrous octopus is a hybrid creature—an oil depot that sprouted tentacles and eyes—and it reaches menacingly for the White House. This representation of the Rockefeller trust's desire to control regulators, suppliers, and competitors casts the modern energy industry as both natural and unnatural, a monstrous exaggeration of organic forces. Like fossil fuels themselves, Standard Oil is both an organic part of the environment and a supernatural force.

In William Randolph Hearst's newspapers, cartoonists such as Gus Mager, Frederick Burr Opper, and Thomas E. Powers routinely caricatured the "Oil Trust" in the first decade of the twentieth century as well. Gus Mager's *"Oily John," the Detective* comic strip depicts a lanky John D. Rockefeller as a detective who repeatedly thwarts the plots of the "small dealer," an independent oilman out to sabotage the trust. In one cartoon, the "small dealer" robs Standard Oil by opening a spigot on the Earth, labeled "Oil," and filling a can (figure 1.7). He rides away on a horse, only to be chased by John D. Rockefeller in disguise. Rockefeller pursues the small dealer in a blimp, then commandeers a car and quickly overtakes the small dealer by ramming his horse. Mager uses the visual language of the comic strip—simple, readily identifiable figure drawing, panel sequence to convey narrative action over time, and explosive, exaggerated action—to parody the power of the oil trust and its products in the early twentieth century. While the octopus motif in Keppler's "Next!" presents Standard Oil as a monster, Mager here presents the oil trust through the genres of the humor comic strip and the detective story. There is no stopping Oily John, a ridiculous miser out to get the little guy. In all of Mager's *Oily John* comic strips, the detective thwarts the small dealer's plans. While the subject of parody, the energy system appears to be unstoppable.

19. Keppler's "Next!" (1904) from *Puck* is available online at the Library of Congress: https://www.loc.gov/item/2001695241/.

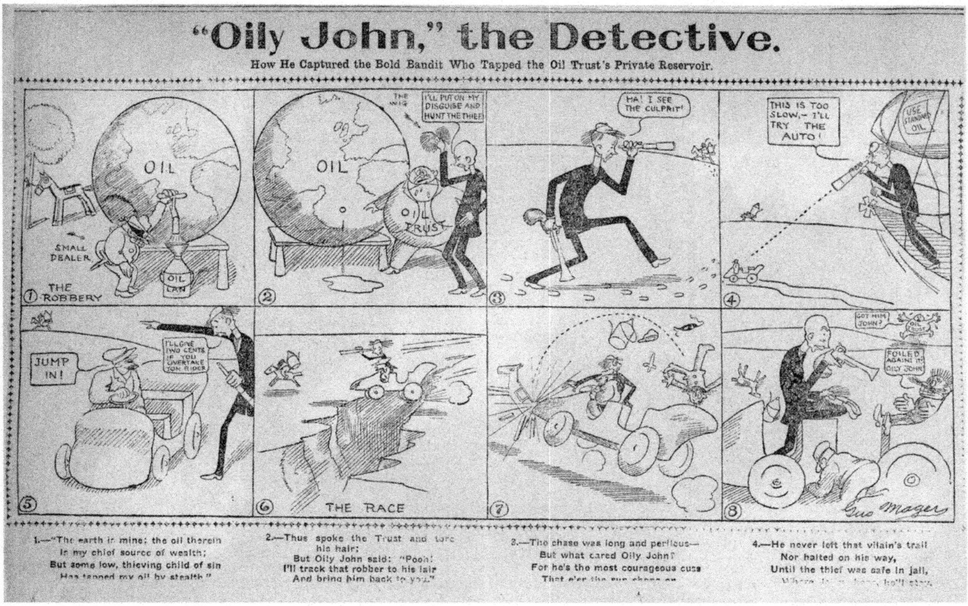

FIGURE 1.7. Gus Mager, *"Oily John," the Detective* ("How he captured the bold bandit"). *New York Evening Journal,* 1905. San Francisco Academy of Comic Art Collection, The Ohio State University, Billy Ireland Cartoon Library and Museum.

In another *Oily John* comic strip, Rockefeller recovers a missing nickel. In preparation for his pursuit of the "small dealer," the oil baron injects himself with a syringe labeled "Standard Oil" and then chases the "small dealer" over a "living bridge" of consumers (figure 1.8). Like Sherlock Holmes's cocaine, Rockefeller's oil acts as a "stimulant," fueling his pursuit of the missing nickel, and the "living bridge" as well as the open-air oil pit in panels 5 and 6 of Mager's comic strip make visual the exploitation of both humans and the environment undertaken by Standard Oil. The detective retrieves his missing nickel at the end of the comic strip, and in the final panel, he removes his disguise and confirms his true identity, backed by a smiling Henry Huttleston Rogers, an early oil industry figure who worked for Standard Oil after selling his business to Rockefeller. Oily John is a stimulant-fueled antihero, determined to run down the competition. Mager's *Oily John* comics are significant both as political representations of the fossil fuel industry and for their adoption and revision of popular tropes to represent the expansiveness of fossil fuels and their attendant economic, industrial, and social systems. Keppler's octopus image harkens back to the maritime imaginary of the whale oil industry, and in *Oily John,* Mager adapts the detective story into an allegory about monopoly capital's control and exploitation of the oil market.

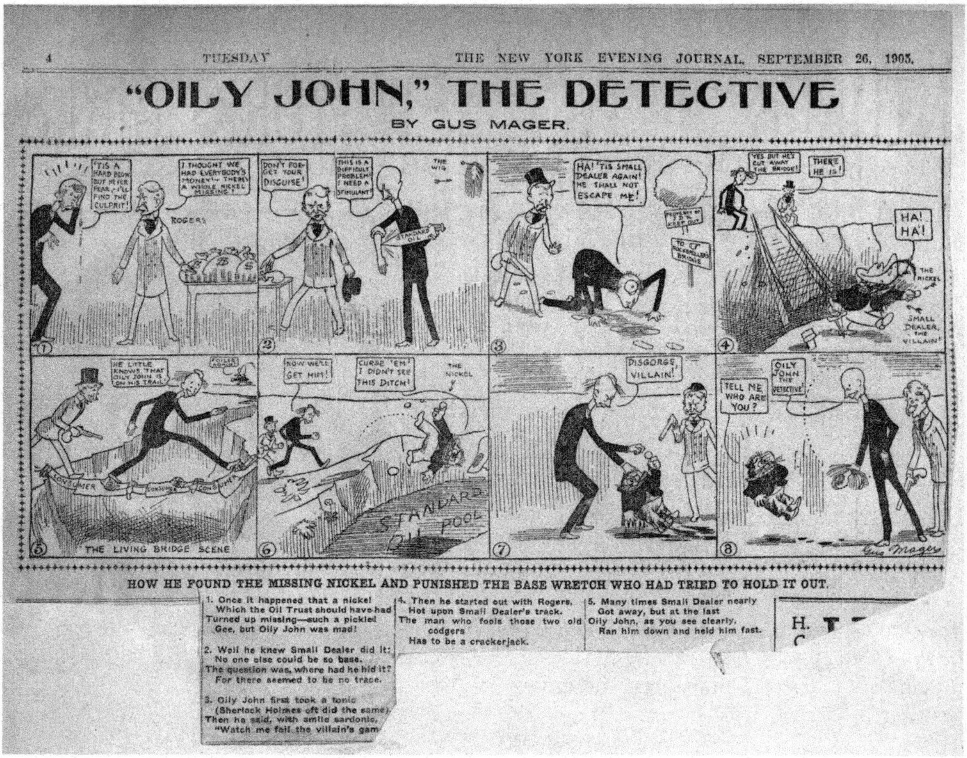

FIGURE 1.8. Gus Mager, *"Oily John," the Detective* ("How he found the missing nickel"). *New York Evening Journal,* September 26, 1905, p. 4. San Francisco Academy of Comic Art Collection, The Ohio State University, Billy Ireland Cartoon Library and Museum.

It is now commonplace to think of the newspaper, the magazine, and the newsstand as products of railroad transportation. A media structure that glommed onto the centralized transit hubs of the street cars, subways, and trains that organized urban space in late nineteenth- and early twentieth-century America, the newsstand both offered a way for an increasing number of urban residents to occupy their time and also fostered a sense of modern, national identity in the reading public. Cartoons and comics documented and expressed the fossil fuel energy regime's developments and values, from coal to petroleum. By using caricature and cartooning to represent the monopolized fossil fuel industries of the late nineteenth and early twentieth centuries, comics artists chronicled the uneven and gradual dominance of fossil fuels in the United States.

Some newspaper comics offer poignant reflections on what we now describe as carbon emissions. One of George Herriman's early comic strips, *Major Ozone's Fresh Air Crusade,* uses the premise of air pollution for humor. Published in 1904, before he developed his long-running *Krazy Kat* comic

FIGURE 1.9. George Herriman, *Major Ozone's Fresh Air Crusade. Washington Times,* March 13, 1904. Chronicling America: Historic American Newspapers, Library of Congress.

strip, Herriman focused the strip on Major Ozone's quest for fresh air, as the title implies. In each strip, after finding a brief moment away from pollution, Major Ozone gets beaten, covered in soot, humiliated, or stranded. In the March 13, 1904, installment, Major Ozone climbs a tall chimney in pursuit of fresh air, and while he sits on the chimney, two workers take down the scaffolding that Ozone climbed (figure 1.9). The strip ends with Ozone spending the night on top of the chimney. With a crescent moon rising behind him, he says, "Oh well I dare say it will do me good." The irony of this strip is subtle, as Ozone sits peacefully on the chimney and enjoys the fresh air that can only be temporary, now that the chimney is complete. A progressive-era environmentalist convinced of the (now disproven) curative properties of ozone, Major Ozone's crusade is destined to fail, as the chimney will soon be spewing smoke and soot. While Currier and Ives documented the emergence of fossil fuel–powered technology as *The Progress of the Century* in 1876, later comic strips like Herriman's *Major Ozone's Fresh Air Crusade* and Mager's *"Oily John," the Detective* question the benefits of fossil fuels, seeing in them less of an efficient than an exploitative, polluted future. As the next chapter details, though, the transition to fossil fuels was eased and made popular in many American newspaper comics of the early twentieth century.

CHAPTER 2

Cars in Cartoons

In 1903 the illustrated magazine *Burr McIntosh Monthly* promoted a print series titled *Buster Brown and His Bubble* by newspaper comics artist R. F. Outcault. The creator of both the Yellow Kid and Buster Brown, Outcault was one of the most well-known comics artists of his time, having reached a massive audience in major newspapers like New York's *Herald, Journal,* and *World* (see introduction). Unlike Outcault's more typical newspaper venues, *Burr McIntosh Monthly* was a magazine that mainly published high-quality photographs suitable for wall display. The magazine printed a selection of three prints from Outcault's series of ten in its August 1903 issue: Buster Brown racing down a city street in a runaway automobile; Buster Brown driving toward a fallen horse that says, "I'm scared to death"; and Buster Brown speeding through a crowd of country folks, with Outcault's Yellow Kid tagging along on the back of Brown's automobile (color plate 2.1). The same issue of *Burr McIntosh Monthly* includes an advertisement for the full print series of *Buster Brown and His Bubble,* noting that this issue's sample "shows three nervous moments. There are ten altogether. 'Dickie' Outcault has unquestionably outdone himself. The regular prints, of which these are reproductions, are 9 × 11½ inches, printed on the best of paper with a three-inch margin, in black, red, green and yellow. Within a month they will be all over the country" ("Buster Brown," Aug. 1903). The prints were also published as postcards, so the advertisement's prediction that Buster Brown would travel "all over the country" was likely true.

Burr McIntosh Monthly sold for a quarter in 1903, contained about forty prints (mostly photographs), and was bound by string so that readers could easily remove images for display. Selling for a quarter per print, or two dollars for the set of ten, Outcault's *Buster Brown and His Bubble* series was likewise printed for wall display, and the cheaper, smaller set of postcards were printed in the same year. This kind of media proliferation was familiar for an Outcault character and comic strip. As Christina Meyer has chronicled of Outcault's earlier creation, "the Yellow Kid operated in a network of different media" in the 1890s, from newspaper comics and illustrated books to children's puzzles and pin-back buttons (46). Buster Brown was a mass-media sensation like the Yellow Kid, and even more so due to the commercial success of Outcault's 1904 licensing deal with the Brown Shoe Company. Buster Brown is a loveable, wealthy kid whose madcap antics undermine his pampered appearance, evocative of the title character in Frances Hodgson Burnett's 1886 novel *Little Lord Fauntleroy.* The title of Outcault's print series, *Buster Brown and His Bubble,* even acknowledges the fanciful extravagance of Brown's wild ride, a path of destruction that winds from the countryside into the city but that nonetheless occurs inside of the safe "bubble" of Buster Brown's comic strip, in which no real harm accompanies the mayhem on the page. Buster Brown brings together the "bad boy" tropes of popular late nineteenth-century novels with the urban escapades of the Yellow Kid.[1] As comics studies scholar Lara Saguisag explains, "In appropriating the bad boy of the countryside and transplanting him into a middle-class home in New York, *Buster Brown* not only provided sentimental attachment to the rural past but also demonstrated that the naughty (white) boy can thrive in the urban present and, potentially, the urban future" (97). The 1903 automobile in *Buster Brown and His Bubble* as well as Buster's own branded footwear in 1904 endow the child character with a sense of intense mobility, reinforcing the fossil-fueled energy and pacing of newspaper comics.

The *Buster Brown and His Bubble* print series concludes with the car in pieces, and in an image also included in the September 1903 issue of *Burr McIntosh Monthly,* Buster Brown paints a sign that reads, "Resolved! I didn't like the old automobile anyway. Walking is better exercise and healthier too." Looking directly at the viewer with wide eyes, shredded tunic, undone bow, disheveled collar, and uneven knickerbockers, Buster Brown

---

1. For a cultural history of the "Bad Boy" in late nineteenth- and twentieth-century American literature, see Kidd 49–85.

has learned from the fossil-fueled wreck, vowing to walk in his soon-to-be eponymous shoes instead of drive. Outcault presents the automobile as an explosive technology, and even the madcap antics of comic strip kids cannot keep up with fossil fuel energy. In the last image of *Buster Brown and His Bubble,* the Yellow Kid floats away with an umbrella while Buster Brown stands next to his wrecked automobile. Icon of cacophonous city streets filled with animals and carriages, the Yellow Kid drifts into the background, and Buster Brown remains in the foreground, the childish icon of the fossil-fueled consumer.

In its December 1903 issue, *Burr McIntosh Monthly* reported that Outcault's *Buster Brown and His Bubble* series had "already reached the sale of over 100,000, and is meeting with tremendous appreciation throughout the country. Forgetting any personal interest, it certainly is a satisfaction to see anything that reflects harmless mirthful good succeed" ("Our Reproductions"). In the March 1904 issue, *Burr McIntosh Monthly* printed an advertisement for Outcault's *Buster Brown and His Bubble* with the slogan "Every Automobilist Should Have These" ("Buster Brown," Mar. 1904). Buster Brown's automobile wreck is oddly projected as an entertaining spectacle, not as a cautionary tale. As Benoît Crucifix explains in his study of turn-of-the-century newspaper comics and "speed machines": "In the first two decades of the century, playfully recuperating stories of havoc-wreaking motorcars that populated the pages of the newspaper, the comic supplement displayed an array of strips representing speed machines that hyperbolically smashed everything up along their way, piling shocks upon shocks." A part of this trend, Buster Brown's wild ride in "the old automobile" conveys the wholesome childhood nostalgia that authorizes and diffuses the chaos that Buster Brown creates in most of his comics. Just as with the Yellow Kid's wild automobile ride in 1899 (see introduction), Buster Brown's automobile adventure emphasizes the populist promise of fossil fuel technology. The car shoots through a rural area, symbolically blowing past older social traditions. Buster Brown represents modern urban America, and in the print series he is gradually accompanied by Black children in a second automobile, as well the Yellow Kid himself, symbol of impoverished youth. Resolving this chaos by swearing off the automobile, Buster Brown retreats to a nostalgic place, reserving the intense energies of the automobile for adults who can properly handle the responsibility of such power. The car is not for joyriding, but even at this early date it is increasingly recognized as a mode of everyday transportation. In the comics, readers experience the vicarious pleasure of wild, fossil-fueled power just as automobiles begin to proliferate around the United States.

Automobility in Comic Strips

Outcault's *Buster Brown and His Bubble* normalizes the automobile as a serious mode of transportation by presenting the automobile in an exaggerated comics scenario. Buster Brown's wild ride channels anxieties about vehicular violence, dispersing them with laughter at the absurdity of cartoon bodies hurtling through space. There were other comics in the 1900s that also presented the automobile as an emergent technology, such as Charles R. Macauley's *Automobiling in the Future* (1901) from the *Philadelphia Inquirer,* Ryan Walker's *The Automopig Family* (1901) from the *St. Louis Republic,* and *Gasoline Gussie* (1904) by John F. Hart and Jack "GAL" Gallagher from the *Philadelphia Evening Telegraph.*

One of Winsor McCay's *Dream of the Rarebit Fiend* comics from 1907 further demonstrates how newspaper comics registered the transition to the automobile as a dominant mode of transportation, easing the rapid shift by overlaying the older transportation means of the horse and the railroad onto the new technology of the gasoline-powered automobile (figure 2.1). One of McCay's long-running comics series, *Dream of the Rarebit Fiend* includes in each installment a fantastical dream sequence brought on by eating the rich cheese dish in the comic strip's title. In a 1907 comic, a driver waits outside a building in an automobile and says, "I'm getting mighty tired of sitting out here waiting for that bunch! Those guys must be hitting it up pretty strong." For sixteen panels of this eighteen-panel comic strip, the driver's automobile bucks like a horse, spins around wildly, flips over and lands upside down, and then spins around to right itself in the final panel, when the driver's passengers finally appear. The automobile in McCay's *Rarebit Fiend* acts in an impossible way, at first like the horse that the automobile replaced historically as transportation, and then in a series of physics-defying moves beyond the kinetic abilities of any vehicle.[2] In his account of Winsor McCay's "animatedness," or his aesthetics of imaginative plasticity, Scott Bukatman posits that *Dream of the Rarebit Fiend* springs from anxieties about modernity and that McCay pushes those anxieties into visible disorder within the structure of the paneled comic strip: "The fixed perspective emphasizes the gradual, if accelerating, metamorphosis. Everything is the same but for that alarmingly animate purse, or the gyrations of an

2. In an insightful essay about early road narratives, Daniel Bowman adopts the term "theriomorphism" to describe turn-of-the-century fictional characters' "tendencies to attribute animal (specifically horse-like) qualities to their automobiles, which in turn affects how they care for their machines" (616). McCay's cartoon (figure 2.2) begins with theriomorphism and then becomes even more fantastical.

FIGURE 2.1. Winsor McCay, *Dream of the Rarebit Fiend: Bucking Automobile,* 1907. National Gallery of Art.

automobile that moves every way but forward. . . . From panel to panel, moment to moment, McCay builds his metamorphoses. The gradual transformation of everyday life continues, building inexorably toward chaos and breakdown" (*Poetics* 62). What McCay illustrates as imaginative play is also clearly made possible by fossil fuels and their energy. When read alongside the frequent stories of railway and automobile accidents that appeared in newspapers at this time, McCay's wild automobile is a threat as much as a pleasant fantasy. The automobile's animated movements in the 1907 comic strip have no utility or purpose, but instead embellish the mechanical function of the gasoline-powered engine with flexibility for its own sake in the interstices of modern life. The springboard for McCay's fantastical figure is the combustion of fossil fuels, an energy that had radically transformed McCay's world during his lifetime and made McCay's media formats possible, from lantern slideshows and animated films to newspaper comics and nationally syndicated editorial cartoons.

As Benedict Anderson influentially argued in *Imagined Communities,* the newspaper produces a sense of national belonging and a sense of simultaneous time in its readers: "the very conception of the newspaper implies the refraction of even 'world events' into a specific imagined world of vernacular readers; and also how important to that imagined community is an idea of steady, solid simultaneity through time" (63). In the late nineteenth-century United States, national identity was diversely represented in the newspapers and illustrated magazines distributed on newsstands and on street corners. In these newspapers, cartoons and comics artists drew stories about the literal technological shifts in this period, from the railroad and the automobile to the dirigible and the airplane, as well as the industrial and systemic shifts occasioned by the use of and increasing reliance on coal, natural gas, and petroleum as fuels. Seeking to represent the centralized industries that structured American economic life, newspaper artists used familiar comics imagery and figuration, thus easing and explaining the transition to fossil fuels. Newspaper comics in the earlier decades of the twentieth century often present the automobile as an ambivalent or even threatening technology, yet as the automobile becomes more common in American culture, many artists draw it as a key feature of both adventure and comedy strips. As Jackson Lears notes, the early "surrealist" period of American newspaper comics that began in the 1890s ends with the increasing standardization of the comic strip under syndication: "Within a few decades, William Randolph Hearst and other newspaper owners had syndicated comic strips and subjected them to corporate market discipline. . . . By the early 1930s, most strips had become comparatively respectable embodiments of petit-bourgeois norms" (330). Bound up in fossil fuel networks for advertising, circulation, distribution, printing, and more, newspapers and their comics increasingly domesticated and romanticized the automobile in the first decades of the twentieth century.

Winsor McCay's fantastical animism is an early petrochemical fantasy. The increasingly passé horse is embodied in McCay's 1907 *Dream of the Rarebit Fiend* by its automobile replacement, lending the fossil fuel tradition a sense of animistic wonder that seems at odds with the more mechanized and standardized systems associated with the automobile. Making fossil-fueled technology seem alive and whimsical was a recurring task for McCay. In the September 6, 1908, *Little Nemo in Slumberland* comic, McCay gives a railroad locomotive the qualities of an automobile (color plate 2.2). Careening through fences, city streets, and a park and eventually landing in a reservoir, the locomotive barrels down on the viewer in each panel, unrelenting in its forward motion as it travels throughout the city. In the penultimate panel, Nemo's impish companion, Flip, comments on the "beauty of this thing" as the locomotive drives into a reservoir. Flip's reference to a beautiful "thing" refers doubly to the beauty of Nemo's dreamscape, where anything can happen, as well as to the beauty of fossil-fueled transportation, a technological wonder that allows you to hurtle though space. As Mina Kaneko has noted, automobiles and railroad cars "frequently malfunction or spin out of control" in *Little Nemo*, yet the frequent wrecks cause no real harm. The otherwise sublime spectacle of a violent train wreck is transformed in McCay's comic strip into a beautiful sequence of plasmatic movements. Nemo's fantastical dream of locomotion is further normalized as mere routine by the comic strip's familiar final panel, wherein Nemo falls out of bed and wakes up, finding himself safe at home with his mother exclaiming, "Come, Nemo! Get up! The tub is ready for you! Come! Take your bath and eat your breakfast, boy!" Paralleling the locomotive's race into the reservoir, Nemo heads into the bathtub, folding the dream into reality. Fossil-fueled fantasy extends into everyday life.

During the first decades of the twentieth century, automobiles multiplied rapidly on American roads. In 1900 there were eight thousand motor vehicle registrations in the United States, and by 1920 there were over eight million ("State Motor"). McCay's comics reflect this transition and the swirl of transportation technologies offering increasing personal power in America. While the automobile provided ample opportunity for fantasy, it was also becoming a part of everyday life and leisure for many middle-class Americans, and newspaper comics reflected this normalization of the automobile in the United States. The newspaper comics in Hearst's and Pulitzer's turn-of-the-century newspapers featured characters like the Katzenjammer Kids and the Yellow Kid, immigrants and orphans at play and work in a New York City where automobiles were scarce novelties. As the comic strip developed into the more formally restrictive, nationally syndicated dailies and weeklies, newspaper comics offered "a pantheon of American types, most of them recognizably urban" according to William Randolph Hearst biographer David Nasaw (109). These syndicated characters were distributed throughout the United States in the first decades of the twentieth century, and as national syndication increased, the "urban" types of early newspaper comics were replaced or revised into types that affirmed the values of the white middle class in America, including the increasing ubiquity of the automobile in everyday life. The connection between newspaper comics and emergent automobile culture in the United States is evident, for example, in the periodicals portfolio of William Randolph Hearst. As noted earlier, Hearst founded the long-running *Motor* magazine in 1903. A glossy magazine filled with photographs, *Motor* catered to an affluent readership of early automobile enthusiasts. *Motor*'s enthusiasm for automobiles is also present in Hearst's more populist newspapers, especially as automobiles become a middle-class commodity in and around 1908, with the manufacture of the Ford Model T. While Hearst's newspapers printed comics critical of the coal, oil, and railroad trusts, the automobile holds out a populist promise of mobility that his newspapers embraced. This increasing endorsement of the automobile entailed the recognition of fossil fuel industries as necessities of American life, distanced from the cluster of economic, environmental, and social problems long identified with fossil fuel industries by Hearst's cartoonists.

In his history of American mass production, David A. Housnell summarizes how the Ford Motor Company used mass production to increase demand for automobiles in the early twentieth century: "Ford sought to manufacture the *lowest* priced automobile and to use continuing price reductions to produce ever greater demand. Ford designed the Model T to be a 'car for the masses'" (9). Ford's strategy of mass production parallels William Randolph Hearst's own populist political platform. A representative from New York to Congress from 1903–7, as well as a Democratic candidate for president, a gubernatorial candidate for New York, and a mayoral candidate for New York City, Hearst ran as an antitrust, prolabor candidate, and this political position coincided with Hearst's media interests. As biographer David Nasaw explains, Hearst campaigned on the idea that "unions were good not only for working people, but for the economy as a whole. The 'prosperity' of the merchant, manufacturer, farmer, book publisher, theater owner, and actor—this was Hearst's list—depended on the purchasing power of the mass of the people" (172). From Hearst's founding of *Motor Magazine* for wealthy hobbyists in 1903 to Henry Ford's mass production of Model Ts for middle-class consumers in 1908, the automobile became another commodity to which Hearst's American masses deserved access, and newspaper comics projected this idea with enthusiasm. For example, in a 1910 single-panel *Mutt and Jeff* comic, the artist Bud Fisher draws himself driving away with his title characters (figure 2.2). Titled "Vacation in an Auto Is the Real Thing," Fisher drives Mutt and Jeff "away from work," clouds of dust and exhaust trailing from the automobile. One of many newspaper comics to boost the idea of automobile tourism, *Mutt and Jeff* also featured in advertisements for the automobile and fossil fuel industries. In 1934 Mutt and Jeff appeared in a Shell Oil advertising campaign that included standees of the comic strip characters for display at gas stations, and artist Bud Fisher was pictured in a 1935 advertisement for Goodrich Tires.[3]

3. For details of the Mutt and Jeff advertising campaign with Shell, see Beerbohm and Olson 298.

FIGURE 2.2. Bud Fisher, *Mutt and Jeff,* August 1910. The Ohio State University, Billy Ireland Cartoon Library and Museum.

FIGURE 2.3. Nell Brinkley, *The Adventures of Cupid. Buffalo Enquirer,* May 10, 1912, p. 5.

In Bud Fisher's "Vacation in an Auto Is the Real Thing," the automobile signifies freedom from work and other social expectations. Other newspaper cartoonists frequently depicted automobiles as a vehicle of modern liberation. In Nell Brinkley's *The Adventures of Cupid* from May 10, 1912, the automobile disrupts social norms (figure 2.3). Brinkley draws a young couple in a speeding automobile driven by Cupid and with "Betty's Daddy tearing through the country behind them." In this and many other Brinkley cartoons, automobile travel is figured as a liberatory escape from traditional gender and sexual roles. As comics historian Trina Robbins has documented, "the Brinkley Girl laughed out loud, with her mouth wide open, her wild hair streaming in the breeze. She leaped through the snow, splashed and swam in the water, ran through the grass. And she often held a job" (39). The automobile was part of the Brinkley girl's modernity, a technology that facilitated the action in Brinkley's art and connoted mobility not just across space but also from social restrictions.

The Time and Space of Driving

Not all comic strips overlaid whimsical invention, national adventure, and everyday speed onto the early automobile. Already noted in chapter 1, *Puck* magazine published a "Motoring Issue" of cartoons about automobile accidents and pollution in May 1910. Five years later, *Puck*'s January 2, 1915, issue was "dedicated to the automobile, and every page bristles with sparkplugs, carburetors, and planetary transmissions" ("Brief Summary"). Among "the artists who give their impressions of motoritis" in the issue was Rube Goldberg, featured in the special "Automobile Number" with a double-page comic strip about an auto mechanic (color plate 2.3). The magazine predicted that "if you've ever paid a repair bill—sure, good cartoonists do—you'll carefully frame this two-page cartoon and present it to your favorite garage for Christmas" ("Brief Summary"). In the comic, Rube Goldberg characterizes the automobile as an unreliable technology that costs more than it is worth. In the first panel, a couple is shown taking their car to a mechanic because of its horn. The mechanic, though, finds a lot more to be wrong with the car. He diagnoses fake problems and takes to the car with a hammer and pickax. In the final panel, the couple sit at a restaurant and order only "three cents worth of orange seeds" because "we're having our car overhauled by an expert, so we'll have to live very simply for a while." The couple accepts the exorbitant and unnecessary cost of the automobile repairs in stride, just another funny facet of modern life in America.

FIGURE 2.4. Orville P. Williams, *Gasoline Gus. Los Angeles Times*, April 11, 1915, p. 104.

This comic was part of a short-lived series announced in *Puck*'s October 24, 1914, issue: "In his new series in color, 'And They Get Away with It,' Mr. Goldberg will take us behind the scene of the various professions, and in his inimitable fashion tell us the tactics adopted by great thinkers to entice the nimble dollar into the till" ("Welcoming"). Goldberg's first "And They Get Away with It" comic is about a lawyer; the December 12, 1914, issue of *Puck* includes a comic about a doctor; and the final installment on February 13, 1915, is about a dance teacher. Best known today for his "Rube Goldberg machine" cartoons, Goldberg's automobile mechanic manipulates the technological complexity of the automobile, prolonging and complicating everyday life in the same manner as the cartoonist's iconic "Self-Operating Napkin" cartoon, originally published in the September 25, 1931, issue of *Collier's* magazine. The automobile does not make life easier for Goldberg's middle-class couple, yet they seem resigned to the car's expense. It is another ridiculous invention of industrial capitalism, a machine more trouble than it is worth but that is everywhere anyway in screwball modernity.

In Orville P. Williams's *Gasoline Gus* comic strip (1913–15), the title character is a madcap jitney driver whose car provides both his livelihood and an excuse to behave recklessly. In the comic strip from April 11, 1915, Gasoline Gus wakes up "two hours before his usual rising hour" and rushes to work (figure 2.4). Picking up a passenger and cramming him into a seat, Gus "shows the proper 'get-the-business' spirit," and he quickly fills his jitney with passengers, the car spewing dust as it speeds along. In the strip's concluding three panels, Gasoline Gus counts his fare money, returns his car to the garage at 3:00 p.m., and arrives at the baseball stadium in time for the first pitch of the new season. A working-class jitney driver, Gasoline Gus achieves some of the trappings of middle-class life through his automobile. It accelerates his workday and facilitates leisure time.

Gene Ahern's *Otto Auto* comic strip (1919–21) typically used three panels to unfold a gag about the titular character's good luck and inextricable connection to his automobile. In an *Otto Auto* comic strip from the *Arizona Republican* on September 10, 1919, Ahern uses a scenario "suggested by 235 and then some, Otto Auto fans": "Engine trouble would stop Otto Auto!" (figure 2.5). In the first panel, placed on the bottom of this vertical comic strip, Otto Auto's car makes strange noises, and Otto says, "Sounds like it's got a fish bone parked in one of th' cylinders." In the second panel, the car erupts with random household objects—a coffee pot, a lawn mower, an umbrella, an alarm clock, a rolling pin, a telephone, and more. In the third and final panel, Otto Auto and his automobile leave the explosion of household objects behind and cruise forward. Otto chuckles to himself, "runs like a four-bit swimmin' suit." Curiously in the background of this final panel, a barn has been knocked onto its side by a horse. The horse seems to be reaching for some flowers to eat from a window. This strange composition fills up what might have otherwise been a blank spot in the comic strip's third panel, and it also juxtaposes the car to the horse. Both seem to bring disorder, yet the automobile moves beyond the domestic space of the home. Otto Auto's car ejects modern household appliances and speeds past a horse and a home in the distance. The driver blissfully leaves domestic concerns behind while traveling through space at fossil-fueled speeds.

Gene Ahern's *Otto Auto* and Orville P. Williams's *Gasoline Gus* were followed by other automotive comic strips, like Frank Beck's *Gas Buggies* (1920–40) and Lee Stanley's *Gassaway Miles—Motorist* (1921–22). These comic strips were among many that featured gag cartoons about mechanics and drivers, and many other comic strips would use automobile-centered gags, as well. Cliff Sterrett's *Polly and Her Pals* frequently involves an automobile, though the car is blended into broader domestic drama. In the May 22, 1933, comic strip, "Paw" Perkins walks by two new automobiles and admires them, exclaiming "Oh, Boy!" and "Hot Dawg!" while sniffing in "that brand new aroma" (Sterrett 139). "Maw" Perkins diagnoses her husband's consumerism, saying, "Oh, [it's] just a touch of his annual ailment . . . Auto-Intoxication!" The four-panel gag strip's concluding pun fully domesticates

FIGURE 2.5. Gene Ahern, *Otto Auto. Arizona Republican,* September 10, 1919, p. 7. Chronicling America: Historic American Newspapers. Library of Congress.

the automobile as a familiar yet dangerous and somewhat illicit pursuit. Printed in May 1933, this installment of *Polly and Her Pals* appeared just months before the repeal of Prohibition in December 1933 following the ratification of the Twenty-first Amendment. Like alcohol, the comic strip implies, automobiles were a public nuisance nonetheless accepted as a part of everyday life, a danger suitable as a consumer choice.

While humor comic strips made automobiles familiar through domestic jokes and explosive hijinks, other comic strips presented automotive and fossil-fuel technology in educational and informational ways. Pete Keenan's *Automotive Oddities* (early 1930s) from the Automotive Industries syndicate, Jack Williamson's *Auto Sense* (1924–27), and E. R. Watkins's *Auto Terms Illustrated* (1922) provided information and instruction about automobiles in comic strip and cartoon form. Similarly, a comic strip titled *Oil Oddities* (1934–37) by Joseph and Sam Kornfeld was syndicated through the Houston-based Oil Features Syndicate; the strip was an illustrated history of the oil industry and petroleum refining. These industry-friendly comics reflected the general acceptance of gasoline-powered automobiles in the United States.

Other comics that were not direct products of the automotive or fossil fuel industries nonetheless became advertising vehicles for them. A celebrity cartoonist who created *Old Doc Yak* and *The Gumps*, Sidney Smith was frequently associated with automobiles. As comics studies scholar Jared Gardner writers, Smith had "outsized personality—matched only by the oversized engines in his many cars," and "his passion for movement and travel [defined] him both as an individual and as a cartoonist until his death in an auto accident in 1935" ("Sidney" 8, 9). In *Old Doc Yak*, the title character, an anthropomorphic yak, often speeds around in automobiles, such as in the Sunday comic strip from May 6, 1912 (figure 2.6). Old Doc Yak appears in the title masthead as a locomotive conductor, speeding while coal flies out of a basket and into the train's wake. In the twelve panels of the Sunday comic strip, Old Doc Yak drives a rental car to a pigs' farm to collect on a bill. The pigs hit Old Doc Yak with a board, tie his automobile to a utility pole, catch him in a rope, crash his own rental car into him while suspended from that rope, and finally eject him off a cliff when his car rams into a roadside barrier. Every panel in the comic strip uses a similar perspective and orientation, and in each panel except the first, motion lines, sound effects, and exhaust clouds abound. The sheer speed captured in the comic strip's panels gives the narrative a sense of powerful forward momentum, even as the actions and intentions of the comic strip's characters are impossible and

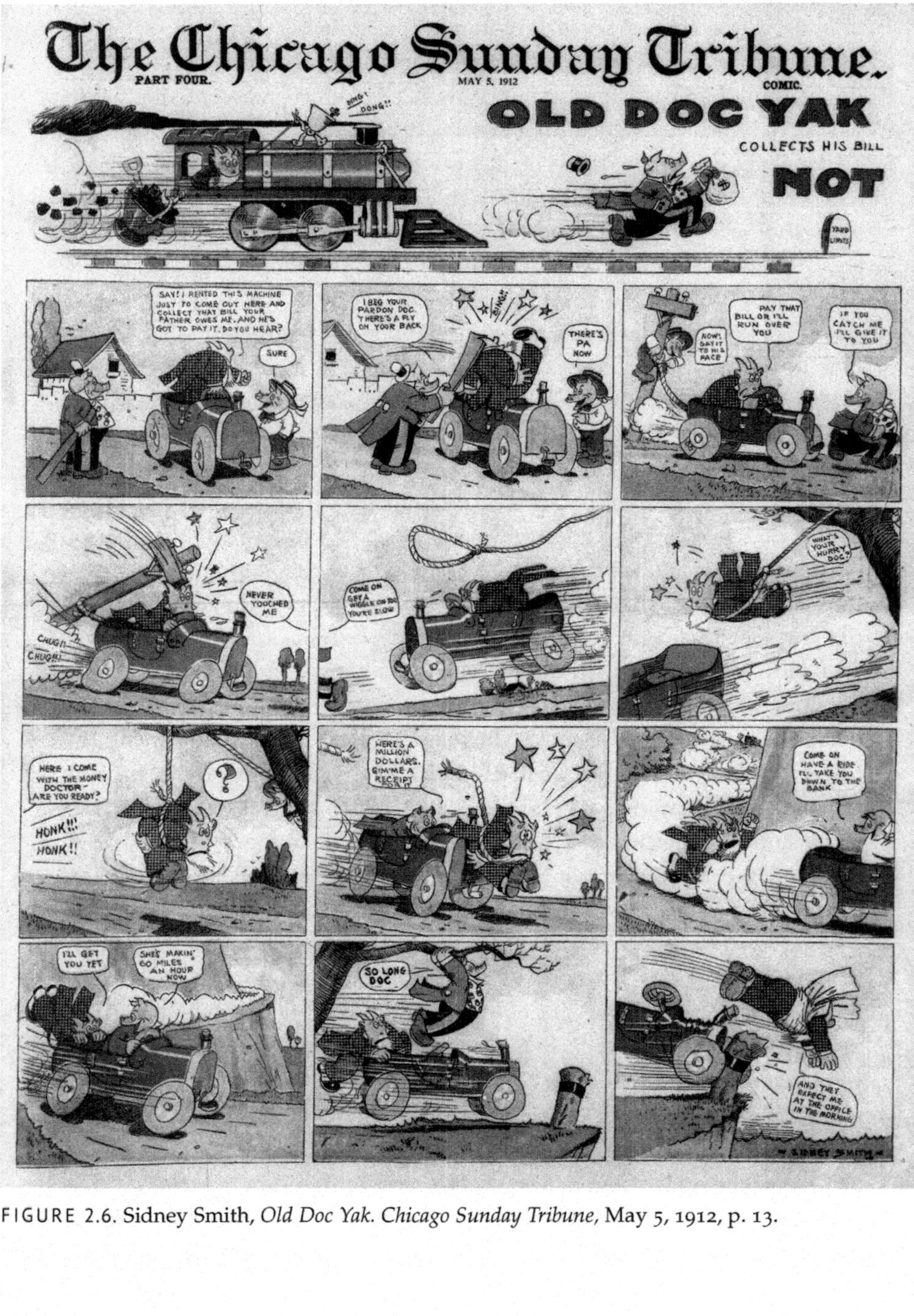

FIGURE 2.6. Sidney Smith, *Old Doc Yak. Chicago Sunday Tribune*, May 5, 1912, p. 13.

confounding. The only logic in *Old Doc Yak* is forward movement, powered by a machine that exceeds the boundaries of biology and physics.

Old Doc Yak glorifies the automobile through slapstick action, and fittingly, the comic's creator, Sidney Smith, endorsed automobiles and identified with them as signs of success. In 1917 Smith and his character Old Doc Yak appeared in an advertisement for Detroit's King Motor Company. Old Doc Yak is drawn sitting atop his roadster, and in the ad's text, Smith praises his King automobile: "It will climb hills on high that even Old Doc Yak's car could not back down" (King Motor). The madcap driving in Smith's comic strips connects quite literally to real-world driving in this advertisement, and Smith concludes his ad copy with jokes that his car "goes so slow on high through congested traffic that the sparrows build nests between the spokes and it is so quiet running that you can hear a pin drop in the mud." This idyllic vision of a quiet, peaceful automobile is as possible as Old Doc Yak's impossibly flexible roadster.

Even in Sidney Smith's comics that do not feature automobiles, the kinetic power of fossil fuels directs the narrative. In the February 9, 1917, installment of Smith's *The Gumps,* for example, the husband, Andrew, tries to light a kitchen stove. When he finally gets it lit, the gas ignites powerfully, blowing him out of the panel with an explosion. In the final panel of the strip, Andrew is surrounded by smoke and clutter, and exclaims, "Oh Min!" (Blackbeard 72). This familiar four-panel sequencing—two panels of buildup, one panel of action, and a final closing joke—depicts natural gas combustion as funny, of course, but also as destructive. It blows the human out of the panel, forcing his body to move at an inhuman speed. Yet, the strip's final panel reassures the reader that it is both possible and funny to live with this kinetic possibility.

In 1923 Sidney Smith's status as a celebrity cartoonist was trumpeted in an advertisement for the *Chicago Tribune* newspapers syndicate. With the headline "Creator of Gumps Signs a Million Dollar Contract and Rides Off in This Car," the text describes Smith's ten-year contract with the syndicate: "It is the highest salary paid by any newspaper to a cartoonist. The contract was sealed by the gift of a Rolls-Royce Automobile" ("Creator"). The luxury automobile connotes the success of Smith's comic strip, as well as its modern pace. Life speeds along for the Gumps, just as it does for Sidney Smith the artist and the daily readers of his comic strip. The artist and the comic strip, along with the newspaper and its readers, are bound together by a shared enthusiasm for fossil-fueled power.

The Domestication of the Automobile

As the above examples show, the automobile featured prominently in American newspaper comics of the 1910s and 1920s, and fossil fuel power is normalized as an energy of everyday life in many American newspaper comics of this time. Benoît Crucifix describes this transition in comic strips' representation of automobiles: "the car as a fantastical attraction would quickly subside as it became more and more common to drive around. And so, simultaneously with the democratization of the automobile, comic strips would increasingly turn to narrative continuity and family melodrama in which the cars take on a completely different role." For example, one of Fontaine Fox's Toonerville cartoons invokes the domestication of the automobile for laughs (figure 2.7). Tomboy Taylor stands on the family's running automobile, letting the car's vibrations assist her in dancing the "shimmy." It is commonplace now for us to think of cars as extensions of human bodies and personalities—so many car narratives, from Hanna-Barbera's *Wacky Races* television show (1968–69) to the *Fast and the Furious* film franchise (2001–present), have relied on the equation of character with car—yet here in this single-panel cartoon, the automobile is not just an extension of the body but a way of remaking the body. The car gives Tomboy Taylor a new way of moving, one that, as her brother remarks in the comics' joke, she would not be able to do by herself. Even the seemingly metabolic act of dancing is here interpreted as the combustion of fossil fuels.

In 1934 the Shell Oil Company printed Toonerville Folks masks and signs for a promotional campaign which made evident a long-running connection between comic strips and fossil fuel industries. Like Sidney Smith's character Old Doc Yak, Fontaine Fox's Toonerville characters connote a folksy past, and customers at participating Shell gas stations could wear the paper face of the Toonerville Trolley's conductor or passenger while driving away, masquerading as figures from a simpler time and place. Mentioned earlier in this chapter, Shell also used Bud Fisher's Mutt and Jeff characters in this campaign, and the act of imaginatively stepping into the role of a comic strip character curiously encourages gasoline consumers to dissociate petroleum from modern technology. Associated with the old-timey qualities of the Toonerville Trolley, gasoline and gas stations become homey mainstays of American life, quaint fixtures of the landscape rather than modern commodities and vertically integrated businesses. As comics historians Robert L. Beerbohm and Richard D. Olson explain, Shell's advertising campaign was extensive:

FIGURE 2.7. Fontaine Fox, *Tomboy Taylor. Toonerville Trolley and Other Cartoons,* Cupples and Leon, 1921, p. 18. The Ohio State University, Billy Ireland Cartoon Library and Museum.

Beginning with the March-April 1934 issue of *Shell Globe,* characters from Bud Fisher (*Mutt & Jeff*) and Fontaine Fox (*Toonerville Folks*) were licensed to sell gas & oil for this company. 52,000 eight foot standees were made for Fisher's Mutt and Jeff and Fox's Powerful Katrinka and The Skipper for placement around 13,000 Shell gas stations. Augmenting them was an army

> of 250,000 miniature figures of the same characters. In addition, more than 1,000,000 play masks were given away to children along with more than 285,000 window stickers. If that wasn't enough, hundreds of thousands of 3x5 foot posters featuring these characters were released in conjunction with twenty-four sheet outdoor billboards. Radio announcements of this promotion began running April 7th, 1934. (298)

In a similar style, Standard Oil commissioned ads from Otto Soglow featuring his *Little King* comic strip character, and Tydol Gasoline also ran advertisements with Soglow cartoon illustrations.[4] Themselves a product of industrial printing and distribution systems, comics domesticated fossil fuels, depicting them as both a natural resource of the traditional American landscape and a consumer product.

Like *Gasoline Gus* and *Otto Auto,* the long-running comic strip *Gasoline Alley* was initially premised on automobile antics, yet the comic strip expanded to include domestic humor and melodrama. In Frank King's *Gasoline Alley* comic strips from 1921, the bachelor mechanic Walt finds a baby on his doorstep. He names the child Skeezix, and for his first weeks of unexpected fatherhood, Walt describes the fussy baby as a malfunctioning automobile. In the February 23, 1921, comic strip, Walt holds the infant Skeezix and remarks that he has "been reading up in the book Skeezix—and I'm getting to be a technical expert. Keep your tank full is the first rule" (King, *Walt and Skeezix*). He goes on to further compare the baby to a car, commenting on his "wheelbase," "body finish," "upholstery," and "three-point suspension." *Gasoline Alley* returns to these kinds of jokes again and again, finding humor in the ironic juxtaposition of automobiles with domestic life, while also reinforcing the automobile's gradual transformation of and absorption into everyday life. Starting in 1918 and still a syndicated comic strip in 2024, *Gasoline Alley* is one of the longest-running newspaper comics in the United States. At more than a century old, *Gasoline Alley*'s shift from automobile-themed comedy during the car's emergence as a mass-market consumer product to a multigenerational family narrative evokes the automobile's imbrication in everyday life. In the January 14, 1921, *Gasoline Alley* comic strip, the polarization that accompanies the automobile is made clear. In the two-panel comic strip, Walt first complains about traffic while he is a pedestrian: "You can't even get across the streets any more. Something ought to be done about it!" (King, *Walt and Skeezix*). In the second and final panel, Walt drives a car, and he complains from the other perspective: "Pedestrians are

4. See Gardner, "American King," 30.

an awful bother! They ought to pass some laws to regulate 'em!" From one panel to the next, automobiles shift from being a modern inconvenience to a normative, even righteous way of moving through space.

Automobiles first appear as a consumer product in early twentieth-century newspaper comic strips, and by the 1920s, automobiles were a facet of daily life in American comics and culture. Comic strips promoted automobile travel and presented fossil fuel consumption as a natural component of domestic life. In *Gasoline Alley,* for example, Walt and Avery go on a transcontinental automobile race that lasted nearly two months in the daily comic strip, from June 18 to August 9, 1923. Readers followed the drivers along their journey "from 42nd and Broadway, New York City," to San Francisco, a trip that promoted tourist travel and car-camping throughout the nation (King, "Gasoline"). This embrace of the automobile in American culture signals a growing reliance on fossil fuels in the United States. As gasoline markets expanded in the first decades of the twentieth century, the American oil industry grew dramatically. A mass media form that helped to facilitate the transition to coal, comics continued to do so as automobiles, petroleum products, and their attendant services proliferated on American roads. As fossil fuels became a fixture of American life, comics visualized the new energy culture that developed with them.

CHAPTER 3

The Petrochemical Origins of the Comic Book

The Anti-Life Equation, the Cosmic Cube, the Infinity Gauntlet, the Speed Force, and Vibranium are just a few of the comic book concepts that make fantasies of fossil fuel energy into powerful narrative devices. These comic book creations represent how fossil fuels facilitate the acceleration of time and manifest forces beyond human abilities. Comics also allegorize oil politics in genre narratives, consolidating fossil fuel's imbrication in global politics through archetypal figures. In DC Comics, for example, a 1980s character named the Duke of Oil is an android with the brain of Texas oil baron Earl Dukeston. He is controlled by stockholders in his oil company who have promised to grow him a new human body.[1] In 1980s Marvel Comics, Sheikh Farouk Al-Fasaud comes from the fictional oil-rich Kingdom of Aqiria, and when his attempt to assassinate a journalist goes awry, he is transformed into Fasaud, a living television signal with a plan to take over global broadcasting.[2] The Duke of Oil and Fasaud are clearly symbols of late twentieth-century oil politics, and they are surface indicators of the dominance of petroleum and petrochemicals in modern American culture. From these

1. The Duke of Oil appears in DC Comics' *The Outsiders* nos. 6–7 (1986) and *Green Arrow,* vol. 3, nos. 47–48 (2005).

2. Fasaud appears in Marvel Comics' *Fantastic Four* nos. 308–10 (1987–88).

1980s oil villains back to the wholesome, automobile-powered families of 1930s gas station giveaway comics, this chapter explores the range of comics that were inspired and sometimes even published by the American fossil fuel industry in the middle decades of the twentieth century.

Starting in the 1930s, the United States used a dramatically increasing amount of petroleum, surpassing coal by the 1950s. Like the transition to coal in earlier decades, the oil transition was not automatic or natural. Oil corporations used advertising and publicity widely in this period of transition, depicting automobiles, gasoline, and petroleum products as part of a happy, healthy American lifestyle.[3] During and after World War II, petroleum products rapidly increased in number and variety. By the late 1950s, as noted by political scientist Adam Hanieh, petrochemicals accounted for "just under 90 percent" of American organic chemical production, an indicator that petroleum had become "the fulcrum of the world's energy regime" (37). This transition to oil was accomplished, in part, through the new medium of the comic book, a print culture innovation that was widely used by oil companies, automobile makers, tire manufacturers, and government institutions to encourage the consumption of oil, gas, and their many by-products. In so doing, the fossil fuel industry's narratives of futuristic technology, primitive exploration, and superhuman power became rooted in the history of comics and inflected the genres, characters, and tropes that took form in American comic books.

Oil Comics

In the early 1930s, Eastern Color Printing Company worked with Standard Oil of Indiana and Gulf Oil to develop comics that connected petroleum and petrochemicals to domestic and fantasy life. As comics historians Robert L. Beerbohm and Richard D. Olson chronicled, the comic book format was "created out of desperation, to keep the printing presses rolling" during the Great Depression:

> Eastern Color printed the comic sections for a score of newspapers along the eastern seaboard, including the *Boston Globe*, the *Brooklyn Times*, the *Providence Journal*, and the *Newark Ledger*. Down-time meant less take-home pay, so [Eastern Color sales manager Harry I.] Wildenberg was always racking his brains for something to fit the color presses. He was fascinated

3. For a cultural history of American car culture, see Seiler.

> by the miles of funny sheets which rolled off Eastern's presses each week, and he constantly sought new ways to exploit their commercial possibilities. If the funny papers were this popular, he reasoned, they should prove a good advertising medium. He decided to suggest a comics tabloid to a client. (298)

Eastern Color printed the tabloid-sized, four-page *Standard Oil Comics* from 1932 to 1934, and the similar four-page *Gulf Funny Weekly* from 1933 to 1941. Originally titled *Gulf Comic Weekly* for its first four issues, *Gulf Funny Weekly* was printed in a smaller, magazine-sized format starting in 1939. "Probably the first tabloid newspaper comic published for American distribution outside of a newspaper in the 20th century," *Standard Oil Comics,* along with *Gulf Funny Weekly,* contributed to the development of the comic book as a commercial product, and as Beerbohm and Olson note, "Wildenberg and Gulf were astonished when the tabloids were grabbed up as fast as Gulf service stations could offer them. Distribution shot up to 3,000,000 copies a week after Gulf changed the name to *Gulf Funny Weekly* with its 5th issue" (298). In 1933 Wildenberg and his Eastern Color Printing colleagues Max Gaines and Lev Gleason (both of whom would become comic book editors and publishers) published a work in the modern format of the comic book, the thirty-six-page *Famous Funnies,* while printing promotional comics like the four-page *Gulf Funny Weekly* and *Standard Oil Comics.*[4]

Standard Oil Comics and *Gulf Funny Weekly* were newsprint advertising pamphlets, and they resemble the Sunday newspaper comics section familiar to millions of American families in the early 1930s. Each issue of *Standard Oil Comics* and *Gulf Funny Weekly* contained original comic strips, along with advertisements, games, and informational features.[5] *Standard Oil Comics* published longtime newspaper comics artist Frederick Burr Opper's *Si and Mirandi* on its cover page, a comic strip about a couple with a stubborn mule named Maud, for a number of issues, and other issues featured Walter Oehrle's comic strip *Goofus McVittle* with the subtitle "He's from the Big City," about the mishaps of the title character when he moves to a farm.[6]

4. For a history of Eastern Color Printing and 1930s comic books, see Gabilliet 7–12.

5. The American Oil Company, known as Amoco, also sponsored an early comic, a 1933 edition of Whitman Publishing's *Mickey Mouse: The Mail Pilot.* Whitman published these "big little books," featuring one image per page paired with text, starting in 1932. Amoco was acquired by the Standard Oil Company of Indiana in 1925, so it is probable that both *Mickey Mouse: The Mail Pilot* and *Standard Oil Comics* were produced from different branches of the same corporation.

6. Information about *Standard Oil Comics* is scarce. According to the Grand Comics Database, there were approximately thirty-three issues published. I have not found any copies of *Standard Oil Comics* in any library or museum as of this writing.

Opper's *Si and Mirandi* comic strip was licensed through Hearst's International Features Syndicate, part of a boom in comics advertising during the early 1930s. As Jackson Lears describes, "national advertisers had used cartoon characters for years, but not until 1931 did they discover the comic strip, when a full-page comics-strip ad for Grape-Nuts, titled 'Suburban Joe,' appeared in Hearst's *Comic Weekly*. Other advertisers quickly followed suit, and soon the funny pages were among the most desirable advertising space in newspapers" (330). *Standard Oil Comics* published comic strips that likewise advertised petroleum products and the lifestyles cultivated with them. In a 1933 edition of *Standard Oil Comics*, for example, a professor tries to blow up Si and Mirandi's cantankerous mule, but the professor is himself blown up when the mule kicks him onto his explosive and Si drops an apple basket on the trigger (color plate 3.1). In the final panel, the professor rests in bed, bandage wrapped around his head, punching a toy mule in the face while exclaiming, "I don't like mules!" (Opper, "Si and Mirandi"). The particular copy of *Standard Oil Comics* in color plate 3.1 is addressed to "Rural Route Box Holder / Gowrie Iowa." A small town in northern Iowa with a 1930 population of 1,059, Gowrie citizens likely used a mix of horses, mules, and gasoline-powered engines for transportation and labor when this comics pamphlet was distributed. Directed at rural readers, *Standard Oil Comics* introduces fossil fuels as a solution to stubborn and unpredictable livestock, demonstrating by counterexample that engines are more reliable than mules. The transition to fossil fuels is accomplished here not by explosive technological innovation but by the daily ubiquity of the comic strip, the creation of fossil fuels as an ever-present reality in rural life. The joke in *Si and Mirandi* hinges on the superiority of fossil fuel energy to comical livestock.

The American comic strip was already structured around fossil fuel tropes by the 1930s, and Opper had even drawn caricatures of John D. Rockefeller and the Oil Trust in the 1900s for Hearst's *New York Journal*. *Standard Oil Comics* uses the explosive, slapstick humor of the comic strip in order to portray the horsepower regime as cruel and inefficient. The message is clear that mules are a waste of time and a danger. By contrast, the interior of this four-page *Standard Oil Comics* pamphlet offers readers a vision of modern transportation in Sid Hix's *Smiling Slim* comic, named after its heroic lead character, a Standard Oil agent who helps to repair a poorly running car with "Iso-Vis 'D' 20-W for moderately cold weather." Unlike the mule in Opper's *Si and Mirandi*, the car is easily serviced with Standard Oil products by Smiling Slim. The car smiles and laughs in the final two panels, providing the kind of amenable companionship that Maud the mule cannot muster.

Standard Oil Comics was published by Standard Oil of Indiana, one of the thirty-four companies created after the breakup of the Standard Oil of

New Jersey trust in 1911. Eight of those thirty-four companies continued to operate under the "Standard Oil" name. As Paul Giddens has documented, Standard Oil appeared and operated as a singular corporate entity after its breakup: "even though the companies were separate and independent, the general public failed to make any distinction and continued to think of them—even to this day—as a single company. The same seven individuals who had held a majority of stock in Standard of New Jersey held a majority of the stock in each [Standard Oil company]. Each of the marketing companies continued to market in the territory originally assigned to it, and for some years they did not actively compete with one another" (355–56). This détente dissolved by the 1920s due to competition from new oil fields in the American West, increased demand for gasoline following the widespread transition to the automobile, and mergers between Standard Oil companies and other oil operators. Giddens reports that in the 1920s, "all former marketing units of Standard not only rapidly expanded their operations within their original marketing territories but sought a share of other potentially rich markets. They invaded the marketing territories of the other Standard companies and competed with Gulf, the Texas Company, Sinclair, Shell, Cities Service, Phillips, and other oil companies" (358). With advertisements for Standard Oil of Indiana's Iso-Vis motor oil, *Standard Oil Comics* is the product of this intensive period of oil expansion and abundance, and just like *Gulf Funny Weekly,* it was published by a vertically integrated oil company that projected affordable and easily available fossil fuels as ubiquitous to a good life.

Distributed at Gulf Oil's branded service stations, *Gulf Funny Weekly* typically contained a humor comic on its front page, an adventure comic on its back page, and a mix of advertisements, humor comics, and nonfiction cartoons on its two interior pages.[7] The January 10, 1941, issue of *Gulf Funny Weekly,* for example, opens with Vic Tor's *Curly and the Kids,* in which Curly and another boy race down a hill on skis. In the bottom two panels, the pair loops through one panel and into the other, traveling between the panels' gutter and ending the page-long comic strip with an explosion of motion lines and sound effects (color plate 3.2).[8] Curly speeds in his comic

7. As with *Standard Oil Comics,* information about *Gulf Funny Weekly* is scarce. According to the Grand Comics Database, there were 422 issues published between 1933 and 1941. There are three issues of the series in the Comic Art Collection at Michigan State University, and there are no other library or museum collections of the title as of this writing.

8. Vic Tor might have been a pen name of Stan Schendel, who was credited with the adventure comic strip *Wings Winfair* that also ran in *Gulf Funny Weekly.* See Adcock.

strip, just as cars speed along on the road. No matter what accident befalls Curly, he will land on his feet, unharmed. It is an exciting yet ultimately therapeutic message for the automobile traveler. In *Gulf Funny Weekly*'s interior, a mix of illustrated features and comic strips present the Gulf brand as a part of everyday life. In the January 10, 1941, issue, an advertisement for Gulf's *Screen Guild Theater* radio show dispenses personal information about famous actors like Joan Crawford and Robert Preston, and Graham Hunter's humorous "Potent Poetry" promotes Gulf's "No-Nox" gasoline. Like its immediate predecessor, *Standard Oil Comics, Gulf Funny Weekly* was designed to give both children and adults something to read during a drive or a stop at a filling station. The promotional comics built an association between automobile travel and the comics medium that was more transparently exuberant and without the editorial context of the newspapers, wherein the fossil fuel industry was often caricatured and critiqued. Gulf's and Standard Oil's comic book pamphlets published comic strips that doubled as petroleum advertisements, directing the fast speeds, exaggerated actions, and fantastic adventures of the comics into the establishment of oil as the dominant energy source of modern America.

The Fossil Fuel Industry's Comic Books

Eastern Color's *Gulf Funny Weekly* and *Standard Oil Comics* are just two examples of industry-sponsored comics that advertised petroleum products. As discussed in chapter 2, *Shell Globe* magazine featured Bud Fisher's *Mutt and Jeff* and Fontaine Fox's *Toonerville Folks,* in conjunction with a 1934 Shell promotional campaign. Published by the Magnolia Oil Company in Texas, the trade magazine *Magnolia Oil News* also included back-cover comics with a recurring character named "Magnolene Mike, D.L." When Magnolene Mike introduces himself in March 1918, he explains that the "D.L." stands for "Dependable Lubricant," and then in April 1918, Mike sets out for France, newly enlisted to fight in the World War. Mike and his trusty can of Magnolia Motor Oil repair the failing engine of a military steamship, a broken-down British tank, and a jammed machine gun. Magnolene Mike appeared on the back cover of *Magnolia Oil News* every month through February 1928, just one month shy of the comic strip's ten-year anniversary.[9]

9. I consulted the New York Public Library's collection of *Magnolia Oil News* for this information. The periodical does not seem to be available through any digital archives as of this writing.

Another early comic book artifact is John Rosenfeld Jr. and Jack I. Patton's *Texas History Movies,* originally published as a newspaper comic strip in the *Dallas Morning News* from 1926 to 1928. The Magnolia Oil Company sponsored the publication of a sixty-four-page paperback edition of *Texas History Movies* in 1932, and this comic was meant to be primarily educational rather than humorous. Reprinted in multiple editions, the book was used in Texas public schools through the 1960s. In *Texas History Movies,* Anglo settlers fight against racist caricatures of Mexicans and Native Americans, ultimately accomplishing the formation of the modern state of Texas. *Texas History Movies* concludes in 1885, without any representation of the oil industry or iconic landmarks like Spindletop, the site of a 1901 oil gusher that led to the formation of Gulf Oil and Texaco. Yet through Magnolia Oil's sponsorship of the comic book, the twentieth-century oil industry itself implicitly continues the Texan "march of progress" initiated by "Spanish priests" and "hardy Anglo-Saxon colonists" (Patton 217).[10]

Texas History Movies is just one example of the oil industry's sponsorship of historical narratives that conclude with fossil-fueled progress. Published by Standard Oil of Ohio in celebration of Ohio's sesquicentennial in 1953, the comic book *Land of the Pioneers: A Story of Ohio* tells the story of the fictional "Goode" family from the Revolutionary War to the 1950s. After learning this history, the recent college graduate Tom Goode declares to his proud family that he plans to work for Standard Oil of Ohio "as a research engineer in their laboratories. You see, I want to be a pioneer, too . . . like the rest of the Goodes!" (14). In the comics' conclusion, the Goode family drives past a new Standard Oil refinery—"There's one of the new frontiers!" exclaims Tom—and the comic book closes with a message that, by juxtaposition, associates democratic values with the availability of fossil fuels: "In America, anyone can build his own future as long as we have freedom and opportunity for everyone! Let's make sure we keep it this way!" (15). Standard Oil of Ohio's assertion that petroleum engineers are "modern pioneers" fuses the colonialist practices of westward expansion to the extraction and refining of fossil fuels. Rather than claiming land as property for US settlements, as the Goode's pioneer ancestors accomplish in the early pages of *Land of the Pioneers,* the Standard Oil Company of Ohio claims mineral rights; constructs drills, refineries, and pipelines; emits pollution; and encourages the consumption of oil. The comic casts these stages of capitalist development in the United States—settler colonialism, fossil fuel extraction, and the creation

10. For a more thorough analysis of Rosenfield and Patton's *Texas History Movies,* see Worden.

of polluted sacrifice zones—as unquestionably good developments that constitute America's upward arc in the twentieth century.

Today, the fossil fuel industry sponsors major museums and other cultural institutions to greenwash their devastating practices.[11] In the middle decades of the twentieth century, fossil fuel companies in the United States also used comics to communicate fossil fuel ideologies. Many fossil fuel–sponsored comics were printed and distributed as single-issue promotional giveaways, like Eastern Color Printing's 1939 *Pure-Oil Comics.* In 1942 Standard Oil published the World War II–themed comic book *Blockbusters from Oil!* celebrating its Toluene petrochemical, used in the manufacture of TNT explosives. In 1946 Standard Oil of New Jersey celebrated the war's end and advertised its refining capacity in *Superfuel for Superplanes.* This comic book was drawn by artist Al Plastino, who would go on to draw *Superman* for DC Comics in the 1950s. In 1951 the Ethyl Corporation partnered with Standard Oil of Kentucky to publish *More Power to You!,* a thirty-two-page comic book encouraging motorists to purchase new cars that take advantage of newer engines and fuel additives. The American Gas Association published a 1947 comic book titled *History of Gas,* drawn by comic book artist Jack Sparling, who would go on to draw *Plastic Man* and many other superhero comics by the 1960s. The comic book features a blue-haired narrator named "Miss Flame," who personifies the domestication of natural gas in American households as a cooking and heating fuel (color plate 3.3). The American Gas Association also published a more straightforward educational comic book titled *The History of Natural Gas* that went through four print editions from 1960 to 1979. In these comics, fossil fuels are both a modern innovation and an ancient energy source, ever-present and available without any long-term consequences for the climate.

The American Petroleum Institute published *The Story of Colonel Drake* in 1954, telling the story of Edwin Drake's famed oil well in Titusville, Pennsylvania. The comic portrays the fossil fuel industry as both historical and modern, a part of America's treasured past that is perpetually driven to remake the world through rail, road, pipeline, and automation.[12] This sense of fossil-fueled progress is portrayed as irreversible and exponential. The comic book's concluding text box states:

---

11. For accounts of the fossil fuel industry's sponsorship of arts and entertainment, see Dahlquist and Vonderau; Evans.

12. Edwin Drake, Titusville, and the visual culture of oil are also discussed in Barrett, "Picturing a Crude Past," and Black.

> Drake's well brought about an immediate revolution in the American way of life, but progress has been even more rapid during the 20th century. Great grandma and granddad thought it was wonderful when they were able to buy kerosene and then gasoline and lubricants at the general store. But TODAY a whole host of new or better oil products, as well as endless services, are provided by a marketing network composed of over 29,400 wholesalers and about 200,000 service stations. In other words: In a thousand ways, all of which grow out of the progressive, competitive nature of the entire petroleum industry . . . OIL SERVES YOU. (15, capitalization and ellipses in original)[13]

The message to readers is that fossil fuels facilitate the midcentury American way of life, and fossil fuel–sponsored comics unsurprisingly present this carbon-intensive way of life as an ideal.

The strong connection between American identity at midcentury and fossil fuel consumption is emphasized in other promotional comics, as well. In *Travel Tykes Weekly,* a newspaper comics pamphlet sponsored by Standard Oil of California, readers are encouraged to follow Mickey Mouse and Donald Duck's race to the Golden Gate International Exposition of San Francisco Bay in 1939. Each issue was published with two cartoons that could be affixed to a large map of the United States to form a comic strip–like border, fusing the cross-country road trip to nationalist pedagogy. Other promotional comics encouraged the consumption of petrochemicals, like the comic books published by B. F. Goodrich that celebrate the increasing reliance on petroleum in rubber manufacturing: *Wonder Book of Rubber* (1947), *Johnson Makes the Team* (ca. 1948–50), *Tommy Gets the Keys* (ca. 1954), and *Tommy Looks at Farming* (ca. 1955). Goodrich's *Wonder Book of Rubber* was updated and kept in print from 1947 to 1971, and the company also published a sales manual in comic book form titled *T. B. Angel in "Take a Little Tip from Me!"* in 1959 that provided "more slants on selling tires, batteries, accessories." Goodrich advertised rubber-soled sneakers in 1962's *P.F. Magic Shoes,* and the United States Rubber Company published comics promoting bicycle tires in 1949's *Bike Comics* and children's shoes in 1965's *Kolonel Keds and His Exciting Bell Rocket Belt.*

Automobile companies also published promotional comics, like the Ford Motor Company's *How to Be an Expert Driver* (1947) and *What One Farm Family Found Out about the New Ford Tractors!* (1955). Other automotive

---

13. The American Petroleum Institute also produced a short film about Drake in 1954 titled *Born in Freedom: The Story of Colonel Drake* and starring actor Vincent Price in the lead role. Drake also features in the French comics series *Lucky Luke,* in a story originally published in 1962 (Morris and Goscinny).

companies published comics, like *Woody Woodpecker in Chevrolet Wonderland* (1954), Dodge Motor's *Roy Rogers and the Man from Dodge City* (1955), and *Walt Disney's Davy Crockett in the Raid at Piney Creek* (1955), advertising Hudson brand automobiles. Mobil Oil published a comic book adaptation of the television Western *The Sheriff of Cochise* in 1957, and similarly associating oil with the Western genre, Richfield Oil published *Rockets and Range Riders* in 1957. Some promotional comics presented a public safety message, like *It's Fun to Stay Alive* (1948), a comic book published by the Ohio Automobile Dealers Association, and the Chrysler Corporation's *Do You Have What It Takes to Drive Like a Pro?* (1961).

In their 1940s and 1950s Adventures in Science series, General Electric published a wide range of educational comics that featured fossil fuel energy, such as *Adventures in Electricity* (1947) and *Adventures inside the Atom* (1948). Best known today as EC Comics, Educational Comics published a series of Reddy Kilowatt comic books promoting electricity, beginning with the film tie-in *Reddy Kilowatt in Reddy Made Magic* in 1946 and continuing through the 1960s. A licensed cartoon character representing the industry, Reddy Kilowatt explains and celebrates the "ready" availability of electricity in the midcentury United States. Created in 1926 by Ashton B. Collins Sr., the commercial manager of the Alabama Power Company, Reddy Kilowatt is anthropomorphic electricity, with a light bulb for a nose and electrical outlets for ears. As Kirstin Moana Thompson has documented,

> with mat or template print advertisements, as well as newsletters, database surveys, mailings and an extensive array of promotional gifts emblazoned with the cheery spokescharacter, by 1938 Reddy Kilowatt was everywhere, appearing on a quarter of 24 million utility customer bills and licensed by over 300 companies worldwide from Australia to Mexico, with the company boasting that their spokescharacter "may even become as popular with [children] as Mickey Mouse or Popeye." . . . Reddy Kilowatt translated the abstraction of electricity into an appealing and highly personable spokescharacter, targeting different rural and industrial workplaces and consumer markets, while also cleverly presenting power bills in labour terms as "cheap wages." As an anthropomorphized, yet gender flexible figure who was also marked by implicit notions of class and race, Reddy paradoxically was both humanized and a mechanical symbol of modernity's values for speed, efficiency and convenience. (128–29)

Widely disseminated through print materials, Reddy Kilowatt was a product of the massive increase in electricity production and usage in the early twentieth-century United States, an intensification of energy consumption that began in major cities and gradually expanded across the countryside. Historian Christopher F. Jones summarizes the rapid expansion of electricity at this time: "By 1930, cheap and abundant energy had transformed the ways millions lived, worked, and played. Energy consumption had increased 250 percent over the first three decades of the twentieth century, more than twice the rate of population growth" (224). Moreover, "the production of electricity grew nearly twenty-fold from 1902 to 1930, supporting a tripling of American industrial output" (225). Reddy Kilowatt, then, expressed this massive increase in electricity through a domesticated cartoon persona.

The Ford Motor Company also published two educational comic books, titled *The Story of Mass Production* (1947) and *The Story of Mass Assembly* (1948). Edited by educational sociologist Harvey Zorbaugh, these comics pamphlets were distributed to Detroit Public Schools in part to recruit students into labor at Ford factories. In 1949 Zorbaugh cowrote an essay with Mildred Gilman in *Family Circle* magazine titled "What Can YOU Do about Comic Books?" Weighing in on the late 1940s comics controversy, Zorbaugh and Gilman argued that comic books were merely a reflection of their historical moment: "The times are out of joint. Aggressive forces let loose in the world have caused two world wars and have started rumblings of a third. How can comic books be blamed—and some blame them almost exclusively—for an increase in violence and delinquency?" (63). Zorbaugh and Gilman argue that comics can in fact remedy social problems and help young readers develop appropriate values: "Our only safeguard to help the young people entrusted to us is to develop an emotional stability, a maturity, and a sense of values that will keep the comics in their place, as entertainment, release, or aid to education, to be outgrown in time for mature satisfactions" (63). Promotional, educational, and public service comic books blend entertainment with education, the energetic sequences of visual images juxtaposed with optimistic messages about triumphant industrialism and the American spirit.[14] For Ford and many other fossil fuel–dependent American companies at midcentury, comic books were less a threat to than a mouthpiece for American values.

Not limited to the newer automobile and petroleum industries, these comic books championed fossil fuels more broadly as well. The Association of American Railroads' School and College Service published at least eleven comic books between 1954 and 1966. *Rails across America* (ca. 1954) is a conventionally educational comic wherein Uncle Sam accompanies a

14. For a study of government-sponsored comics, see Graham.

boy named Jimmie Wilson on a tour through railroad history. 1958's *Special Agent: A Picture Story about the Railroad Police* uses the genre conventions of crime and detective comics to heroize "the saving of lives and property and the prevention of crimes" accomplished by the railroad police, who "safeguard more than 233,000 miles of road and 389,000 miles of track operated by the railroads—and the more than 400,000,000 passengers as well as the billions of dollars' worth of freight transported by the railroads annually."[15] The miles of road and track, the number of passengers, and the piles of freight are vast yet under control, rationalized and overseen by well-trained officers who were once, perhaps, much like a young reader of the 1958 *Special Agent* comic book. Comics romanticize and glorify the dominance of coal and oil in midcentury America through narratives that instruct young readers to consume, value, and work with fossil fuels.

Fantasies of Power

From *Standard Oil Comics* and *Gulf Funny Weekly* to a wide range of promotional giveaways throughout the 1940s and 1950s, comic books circulated through the fossil fuel industry, its customers, and its employees. Yet comics also circulated through newsstands at an increasing rate in the 1930s. In 1934, just one year after launching *Standard Oil Comics,* Eastern Color Printing published *Famous Funnies* #1, a comic book that sold for ten cents. As Jean-Paul Gabilliet states in his cultural history of American comics, the number of comics publishers rapidly increased, from just one publisher in 1933 to "more than fifty in 1939," and "even more significant was the evolution of the number of releases: 3 comic magazines appeared in 1933, 16 in 1934, 19 in 1935, 79 in 1936, 163 in 1937, 224 in 1928, and 322 in 1939" (17). During the Great Depression, the increase in inexpensive comic books was possible due to the increased production capacities of fossil-fueled printing and transportation. *Famous Funnies,* for example, would run for 218 issues, ending in 1955 at the end of American comics' "Golden Age."[16] *Famous Funnies* #1 reprinted, among other newspaper comic strips, a series of *Hairbreadth Harry* comics. An adventure comic strip originally created by C. W. Kahles in 1906, *Hairbreadth Harry* was written and drawn by F. O. Alexander in 1934, and it featured recurring damsel-in-distress scenarios. One of the

15. *Special Agent: A Picture Story about the Railroad Police* is attributed to Bill Bunce by the Hagley Museum and Library.

16. For a concise history of comic book publishing, see Hatfield, "Comic Books."

Hairbreadth Harry comics pages to appear in *Famous Funnies* #1 invokes the ways in which comics were buoyed by fossil fuel power.

Set in the fictional nation of Blotskia, the first installment of *Hairbreadth Harry* in *Famous Funnies* begins with the strip's titular hero Harry working "to bring in an oil gusher" (color plate 3.4).[17] The comic strip's perpetual damsel-in-distress, Belinda Blinks, plans to "christen" the new oil well, but she is abducted, in typical fashion for the comic strip, by the mustachioed villain Rudolph Rassendale. When Rudolph throws Belinda out of a flying plane, Harry brings in his oil well with a "depth bomb," and the resulting oil geyser catches Belinda midfall. In the strip's final panel, Harry exclaims, "There, skeptics! Your oil! Shut in the flow slowly so as to lower the girl gently," while Belinda exclaims, "A pretty bum way to christen an oil-well, if you ask me!" A silhouette in a cloud-like geyser of oil, Belinda has been saved by Harry's masterful control of fossil fuel resources. A heroic pulp adventurer, Hairbreadth Harry is a fantasy of not just masculine power but also geological control. In this comic strip, the explosive power of fossil fuels is wielded safely and confidently by a hero, typically white, male, and American. With a name that denotes his precise timing of the oil gusher, Hairbreadth Harry saves the damsel in distress with oil.

By the late 1930s, the number of comics titles increased significantly, and publishers like National Allied (later known as DC Comics) began printing original, multipage comics stories in their comic book periodicals, similar to the pulp magazines that were already well established on American newsstands.[18] In the iconic *Action Comics* #1, Superman consolidated heroic tropes from pulp magazines, mythology, and popular culture into what is widely regarded to be the first superhero character in comics.[19] Superman appears in 1938 in direct relation to fossil fuel power. On the cover of *Action Comics* #1, the costumed hero lifts a car and smashes its front end, while three male figures cower and run away (color plate 3.5). The interior page introduces Superman in a sequence of explanatory panels, and his powers include the ability to "run faster than an express train" (Siegel and Shuster, "Superman" 8; see figure 3.1). Shuster's illustrations of Superman typically position the figure in motion, often lunging or lifting something toward the right-hand

17. This installment of F. O. Alexander's *Hairbreadth Harry* comics strip is the first of four *Hairbreadth Harry* comics that were reprinted in the July 1934 issue of *Famous Funnies*. Distributed through the Ledger Syndicate, the strip was originally published in newspapers on Sunday, April 8, 1934.

18. For accounts of comic book publishing in the United States, see Dauber, Gabilliet, Gardner's *Projections*, Hatfield, "Comic Books," Kidman, and Wright.

19. For a scholarly account of Superman, see Gordon's *Superman*.

FIGURE 3.1. Panels from Jerome Siegel and Joe Shuster, "Superman." *Action Comics* no. 1, DC Comics, June 1938.

side of the panel or page. Reading Superman comics and looking at Superman's figure encourages forward momentum, as the reader follows Superman into the next panel and the next page.

A new media form that flourished alongside film, magazines, newspapers, and photography, comics have both historical and ideological connections to the aesthetic theories that propelled formal and narrative experimentation in twentieth-century modernism. Accordingly, comics in the United States extend the artistic representation of modernity and its fossil-fueled exuberance, also captured in works of fine art as varied as J. M. W. Turner's Romantic painting *Rain, Steam, and Speed—The Great Western Railway* (1844), with its landscape occluded by hazy smog, and Joseph Stella's multiple paintings of the Brooklyn Bridge that denote a futuristic city of abstract shapes from 1919 through the 1930s.[20] 1938's *Action Comics* #1 introduces Superman as an impossibly strong figure. Joe Shuster's cover illustration itself reflects the influence of modernist aesthetics on superhero comics. Lifting up an automobile and smashing it into a boulder, Superman's heroic pose and superhuman strength partake of a modernist visual iconography

20. Joseph Stella saw the Brooklyn Bridge as "the shrine containing all the efforts of the new civilization of AMERICA," and standing on the bridge, he feels the "underground tumult of the trains in perpetual motion" to be "like the blood in the arteries" (Stella 87–88). For accounts of oil, exuberance, and other feelings in American literature, see Buell; LeMenager, *Living Oil.*

evident in many works of Futurist art, including Umberto Boccioni's 1913 sculpture *Unique Forms of Continuity in Space.*[21] Lunging forward like Boccioni's geometrical strongman, Superman on the cover of *Action Comics* #1 is more than human, terrifying the fleeing bystanders. Described on the first interior page of *Action Comics* #1 as a "champion of the oppressed," Superman in this first issue overcomes industrial technology and biological limitations to serve as an icon of utopian powers and possibilities, much in keeping with modernist ideas about aesthetic and technological transformation. As Caroline Tisdall and Angelo Bozzolla explain, Boccioni's sculpture realizes the futurist ideal of bodily transformation: "Human features made way for a synthesis of every kind of machine the Futurists ever depicted, his chest swelled out into the shape of the 'non-human model' envisioned by Marinetti in 'War, Sole Hygiene of the World' . . . as if in flight, the thigh and calf muscles of this monstrous mechanized mannikin, all the more alarming for being half-size, are pushed back as if by the pressure of air as it cuts through space" (81). What Boccioni figures as aggressive, fast, and mechanized armor in *Unique Forms,* Siegel and Shuster fashion as a superhero costume, the "S" signifying his status as "the future man."

Superman's resemblance to Boccioni's *Unique Forms of Continuity in Space* is just one visual connotation at work in the cover image. *Action Comics* #1's cover illustration has a background filled with lines that emanate from a yellow center. These lines and colors create a sense of explosive action. The bright center of the composition radiates in a way that evokes another Futurist work, Giacomo Balla's *Street Light* (1910–11).[22] In *Street Light,* Balla paints luminescence as a series of curved lines extending from a central, bright bulb. This intense burst of light is occasioned by fossil fuels, and the light radiates out as almost material waves of energy. On the cover of *Action Comics* #1, Superman creates the same visual effect as Balla's electric streetlight, producing energy that radiates outward through black lines on a yellow-then-red burst of energy. Iconic yet not singular, Balla's *Street Light* is part of a more generally modernist interest in technology's supersession of nature. In the painting, the light bulb outshines and almost covers over the moon in the background. The tension between streetlight and moonlight in the painting is one example of what Amelia Jones has identified as a central theme in New York's Dadaist movement. The "machine works" of modernists like Marcel Duchamp, Jones argues, "are extremely complex and can

---

21. An image of Boccioni's *Unique Forms of Continuity in Space* (1913) is available online at: https://www.metmuseum.org/art/collection/search/485540.

22. An image of Balla's *Street Light* (1910–11) is available online at: https://www.moma.org/collection/works/78382.

most productively be viewed as incomplete negotiations of the violent challenges to the masculine subject in urban industrialism" (125). While Balla's *Street Light* itself may offer either a sense of masculine virility (the power of electricity!) or a sense of loss (the moon pales in comparison!), the luminous, explosive energy in the painting becomes background for Superman's own assertion of masculine power in *Action Comics* #1. The superhero resolves the modernist tension between machine and nature, industry and agency.

Superman's costume also has notable overlap with Futurist art. The painter of *Street Light,* Balla, also designed clothing for the new, modernist age. "Considered the father of Futurist fashion," Emily Braun writes, "Balla began designing textiles and suits in 1912–1913. With asymmetrical cuts and diagonal surface patterns, the brightly colored outfits were a direct translation of the dynamic 'force-lines' of his painted canvases" (36). The brightly colored, simple outfits of Futurism were meant to facilitate dynamic action, and the cotton, latex, leather, and spandex outfits of superheroes continue Futurist ideas of fashion's form brightly announcing its function. As with Balla's fashion and the superhero's costume, the functionality of the leotard is just one of its appeals. Both the futurist's and the superhero's costumes present the body as spectacle. As Scott Bukatman has argued, the urban superhero is a dandy, taking to the night in a flamboyant costume: "superheroes don't wear costumes in order to fight crime, they fight crime in order to wear the costumes" (*Matters of Gravity* 216). The superhero dons a costume that transforms a person into a concept, a body into a symbol. Accordingly, the superhero becomes a figure that can manifest fossil-fueled power without the cumbersome infrastructure of fossil fuels.

In addition to Superman's pose, the light, and the costume, the damaged car on the cover of *Action Comics* #1 has a distinct symbolic meaning in the context of modernism. In his "Foundation and Manifesto of Futurism," F. T. Marinetti details how a car wreck inspired his aesthetic ideals. In his car, Marinetti "sped on, squashing beneath our scorching tires the snarling guard dogs at the steps of their houses, like crumpled collars under a hot iron" (12). Marinetti then describes how he makes an irrational U-turn, almost hits some cyclists, and then crashes in a ditch. Everyone thinks the car is totaled, but it turns out that Marinetti's "gorgeous shark" of a car comes "back from the dead, darting along with its powerful fins!" (13). Marinetti's fetishistic shark-car is just part of the transformation occasioned by the car crash. Marinetti himself is also transformed, "with my face covered in repair-shop grime—a fine mixture of metallic flakes, profuse sweat, and pale-blue soot—with my arms all bruised and bandaged, yet quite undaunted" (13). Marinetti's transformation might be familiar to fans of superhero comics, since

FIGURE 3.2. Panels from Jerome Siegel and Joe Shuster, "Superman's Phony Manager." *Action Comics* no. 6, DC Comics, November 1938.

the artist effectively becomes a superhero: costumed, shiny blue, covered in semimysterious substances, battle-tested, and stronger than ever. Clark Kent's meek journalist persona is preceded here by the avant-garde poet, both of whom have a secret life of explosive action. The automobile is a symbol of technological advance, mechanized speed, and human potential that extends petrochemical fantasies of superhero bodies.

Jerry Siegel and Joe Shuster's Superman story in November 1938's *Action Comics* #6 invokes the connections between superheroes and fossil fuels. In the story, Clark Kent meets Nick Williams, a con man claiming to be "Superman's personal manager" (Siegel and Shuster, "Superman's Phony Manager" 74). Williams trumpets his business acumen and proudly points out a blimp towing a banner that reads "Use Superman Gasoline for Super-Power!" (75; see figure 3.2). On the next page, Williams points out a billboard advertising "The Superman Streamline Special, America's Favorite Automobile" (76). Williams offers Clark Kent the chance to have a "personal interview with Superman" in exchange for positive press, and after hearing about this exchange in the *Daily Star* newsroom, Lois Lane invites herself along to get the scoop (76).[23] Lois slips Clark Kent a sleeping pill at dinner and goes to the Superman interview by herself, where she exposes Williams's fake Superman as an actor. Williams and his crony toss Lois out of a

23. The name of Metropolis's newspaper changes from the *Daily Star* to the more familiar *Daily Planet* in *Action Comics* no. 23 (1940).

window, and the real Superman arrives just in time to catch her. Superman saves Lois and delivers the frauds to the police.

In this story, Siegel and Shuster differentiate Superman from the comics characters who routinely appeared in advertisements during the 1930s. Not a spokesperson for fossil fuel companies, Superman instead internalizes the power, speed, and strength of fossil fuels. Rushing to Lois Lane's rescue, Clark Kent "sheds his garments and glasses, and stands revealed in the Superman uniform!" and Superman is then described as "speeding off into the night like a living projectile!" (Siegel, "Superman's Phony Manager" 81). Superman is not a spokesperson for fossil fuels but is instead an embodiment of fossil fuel energy itself.

The imaginary attribution of fossil fuel power to a human form is pursued even further at the end of the Superman story in *Action Comics* #6. At the bottom of the story's final page, there is a comics sequence titled "Acquiring Super Strength" (86). This supplement to the Superman story instructs readers to do a wrist exercise that "will eventually impart to you a crushing hand-grip!" (86). Superman models a power that is transferable to the comic book's readers, at least according to this feature and many other comic book advertisements for bodybuilding manuals, X-ray spectacles, and means of self-empowerment. In self-reflexive superhero stories like those in *Action Comics,* the connections between superheroes and fossil fuels are made visible even at the level of plot. Superman's personal integrity differentiates the character from the otherwise crude commercialism of American culture. Rather than advertise automobiles and gasoline, Superman acts as a free individual, serving the greater good by choice and not for profit. However, the *Action Comics* #6 story about fraudulent Superman advertisements belies the fact that DC Comics pursued licensing deals for Superman starting as early as 1939. As Ian Gordon notes in his study *Superman: The Persistence of an American Icon,* the antilicensing story in *Action Comics* #6 might not have been as clear as it seems: "In a 1983 interview, Jerry Siegel remembered this story in a more positive light, omitting any mention of Superman's name being stolen and his likeness exploited. Instead, he suggested that the story inspired DC to look for licensing opportunities" (21).[24] This retrospective change from an anticapitalist Superman to a commodified Superman entailed a reorientation of the character's relationship to consumerism, an increasingly central facet of American life and industry. As Gordon explains, Superman began as "somewhat of a reformist liberal, albeit one given to direct action" in the

24. For a history of American comic books that foregrounds licensing, see Kidman.

late 1930s but would transform "into a symbol of more general American cultural values in that his individualism was tied to consumerist values" in the 1940s and 1950s (18).

During World War II, Superman and many other superheroes symbolized American nationalism, and Superman's identification with American values was also an identification with American's rampant consumption of fossil fuels. The cover of *Superman* #19 in November and December 1942, for example, depicts Superman lifting a car above his head. The car has no tires, and Superman is helping the passengers by flying them around. In late 1941, the United States began rationing automobile tires due to a severe rubber shortage, a shortage overcome by the use of petrochemicals to manufacture synthetic rubber. In this cover illustration, Superman works as the literal engine of American everyday life, a figure that instills confidence in fossil-fueled systems even during times of austerity. Superman is a petrochemical fantasy, as he embodies the promise of fossil fuels in midcentury America. He does what fossil fuels do, but without the realities of emissions and extraction.

Other midcentury American comics participated directly in the military-industrial complex. Comics artist Will Eisner made comics for *Army Motors* magazine in 1944, and then starting in 1951 at the beginning of the Korean War, Eisner produced *PS: The Preventive Maintenance Monthly,* an illustrated magazine that provided technical instruction about military equipment repair in a comics format. *PS: The Preventive Maintenance Monthly* has been continuously in publication and is now a digital magazine, a stalwart component of military-industrial pedagogy for decades. Political scientist Neta C. Crawford explains the substantial role that the United States military has played in maintaining American access to fossil fuels around the globe:

> As the U.S. military grew increasingly dependent on coal, and then oil, in the nineteenth and twentieth centuries, it focused on developing the tactics, strategies, and military bases and equipment necessary to ensure easy access to a secure supply of fossil fuels. Indeed the U.S. armed forces and other militaries have, at times, shown flashes of tactical brilliance in ensuring that they would have a steady supply of fuel. This was the institutionalization of fossil fuel demand and use, which then resulted in past and current military greenhouse gas emissions. (11–12)

As Crawford notes, the US Department of Defense "is the single largest energy consumer in the United States," and thus, comics like Eisner's *PS: Preventive Maintenance Monthly* as well as DC Comics' *Superman* established the habits, knowledge, and values of fossil fuel culture in a mass of American readers.

Super Fuel

Superman is a petrochemical fantasy, a figure who has access to the intense energy of fossil fuels but without any of the costs to environment, society, or the future of the planet. The connection between the power of fossil fuels and the power of the human body is also clearly made in oil industry publications like the 1950s giveaway comic book *RD-119: The Miracle in Your Gas Tank,* published by Sinclair Oil to promote their RD-119 fuel additive (color plate 3.6). The Sinclair product is promoted by the "Miracle Man," a cape- and tights-wearing superhero, who cries out "Sinc-Lair!" to do magical things like shrink down into an engine or drive a flying car over the Sinclair oil refinery and pipeline system (*RD-119*). At the comic's end, Sinclair's Miracle Man turns out to be a Sinclair gas station attendant who is happy to sell "a gasoline with RD-119 that works like magic." By the 1950s, the superhero's connection to fossil fuels is so apparent that Sinclair Oil's Miracle Man appears on the cover as an emanation from the automobile's gas tank. The "miracle" in Sinclair's comic book is gasoline, no matter if it is dressed up in a superhero costume or just paid for at the pump.

As the Miracle Man makes evident, the sleek experience of driving an automobile coextends with the powers of comic book superheroes. Both conjure a sense of technological sophistication and the seamless expansion of human power, evident not just in comics, of course, but in other public installations like General Motor's *Futurama* exhibit at the New York World's Fair in 1939. Comics participated in the popularization of modernist aesthetics and design in midcentury America, and comics creators incorporated material from modernist art into their popular images. For example, Joe Shuster attended the Cleveland School of Art in the early 1930s, so he was likely exposed to modernist art before creating Superman. Moreover, Boccioni's *Unique Forms of Continuity in Space* was one of many Futurist works included in the Museum of Modern Art's *Cubism and Abstract Art* exhibit in 1936, just two years before Superman appeared in a similar lunging pose on the cover of *Action Comics* #1 ("Cubism"). It is plausible to read a popular renaissance of futurist aesthetics in American comic books, even if that revival was less an intentional return than an effect of modern style. But perhaps more important than any avant-garde ideology was Shuster and Siegel's involvement in print culture of the 1930s. They actively published and contributed to science fiction fanzines in the 1930s and set out to work for hire as a freelance comic book team. The visual markers of modernism evident on the cover of *Action Comics* #1 are emblems not necessarily of direct influence or self-aware referencing, as we may expect of postmodern artists, who often signal or cite their influences, but are instead signs of modernism's transformation into a series of tropes that signify explosive action and iconic meaning in America's midcentury fossil fuel culture. Futurism's idealistic heroism is visible in *Action Comics* #1 immediately, in part because by the late 1930s, futurism as an aesthetic style had entered the popular lexicon of visual iconography. Modernism had become familiar, and through that entrance into popular culture, superhero comics blended the experimental styles of modernism with those of adventure stories to represent a culture powered by massive amounts of oil and gas. The superhero consolidated fossil fuel energy into a recognizable set of tropes and types, bringing modernism's techno-utopianism into serial narratives about American values.

The association of comic books with the modern energy source of petroleum was seemingly ever present, even in the title of the first Marvel comic. Published in 1939, *Marvel Comics* only lasted one issue before its publisher, Martin Goodman, changed the title to *Marvel Mystery Comics.* Longtime Marvel Comics writer and editor Roy Thomas has asked, "did the name change [to *Marvel Mystery Comics*] really, as a few people seriously believe, have something to do with an automotive product on the market named Marvel Mystery Oil? Hard to believe, and yet . . . !" (26, ellipses in original). No matter the intention behind the change from *Marvel Comics* to *Marvel Mystery Comics,* it "inevitably evoked the name of the popular and highly advertised fuel additive" (Bell and Vassallo 55). Comics traffic in these nebulous but evocative associations and connotations.

The "Secret of the Iron Jungle" story in *Batman* #6 (1941) is a more direct statement of the superhero's support of fossil fuels. In the story, Batman and Robin save the Page Oil Company by fighting off a corrupt business partner and detonating an explosive to open up an oil well. The comic book contains an explanatory footnote for the term "gusher," in case readers need context: "A gusher is a monster spout of oil that often brings untold wealth—shooting thousands of feet from below the Earth, hundreds of feet into the air, gushers have been known to pour out oil at the rate of two million gallons a day" (Finger et al. 294). At the story's end, the oil workers exclaim, "Look at that darn gusher—going to bring millions of gallons of oil—whee—harrah!" and Batman and Robin smile as they walk away from the scene (305). The superheroes save the day again and ensure the future of fossil fuel extraction.

In the February and March 1942 issue *All-Star Comics* #9, written by Gardner Fox and drawn by a number of artists, the Justice Society of America travels to Latin America in order to protect American fossil fuel and mineral resources from Nazi saboteurs. In this wartime adventure story, the superheroes are agents of America's fossil fuel regime. Each member of the Justice Society goes on a unique adventure, and Hawkman begins the issue in Mexico, where "black gold flows deep . . . Its oil wells contribute greatly to this country's prosperity" (Fox et al. 6). Hawkman breaks up a Nazi spy ring plotting railroad sabotage, and later in the issue, Sandman travels "to the city of Caracas, Venezuela, birthplace of Simon Bolivar, the great liberator. . . . In Lake Maracabo [*sic*], the fertile oil region, wells are sunk in the lake itself!" (26; see color plate 3.7). In the Sandman story's opening panel, the masked superhero swings toward a cluster of oil derricks, and he learns from a Venezuelan secret service officer that "Venezuela leased her oil fields to Britain and the United States. Now the fascists are attempting to sabotage those wells in an effort to slow up production or take complete control over their output!" (26). The other Justice Society members adventure elsewhere: the Spectre fights against Nazi airships in Argentina; the Atom travels to Chile, "rich in nitrates, gold, and copper" (20); Johnny Thunder goes to Cuba, prized as "a mighty vacation resort for all America" as well as for its "valuable mahogany and cedar . . . the finest tobaccos, and its great sugar plantations" (33); Doctor Fate goes to protect Brazil, "gifted with rich coffees and fine rubber" (40); Starman flies to Bolivia, "a mighty mining nation, producing one-fourth of the world's tin, and being rich in tungsten, silver, lead, zinc, antimony, copper, and gold!" (47); and finally, Dr. Mid-Nite exposes "an epidemic of mass hypnotism" in Colombia (53). At the end of this tour of the Americas, the Justice Society enjoy a "victory ball" to "[celebrate] our freedom from all fifth column activities and also [cement] the ties of friendship with all the Americas!" (61). While Martin Goodman's *Marvel Mystery Comics* took advantage of name recognition through its alliterative twin product Marvel Mystery Oil, other early superheroes like Batman, Robin, and the Justice Society of America more directly secure fossil fuels for American consumption in their adventures.

Much later in superhero comics history, the 1980 *The Brave and the Bold* #163 presents an updated perspective on the link between superheroes and petroleum that reflects the shifting economics and politics of fossil fuels of its time. The story features the DC Comics superheroes Batman and Black Lightning, who are both investigating recent gasoline truck hijackings in their respective home cities of Gotham and Metropolis. Batman and Black Lightning meet up at an oil storage facility controlled by General Hargrave, who is plotting a military takeover of Middle Eastern oil fields. The warmongering General Hargrave speaks at length about his evil plan while Batman and Black Lightning listen, surrounded by goons: "Our country's become a laughingstock in the eyes of the world because of the energy crisis—because they see we're no longer strong! And the only way America will ever regain its position as world leader is to cease allowing the oil-producing nations to dictate policy to us—and for the USA to take control of the Arab oil fields!" (Kupperberg et al. 15). Written in the wake of the 1970s oil crisis, this issue of *The Brave and the Bold* positions superheroes as rational protectors of fossil fuel infrastructure in a more complex political context.

As Timothy Mitchell explains, the 1970s oil crisis led to a widespread recognition that petroleum was limited, finite, and even harmful, rather than an abundant resource: "Public debate contributed to the sense of threat, linking the [1973] oil embargo to a wider 'energy crisis,' a problem of the 'limits to growth,' and the vulnerability of 'the environment'—a word that had previously meant milieu or surroundings, but had recently come to be used with the definite article . . . to designate an object of widespread political concern" (175). When petroleum seemed abundant and cheap to Americans in the 1930s through the 1960s, comic books emerged, and their narratives take place in an increasingly petroleum-fueled United States. In characters like Superman, comics artists, writers, and publishers represent what Mitchell describes as "energy and the forms of life that were increasingly dependent of that energy" with stories of superhuman powers, global threats, and astonishingly fast movement (42). As energy culture changed in the 1970s, later superhero stories like Batman and Black Lightning's oil crisis adventure telegraph fears of peak oil and predict American-launched wars over fossil fuels in the Middle East. At the end of *The Brave and the Bold* #163, Black Lightning jokes with Batman about the price of gas: "I figure with gas goin' for better'n a buck a gallon these days, no way could I let 'im blast them storage tanks!" (Kupperberg et al. 17). Superheroes continue to protect fossil fuels and to preserve access to them as a fundamental right of American life. Fossil fuel realities modulate the superhero's adventures.

Concerned with oil prices as they are, Batman and Black Lightning nonetheless do not acknowledge that the fossil fuel industry and the culture that it has helped to create damage the environment and countless lives. Instead, the fault lies with one evil individual, unjustly marshaling military resources to control access to petroleum reserves. This moral allegory fails to capture the true scope of fossil fuels and carbon emissions in the United States. By burning fossil fuels, Americans have released over 400 billion tons of carbon dioxide into the atmosphere, a full 25 percent of global emissions. Today, it is clear that the burning of fossil fuels has changed the Earth's climate and put millions in crisis. This fossil fuel reality appears in comics too, though often in fantastical form. In *Strange Adventures* #120, published by DC Comics in September 1960, the cover story "The Attack of the Oil Demons!" depicts subterranean oil creatures who travel to the Earth's surface through a well (color plate 3.8). Written by Gardner Fox and drawn by Sid Greene, the story's human protagonist figures out how to communicate with the oil demons, and he sends them back below ground in steel drums. In exchange for this good turn, the oil demons endow the story's hero with "an uncanny ability to sense exactly where to drill for oil!" (Fox and Greene 9).[25] With its opening chaos and terror, "The Attack of the Oil Demons" presents oil as a dangerous, uncontrollable, toxic force, and in resolving the chaos, the comic book's oil worker hero learns to control the harmful effects of fossil fuels. Like the "Miracle Man" who emerges from the gas tank in Sinclar Oil's 1950s promotional comic book, *Strange Adventure*'s oil demons bring with them comforting knowledge about fossil fuels and their continued abundance. Reassuring narratives about explosive energy and strong men, these comic book adventures resolve the violence of fossil fuels with magical abilities and technological fantasies. Comic books elaborated fossil fuel ubiquity, and the medium represented the newfound powers that had become common to fossil fuel consumers in midcentury America.

25. *Strange Adventures* no. 120 also contains a story featuring the Atomic Knights by John Broome and Murphy Anderson. The Atomic Knights are sci-fi heroes who adventure in World War III's nuclear fallout, so the menace of the oil demons is paralleled by the dystopia of the Atomic Knights in this comic book.

CHAPTER 4

Plastic Man and Other Petrochemical Fantasies

In 1933 the American Petroleum Industries Committee published an accordion-fold pamphlet titled *The Clean-Up: A Moving Picture of Science, Industry, and Taxation Featuring Petroleum Pete* (figure 4.1). The pamphlet is a continuous, eight-page illustrated narrative, with a prose piece titled "Short Story of the Petroleum Industry" on the reverse side. In the pamphlet's "moving picture," the titular character, Petroleum Pete, "just a drop of crude oil," goes on an "exciting journey" from his "family home" in "subterranean sands and porous rocks" to a consumer's automobile. At the end of the lengthy refining process, and underneath an illustration of Pete in a gas pump, the caption reads:

> You know the rest of Pete's life story. He is potential power, he and innumerable millions of other drops that once were crude oil. Thousands of miles they were transported, many and varied treatments they were given to make then [*sic*] clean and refined, and then they were placed within easy reach of the motorist—all in preparation for that brief moment when, mixed with air, they were exploded and their power used to move a vehicle for pleasure or for business.

The pamphlet's "moving picture" format blends together elements of film and comics, juxtaposing image and text in sequences that unfold

FIGURE 4.1. *The Clean-Up: A Moving Picture of Science, Industry, and Taxation Featuring Petroleum Pete.* American Petroleum Industries Committee, 1933. Special Collections Research Center, University of Chicago Library.

continuously on the page. The depiction of Petroleum Pete's long journey from extraction through refining and finally to combustion stretches out in time and space, creating the sense that oil production is a difficult, complicated, and technical business unfairly taxed by the United States government. As the pamphlet's final scene emphasizes, Petroleum Pete's major difficulty in getting from underground to a gas tank comes from government regulation and taxation: "from the time Pete left his underground home until he found his job in that automobile, he encountered many strange persons enroute. At every turn they met him, all in uniform and remarkably alike in that always they had one hand out and one word to say, 'Gimme!' Pete quickly learned that these were tax collectors."

Advocating for fewer taxes on petroleum and its industries, the American Petroleum Institute's pamphlet emphasizes the complexity of the refining process, noting that petroleum's widespread and historical uses as an illuminant, a machine lubricant, and a fuel "represent only an infinitesimal few among the thousands of ways in which petroleum and its derivatives, either alone or compounded, daily are used in some form by every person in the civilized world" (*Clean-Up*). Petroleum Pete is everywhere, the fuel of modern life. Like petroleum, comics also became widespread in the 1930s through the 1950s. During this period, the fossil fuel industry widely expanded the use of petrochemicals and other petroleum by-products in all kinds of manufacturing and especially in the making of plastics. The use of petrochemicals contributed to what J. R. McNeill and Peter Engelke describe as the "great acceleration": "Global plastic production exploded at midcentury. World production rose from less than 50,000 tons in 1930 to 2 million tons in 1950 and 6 million tons a decade later. New types of plastics flooded the marketplace. Plastics substituted for materials such as glass, wood, and paper in existing goods or became the key substance in a huge array of new consumer goods" (137). This growth in petrochemical plastics occurred alongside the emergence and proliferation of the superhero in US comic books, resulting in a conception of both infinitely flexible and invincible bodies that replicate the qualities of midcentury plastic materials.

Plastic Aesthetics

Plastic bodies abound in comics. The rendering of impossible bodily actions, contortions, and expansions is a hallmark of the medium, from Rodolphe Töpffer's quick caricatures to Jerry Siegel and Joe Shuster's leaping and, ultimately, flying "man of steel." Closely related to comics in historical origins and content, animated film has even been described by film director and theorist Sergei Eisenstein as "plasmatic," a term that conjoins the colorful play associated with plastics to the neither-matter-nor-liquid viscosity of plasma (32). For Eisenstein, Disney's plasmatic cartoons from the 1930s and 1940s offer "a complete return to a world of complete freedom," a vision that emerges "at the very summit of a society that had completely enslaved nature—namely, in America" (7). While plasmatic cartoons provide relief, in Eisenstein's view, from the exploited lives viewers lead under capitalism, they draw on a set of animistic, primal ideas about nature. As such, for Eisenstein, the political capacity of the plasmatic is limited, as it lacks a dialectical opposite and thus provokes merely pleasant nostalgia for a more natural condition. In animated films as well as in the Amoco Oil–sponsored picture book *Mickey Mouse: The Mail Pilot* (1933) and Standard Oil of California's illustrated newspaper pamphlet *Travel Tykes Weekly* (1939), Disney characters enfold plasmatic play within fossil fuel industries.[1] From our con-

1. As noted in chapter 3, the 1933 Amoco edition of *Mickey Mouse: The Mail Pilot* is one of Whitman Publishing's "Big Little Books." It contains a single narrative with text and full-page illustrations. The back cover of the Amoco edition is an advertisement for Amoco and American Oil gasoline, "from Maine to Florida . . . Each the best in its price class." *Travel Tykes Weekly* was a broadsheet with illustrations, comics, and prose stories.

temporary vantage point, the plasmatic and its expressive fluidity seems less of an expression of primal nature trapped within industrial capitalism than an expression of how fossil fuel capitalism transformed life in midcentury America.

As environmental humanities scholar Ursula Heise has argued, plasmatic animation's ability to morph and reshape subjects, objects, and settings gives it a unique ability to imagine the environment: "Speaking and acting animals, plants, and objects invite the viewer to see humans as only one of many manifestations of liveliness, intentionality, and agency in the fictional worlds of animation" (305). Along with this expanded view of life, "plasmatic bodies, both human and nonhuman . . . playfully explore ecological adaptation, resilience, and the synthetic, human-made ecologies that define the future of nature in the Anthropocene, the age in which humans transform even the most basic structures of their planet" (305). Plastics are one of the major ways that humans have transformed the environment, and the concept of the "plasmatic" names the quality of colorful, even infinite flexibility that plastics introduced. The plasmatic expansion of boundaries that Eisenstein and Heise attribute to the medium of animation has also long been a quality of comics, and in comics, it is evident that the plasmatic expansion of boundaries is facilitated by fossil fuels. The emergence and ubiquity of plastics by the mid-twentieth century in the United States is thematized in comic books, as a site of expansive possibility and as a force that fundamentally reshapes the human and the environment.

In cultural theorist Scott Bukatman's adoption of the concept, plasmatic arts like comics and animation once presented an unbounded field of representation: "forms were dynamic and mutable; all things were possible" (*Poetics of Slumberland* 13). The infinite flexibility of an illustrated world is a central component of comic books. While plasmatic intensity and play has been tracked in animation and linked historically with the advent of modernism and technological innovations in film, photography, and printing, the aesthetics of plastic have shaped American comics and the comic book superhero as well, especially through the conceptual link between plastic flexibility and petrocultural power. As Bart Beaty notes, "comics—and superhero comics in particular—have placed a greater premium on the visualization of energy than other forms" (337). If plastics are, as in Amanda Boetzkes and Andrew Pendakis's analysis, "valueless, infinitely transposable, and therefore seemingly voided of ontological stability," then superhero comics articulate a worldview that blends the energy of petroculture

---

According to the Grand Comics Database, there were at least seventeen issues of *Travel Tykes Weekly* published in 1939. See https://www.comics.org/series/98599/.

with the ephemerality of plastics, a world of superhuman possibility that strives to transcend material limits. Yet, plastic's often zany possibilities also make clear the limitations of not only aesthetic forms—only so much stretching of the world can occur on a piece of paper with finite dimensions—but also narratives. Plastic heroes in comic books remain relatively singular, existing as anomalies within a less fluid world. In comics, as in polluted environments, plastics promise an infinite fluidity that they cannot deliver.

Plastics are a part of superhero comics, just as they are a part of America's everyday environment, and plastics were becoming newly meaningful in American culture at the time of the superhero's emergence on the newsstand. As Jeffrey L. Meikle posits in his history of plastics, there were two conceptions of plastics by the 1940s, one stemming from early plastics like Celluloid and Bakelite, and the other from newer thermoplastics. While early plastics were represented and even designed as "an extension of natural materials" such as wood or metal, the new conception of plastics envisioned an "expansive culture of impermanence," in which Americans enjoyed "an irrational phantasmagoria of ungrounded images, all in brilliant synthetic colors, a carnival of material desire" (Meikle 64, 68, 67). As political scientist Adam Hanieh describes, the adoption of petrochemicals changed everyday life significantly through abundant fossil fuel derivatives:

> From the 1950s onwards, a wide array of naturally derived substances—wood, glass, paper, natural rubber, natural fertilizers, soaps, cotton, wool and metals—were systematically displaced by plastics, synthetic fibres, detergents and other petroleum-based chemicals. This "petrochemical" revolution enabled the *syntheticization* of what had previously been encountered and appropriated only within the domain of nature; the very substance of daily life was transformed, alchemy-like, into various derivatives of petroleum. (27)

This transition from a natural to a synthetic world is articulated in midcentury American superhero narratives, which often feature heroes who strive to preserve order with fantastic powers. Plastic in these superhero narratives, then, is the occasion of both immense freedom and profound stasis. Like plastics themselves, superhero stories about plastic heroes create the appearance of limitless freedom, with the ironic effect of preserving habits of life, such as the casual consumption and disposal of petrochemical plastics, that have become so natural as to seem neutral.

One of the many superheroes to appear on US newsstands in the wake of Superman in 1938, Plastic Man is a minor figure if judged by the number of comic books published since the 1940s that bear the character's name. But Plastic Man's superpowers and frenetic energy resonate across the superhero genre. The contorting and stretched body figures in earlier comics like Winsor McCay's *Little Nemo in Slumberland* (1905–11 / 1924–27), and Plastic Man's superhuman elasticity adapts the visual effects of funhouse mirrors into a central narrative device. As Scott Bukatman argues, "Plastic Man, with his morphing morphology . . . serves to demonstrate the plasmatic fantasy that underlies the entire superhero genre, with its transformative bodies, split identities, and infinite adaptabilities" (*Poetics of Slumberland* 19). Moreover, Plastic Man works in the intricate and imaginary connection between superhero bodies and petroculture, forging a link between the imaginary possibilities of the plasmatic and the material reality of plastics. In his essay about Plastic Man's creator, Jack Cole, Art Spiegelman describes not just the character Plastic Man but also the comics pages themselves on which he appears, in terms of energy and force:

> Each panel seems to swallow several separate instants of time whole, as if the page were made up of small screens with different, though related, films whizzing by at forty-eight frames a second. Jack Cole's is an amphetamine–riddled art: Tex Avery on speed! And it's not just Plastic Man who bounces and twists; any one of Cole's incidental figures would seem as kinetic as Plas if it were transplanted into someone else's comic book. Each page is intuitively visualized to form a coherent whole even though the individual panels form a narrative flood of run-on sentences that breathlessly jump from one page to the next. The art ricochets like a racquet ball slammed full force in a closet. Your eye, however, is guided as if it were a skillfully controlled pinball, often by Plastic Man himself acting as a compositional device. His distended body is an arrow pointing out the sights as it hurtles through time. (Spiegelman and Kidd 37)

Spiegelman's metaphors for Plastic Man are mixed, and he avoids reference to nonhuman energy sources. This is perhaps because of Spiegelman's interest in projecting Jack Cole's work as art, and therefore organic, rather than the industrial product that comics have been framed as for most of their history in the United States. Interestingly, though, Spiegelman's emphasis on the unity of form and content in Plastic Man comics—the way in which Plastic Man's kinetic speed and flexibility is captured not just in narrative but in the composition of the comics page itself as a "coherent whole"—shares in the understanding of abstract art articulated by painter Barnett Newman in his influential 1945 essay "The Plasmic Image." In that essay,

Newman makes a distinction between the "plastic" qualities of a painting—its use of color and compositional structure—and the "plasmic image," which incorporates these plastic elements not just as surface features but as expressive content: "the plastic elements of the art have been converted into mental plasma" (141). While Newman envisioned and advocated for a mode of abstract painting that sought to convey abstract truths, the inherently narrative art of the comic book page in *Plastic Man* conveys not an abstract, transhistorical truth but an expression of the condition of the petrochemical age, moving at unprecedented speeds and reshaping bodies. In Plastic Man and related stretchy superheroes, the speculative ideologies of plastics project safely consumerist yet pleasantly flexible utopias.

As mentioned above, Plastic Man was created by the artist Jack Cole, and the character first appeared in *Police Comics* #1 in 1941. As Art Spiegelman notes, Plastic Man's original name was "India Rubber Man," yet Cole's editor felt that the term "plastic" captured the excitement associated with the new wave of plastics emerging in the 1940s (Spiegelman and Kidd 15). Among these new plastics, synthetic rubbers were manufactured with the use of petrochemicals, and they touted better elasticity and durability than natural rubber while also being less prone to the economic volatility, price spikes, and wartime shortages of the natural commodity. Plastic Man's polymorphic body, which can stretch in seemingly infinite directions, is routinely likened to "rubber" in his 1940s comics, and in *Police Comics* #1, the United States Rubber Company even placed an ad boasting the superior qualities of the US Royal Rider bicycle tire, made with material also used in Navy "torpedo planes." The ad's juxtaposition of bicycles with fighter planes domesticates Plastic Man's superheroic fantasy, grounding synthetic rubber in a mundane activity that nonetheless connotes high-speed adventure.

Police Comics #1 tells Plastic Man's origin story. A criminal gang robs the "Crawford Criminal Works," and gang member Eel O'Brian is shot by a security guard and doused in a "vat of acid" (Cole, "Plastic Man" 32). Left for dead by his fellow criminals, Eel stumbles through a swamp and up a mountain before passing out. He wakes up in a mysterious mountain retreat, Resthaven, where he is nursed to health by a monk. While at Resthaven, Eel realizes that his body is "stretchin' like a rubber band!!" (34; see figure 4.2). In a three-panel sequence, he stretches his arms, cheeks, and head, reaching outside of the first panel border, becoming an abstract triangle in the second, and rounding out in the third panel through a peephole frame. This sequence emphasizes the new stretchy possibilities realized in the comic, a world where, as will become evident in later Plastic Man stories, plasticity becomes a feature not just of one unique individual but the

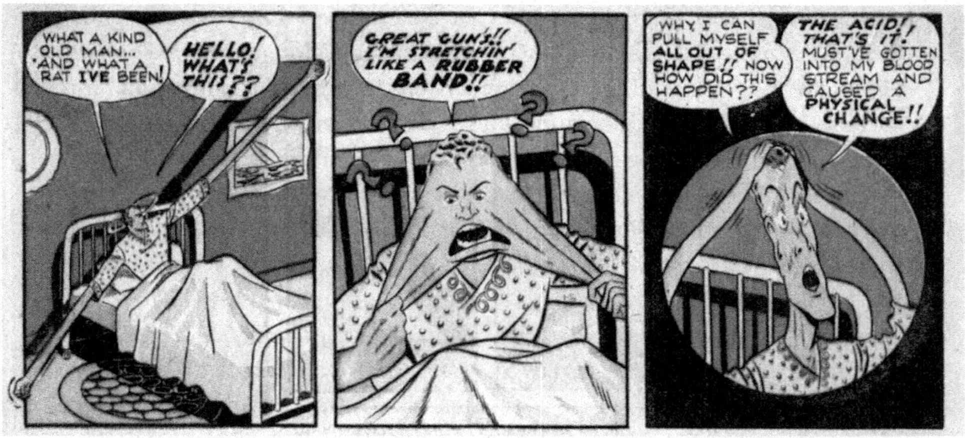

FIGURE 4.2. Panels from Jack Cole, "Plastic Man." *Police Comics* no. 1, Quality Comics, August 1941.

world itself. Eel goes on to fight crime with his newfound abilities as Plastic Man. The character's dual identity offers a glimpse into what makes Plastic Man emblematic, as he is bound to the very criminal world he fights against. While he embodies the posthuman possibilities of new plastics in the mid-century, Plastic Man also seeks to contain and curtail the spread of plasticity, which the comic often figures as monstrous and villainous.

Plastic Man's adventures often pit him against other energy sources. In *Plastic Man* #7 (the character got his own series in 1943, two years after his introduction in *Police Comics*), Plastic Man confronts Dr. Volt, who has invented a box that shoots lightning bolts. Plastic Man foils Dr. Volt's attempt to break into a bank safe by stretching out in front of a lightning bolt, which Plastic Man is "insulated against" because of his chemically enhanced body (Millard and Spranger 5). Dr. Volt eventually blows up his own lair, and he is crushed while fleeing the scene when a bolt of lightning topples a tree. This moment of "poetic justice," as Plastic Man's sidekick Woozy Winks describes it, positions Plastic Man alongside natural forces (12). He is a crime-fighter, enforcing the social order, and for Dr. Volt, the natural order also enforces itself, punishing him for manipulating lightning with, in Plastic Man's words, "genuine lightning" (12). As the cover of the issue makes clear, Plastic Man is figured as lightning itself, a naturally occurring phenomena transformed into a superhero with plastic powers (color plate 4.1).

This ambivalence between figuring Plastic Man as artificial and synthetic or as natural and organic is even more evident in *Plastic Man* #3 (1946). In a convoluted story titled "A Whale of a Tale," written by Gwen Hansen and drawn by Jack Cole, Plastic Man is asked by the FBI to investigate the Strumby gang, which is smuggling precious materials into the United States. Simultaneously, Woozy Winks is convinced that Plastic Man is ignoring him because he smells bad. Woozy goes to a perfume store to buy a bottle of "Correcto," and finds the owner on the verge of committing suicide because he can no longer buy ambergris, due to the Strumby gang's monopoly on the precious material. Woozy then gets in a rowboat to go whaling and is shortly swallowed by a whale that is actually a submarine in disguise. Plastic Man flies overhead and sees this strange whale, which, it turns out, is the Strumby gang's secret hideout. A confrontation ensues, resulting in the capture of the gang and the release of their stockpile of ambergris. Both Plastic Man and Woozy get what they were after. Like in the Dr. Volt story, Plastic Man is likened to the whale and its oil, yet the superhero is also strangely other to organic matter. Plastic Man takes the form of a red whale in the comic, and then hugs the criminals' whale submarine. Plastic Man is sweetly natural and disturbingly alien, morphing in the next panel from a whale to something that "looks more like an octopus."

As an embodiment of the possibilities of plastics, Plastic Man stands in for the both the promise of this material—it will transform what is possible in everyday life—and its threat to human autonomy: Plastic Man's body becomes estranged from natural limits, a product of petrochemicals that can surpass physical and social boundaries. In *Plastic Man* #22, an entire city gets his stretchy powers, after a criminal accidentally dumps a chemical agent in the water supply. Titled "Plague of Plastic People," the story presents plasticity as a threat to the social order. Plastic Man and his FBI boss strive to stop the menace of plastic people, even though the plastic people are not criminals but do-gooders. A prison guard uses his stretchy powers to prevent a jailbreak, and citizens offer to help Plastic Man fight crime. When the plastic powers wear off as the chemical works its way out of people's systems, Plastic Man is relieved that everyone "will go back to normal" (Cole, "Plague" 13). In keeping with the discourse around plastic in midcentury America, these new plastic objects were, on the one hand, positioned as extensions of natural products, meant to bring order to domestic and industrial space, and on the other, presented as radically new materials that would remake everyday life.[2] Plastic Man embodies these tensions, and holds widespread radical transformation at bay through his own polymorphous flexibility.

---

2. For accounts of plastics, the environment, and culture, see Boetzkes; Davis, *Plastic Matter,* and "Imperceptibility"; Irr.

Jack Cole's dynamic Plastic Man illustrations push the boundaries of the comics page, and his stories often involve madcap action and waste. As in Plastic Man's origin story and in "Plague of Plastic People," chemical spills and wild energetic explosions are a mainstay of these early comics. Coupled with the frenetic pace of action and motion associated with Plastic Man, there is something of what Sianne Ngai has described as the "zany" in these stories. The frenetic energy expenditures of Plastic Man offer a striking example of "zany performance," which "involves a certain deformation of the forms of activity, a certain indifference to their qualitative differentiation" (Ngai 197). Plastic Man's continual shifting—he routinely transforms into rugs, boats, fire hydrants, even other people—undoes the very stability of personhood. Ngai associates this aesthetic mode with gendered and racialized modes of labor that blur the distinction between play and work. In Plastic Man comics, this erosion of stable character is clear, as the character becomes flexibility in essence. In early issues of *Police Comics,* Plastic Man routinely appears as the small-time criminal Eel O'Brian, an identity that allows him to infiltrate criminal gangs. This grounding quickly disappears in Plastic Man comics, though, and Plastic Man eventually jettisons his "real" identity. Indeed, in a 2004 *Plastic Man* miniseries by Kyle Baker, the character's origin as Eel O'Brian is described as an "exhausting backstory," something that haunts the superhero Plastic Man, better to be forgotten.

Plastic Man, then, aspires to be a character without a history or personality, defined only by an ability to stretch, flex, and reshape. He is a symbol both of the ephemerality and substancelessness of plastics and of a zany embodiment of labor as joyous play. As Amanda Boetzkes has argued about contemporary art that uses plastics, the very foregrounding of plastics as a material produces a kind of stasis: "Plastic is amoral, atemporal, sensorially rich, and yet a profoundly anxious substance. The ubiquity of plastic is evidence of the state of paralysis in the face of the ecological condition. It airs a negative dialectic: what art reveals is precisely the inefficacy of acts of revealing" (184). The spectacle of Plastic Man's plastic body, in this regard, both enforces the "normal" operations of society, as Plastic Man fights crime, and naturalizes the ways in which plastics reshape our bodies, economies, and ecosystems. This curious duality is transplanted onto the stretchy superheroes that follow Plastic Man, all of whom represent both a strange future and a status quo.

Plastic Man's followers in superhero comics include the Elongated Man, Mister Fantastic, and Ms. Marvel. In each of these characters, one finds the trope of bodily plasticity, along with triumphalist imaginaries of a world remade. What plasticity in comics ultimately demonstrates is how plastics became not just a metaphor for thinking about bodies and actions but also a framework for the remaking of bodies and actions themselves in the petrochemical era. Moreover, in these later comics, plastic becomes expressive not just of midcentury consumerist ideology but also of material limits to consumption and economic growth.

Motion Lines

By 1956 comics had shifted considerably as a popular medium in the United States. After a publishing boom in the 1930s and 1940s, a postwar downturn pushed many comics publishers out of the marketplace, and many remaining comics publishers shored up their place on American newsstands by forming the Comics Code Authority, which ensured that comic books stamped with the CCA seal were appropriate for children.[3] Under these new conditions, the superhero's previous ties to real-world political events, such as warfare in Germany or Japan, receded, and a new level of often goofy abstraction entered into comics narratives. On the cover of DC Comics' *Showcase* #4 (1956), for example, the Flash races out of a filmstrip, surpassing the speed of projection through his immediate, explosive presence on the comics page. This "Silver Age" Flash aims to surpass the limits of media itself, to jump out of the moving picture and the page. The cover suggests an avant-garde aspiration, the destruction of the barrier between art and everyday life, as the Flash runs out of unspooling film, into a color comics illustration, and toward the reader.

DC's *Showcase* #4 introduced the character Barry Allen, who becomes the Flash when he is soaked in chemicals and struck by lightning. When drawing the Flash, penciler Carmine Infantino and inker Joe Kubert use generous amounts of speed lines, also referred to as motion lines, to signal the superhero's rapid movements across the page. There is a distinct similarity between the speed lines that are ubiquitous in comics illustration and the representation of motion and movement in Marcel Duchamp's 1912 painting *Nude Descending a Staircase (No. 2)*.[4] Notable, in part, because it was a

3. For accounts of the comics code, see Kidman 46–90; Nyberg; Tilley.

4. An image of Duchamp's *Nude Descending a Staircase (No. 2)* (1912) is available online at: https://www.philamuseum.org/collection/object/51449. Emblematic of Duchamp's importance to comics are Bill Watterson's invocations of Duchamp's *Nude Descending a Staircase (No. 2)* in two separate *Calvin and Hobbes* comic strips. See the November 3, 1993, comic strip at https://www.gocomics.com/calvinandhobbes/1993/11/03, and the January 24, 1995, comic strip at https://www.gocomics.com/calvinandhobbes/1995/01/24.

part of the 1913 Armory Show in New York City, Duchamp's well-known composition represents time in the static space of the painting. Comics introduce time into the fixed space of the printed page too, and while comics also use panels, text, and other elements to convey sequence, the representation of a single figure in motion, in a single illustration, is a common practice. In *Showcase* #4, for example, the Flash races down the side of a skyscraper, his "fantastic speed" represented by speed lines in a ribbon-like formation evocative of motion-blurred photography (Kanigher 8; see color plate 4.2).[5]

The speed lines that denote the Flash's superheroic movement trail behind the figure, though they have the visual effect of propelling the figure forward. The Flash's speed-line panels epitomize how comics represent time in space. As the cover of *Showcase* #4 itself demonstrates, the Flash captures the movement of film in a print format. Stephen Kern has noted that Duchamp's *Nude Descending a Staircase (No. 2)* is part of a broader modernist interest in motion, inspired by developments in media technology. Kern writes, "Marcel Duchamp observed that 'the whole idea of movement, of speed, was in the air,' and acknowledged that his *Nude Descending a Staircase* was inspired by chronophotographs and motion pictures. The cinema reproduced the mechanization, jerkiness, and rush of modern times" (117). With the Flash, this aesthetic interest in speed becomes a narrative theme as well as a formal structure for image-making. Less about speed itself than about heroic fantasy, the Flash embodies the speed and fragmentation occasioned by modernity in a heroic icon. In the 1910s, Duchamp's figuration of modern speed distorts and disfigures the human body, rendering it as a series of lines and shapes cascading across the image. This interest in speed was also prevalent among the Futurists, in works such as Giacomo Balla's *Dynamism of a Dog on a Leash* (1912) or Anton Bragaglia's works of photodynamism (1911–14). In *Showcase* #4, Carmine Infantino prioritizes the individual figure; at the end of every speed line is a heroic individual, not a blur of shape and color. The superhero contains and realizes petrochemical powers, suited up in synthetic fabrics and moving in incredible ways. In petrochemical fantasies like the Flash, individual humans command energy not through carbon-emitting systems but instead through their superpowered bodies.

Plastic Man's original publisher, Quality Comics, went out of business in 1956, and the character did not appear in comics again until 1966. In the meantime, DC Comics created another stretchy character, the Elongated Man. While DC Comics' Elongated Man has similar powers to Plastic Man,

5. Comics have many connections to a figure like Duchamp, whose well-known readymade *Fountain* (1917) bears a reference to the comic strip *Mutt and Jeff*, created by Bud Fisher in 1907.

the origin of his powers lies not in a mysterious chemical process but in the consumption of the fictional "gingo" fruit. Originally appearing in *The Flash* comic book in 1960, Dibny is a clearly goofy figure, in the zany tradition of Plastic Man.[6] In *Flash* #115, Dibny is working as a circus act, stretching to catch a woman launched out of a cannon. He then takes a vacation to the "Mexican wilderness" to find the gingo plant: "The fruit of the gingo is the basis of the chemical which I isolated and gave me my extraordinary ability to stretch myself almost without limit!" (Broome et al., "Elongated Man's Secret Weapon" 3). When Dibny finds a gingo tree, though, he is immediately distracted by a bright red light. The light turns out to be a shrink ray brought to Earth by aliens. The aliens plot to take over the planet once they have shrunk the world's inhabitants. While the 1940s Plastic Man engaged in adventures that pitted him against energy inventors and chemical polluters, struggles which allegorize Plastic Man's imbrication in petrochemical plastics and pollution, Elongated Man's encounter thematizes the colonial extraction of rubber. Dibny's gingo fruit gives him flexible powers, figuring both the role natural rubber played in the growth of consumer capitalism and the persistence of materials like natural rubber even within the petrochemical plastics regime of the mid-twentieth century.[7] In the story, the alien's shrink ray ultimately fails once Elongated Man and the Flash team up, combining their flexibility and super speed. Dibny and the Flash's reworked bodies give them heroic powers, while the alien's reworking of bodies poses an existential threat to humanity. Like Plastic Man, Elongated Man poses a dichotomy between the flexible and pleasurable use of plastics and the monstrous, villainous use of technology to reshape the world. The stretching superhero enforces limits, though he has none of his own.

A year after the appearance of Elongated Man in DC Comics, Marvel Comics introduced a plastic hero too. The patriarch of the Fantastic Four, Reed Richards, a.k.a. Mister Fantastic, is also stretchy and flexible (color plate 4.3).[8] While Plastic Man is doused by acid and Elongated Man consumes an exotic fruit to become plastic, Reed Richards is, like many of Marvel's nuclear-age heroes, exposed to cosmic rays that endow him with

6. The Elongated Man first appears in Broome et al., "Mystery."

7. Stephen L. Harp's history of rubber documents that material's crucial role in the making of consumer capitalism: "During the late nineteenth- and early twentieth-century consumer-oriented industrialization—often called the Second Industrial Revolution—rubber was what sugar and cotton had been to the early, or 'first,' Industrial Revolution" (4).

8. The Fantastic Four were originally cocreated by Jack Kirby and Stan Lee. The superhero team first appeared in *Fantastic Four* no. 1 (November 1961).

powers. In "Fantastic Four Feature Page" from *Fantastic Four* #16, Richards explains:

> The shapes which I can mold my pliable body into are virtually limitless! I can shape myself into anything from a spare auto tire to a delicate, life-saving parachute! These shapes can be assumed with the speed of thought, but only because I have spent long hours practicing and developing my agility! Due to the extreme flexibility and elasticity of my molecular structure, I can absorb the impact of any type of shell (except an atomic missile) without suffering any physical harm! Naturally however, this can be extremely exhausting and leave me in a weakened condition for hours! (Lee and Kirby 419)

Atomic-era superheroes like the Fantastic Four are empowered by what historian Paul S. Hirsch has described as a "benevolent form of atomic energy . . . radiation exposure granted new and remarkable powers to humans, rather than incinerating them" (29). These nuclear-powered superheroes are evidence of how "the Cold War revitalized" comic books in the 1950s and 1960s by dramatizing how "Americans once again became heroes, not targets; active cold warriors instead of cynical victims" (Hirsch 29). While this Cold War triumphalism is certainly apparent in the Fantastic Four, Reed Richards's theoretically limited powers—he cannot withstand an atomic bomb—also express the fragility of an organic body, even from within the fantasy of plastic powers. Human weakness is a recurring trope in the Fantastic Four comics, as the heroes struggle with their newfound powers and responsibilities. Richards, especially, becomes absorbed with science and technology, isolating himself from his family and friends. Marvel's Mr. Fantastic registers not just the zany heroism of the Cold War superhero, but also the ways in which plasticity pushes the human body beyond its limits.

In *Action Comics* #1, Superman is faster and stronger than machines. An alien from another planet, his blue and red leotard as well as his alter ego, Clark Kent, confirm his status as an "ideal" American individual, an emblem of national identity. This humanist logic is a hallmark of popular modernism, which in the pages of middlebrow magazines, pulps, and comic books adopted modernist styles while reinforcing the social norms that many modernists bristled against. The same structure is evident in *Showcase* #4, in which the Flash retains his individuality even as he traverses the boundaries of time and space, and in Marvel's *Fantastic Four* series, where bodily mutations expand the capabilities of the "nuclear" family. The modernist visions articulated by the futurists earlier in the twentieth century often read like superhero stories, complete with visions of mutations, powers, and self-propulsion, though the political ideals behind either are quite different. Marinetti wrote in the futurist manifesto "Extended Man and the Kingdom of the Machine" (1915) about his vision of a superpowered future:

> We believe in the possibility of an incalculable number of human transformations, and we are not joking when we declare that in human flesh wings lie dormant.
>
> The day when it will be possible for man to externalize his will so that, like a huge invisible arm, it can extend beyond him, then his Dream and his Desire, which today are merely idle words, will rule supreme over conquered Space and Time.
>
> This nonhuman, mechanical species, built for constant speed, will quite naturally be cruel, omniscient, and warlike.
>
> It will possess the most unusual organs; organs adapted to the needs of an environment in which there are continuous clashes.
>
> Even now we can predict a development of the external protrusion of the sternum, resembling a prow, which will have great significance, given that man, in the future, will become an increasingly better aviator. (86)

Marinetti's descriptions of bodily transformation read uncannily like a rubric for creating your own superhero—from winged heroes like the Justice Society's Hawkman or the X-Men's Angel, to the invisible, stretchy, indestructible, or fiery bodies of Marvel's iconic superhero team, the Fantastic Four. Marvel's Fantastic Four realizes Marinetti's vision of human transformation through the fusion of aesthetic experimentation with Cold War American values.

Created by Jack Kirby and Stan Lee and published in 1961, *Fantastic Four* #1 introduced the superhero team composed of Mister Fantastic (Reed Richards), the Invisible Girl (Sue Storm), the Human Torch (Johnny Storm), and the Thing (Ben Grimm). Endowed with superpowers when exposed to "cosmic rays," the Fantastic Four are a group of do-gooders who operate out of the top floors of the Baxter Building in Manhattan (Lee and Kirby 18). The Fantastic Four's earliest adventures include struggles against the world-domineering plans of the Mole Man, Doctor Doom, and the Puppeteer, and the stories typically involve travel to other planets, dimensions, and temporal realms, a hodgepodge of mystical and pseudoscientific settings. These adventures might seem at odds with the often nonnarrative art produced by Marinetti and other futurist artists, yet as Richard Humphreys has argued, "Futurism seems to come with Darwinian evolution, evoking a sci-fi fantasy of 'Things to Come,' with intergalactic travel, alien encounters and extraordinary transformations of the human mind and body" (222). Indeed, the transformation of the Fantastic Four is an emblem of the futurist notion that "movement and light destroy the materiality of bodies" (Boccioni et al. 30). The comic series explores what could happen in a world of heroic dematerialization, where heroes wear "unstable molecules" to cover their unstable, irradiated bodies. The Fantastic Four make literal the avant-garde aspirations of the futurists, rendering acceleration, evolution, and technological progress into humanoid forms.

Futurism itself would eventually be directly invoked by a Fantastic Four character, the Futurist, who appeared in a two-issue storyline in 1980. In *Fantastic Four* #215, a scientist named Randolph James is assaulted by a group of "punks" looking for money (Wolfman et al., Feb. 1980). Suffering from his injuries, Professor James uses his experimental "evolution-accelerator" on himself, hoping that it will heal him. In a typical scientific, superheroic twist, the "evolution-accelerator" turns the scientist into the Futurist, an advanced humanoid with immense powers and a neoclassical toga. By the next issue, the Futurist has teamed up with the villain Blastaar, who entered Earth through an interdimensional portal. The duo fight the Fantastic Four, and the Futurist inevitably realizes that the Fantastic Four are not his enemies after all. Ultimately, Reed and Sue Richard's son Franklin saves the day by defeating Blastaar. As a child anchor of the Fantastic Four's normative family unit, Franklin plays an instrumental role in redeeming the Futurist, thus preserving the experimental spirit powered by cosmic energy so central to this comics series. Blastaar gets sent back through the interdimensional portal, and the Futurist journeys into the cosmos, set to explore "the supreme vastness of the universe" (Wolfman et al., Mar. 1980). The avant-garde is personified and reworked into a popular shape.

On the one hand, the *Fantastic Four*'s Futurist story is emblematic of the speed of superhero comics—both the speed of narrative pacing, as a character like the scientist Randolph James undergoes a rapid series of transitions in mere pages of a comic book, and the speeds available to superheroes and villains through speculative technologies and energy forms, as when the Futurist speeds into the cosmos in a bright flash of motion lines. Cosmic rays, chemical spills, radiation exposure, and genetic mutation all introduce petrochemical powers—speed, strength, and the sensation of human extension into machine, so emblematic of driving. As Marshall McLuhan remarked in 1964's *Understanding Media*, an automobile "turns the rider into a superman," and superhero comics elaborate on that extension of power (221). The fittingly named "Futurist" character makes apparent an aesthetic allegiance to modernist technological utopianism that runs throughout many superhero comics, beginning even with the superhero's predecessors in science fiction newspaper comic strips like *Buck Rogers* (1929–67) and *Flash Gordon* (1934–2003) and early comic book characters such as the original Human Torch featured on the cover of *Marvel Comics* #1 in 1939. In their late-modernist incarnation in post-1960s Marvel Comics, characters like the Futurist represent the aesthetic possibilities of technology as a disruptive and expansive force, with the same tropes of bodily transformation, inhuman violence, and high-speed travel that informed modernist movements like Futurism. Yet, as Alan Nadel has argued about Cold War American culture generally, these tropes are "contained" in superhero narratives that reaffirm the moral righteousness of United States liberalism and the sanctity of the normative white American family. Superhero comics are a mode for the articulation and expression of petrochemical fantasies as allegories of domestic, political, and social struggle.

Contemporary Petrochemical Superheroes

In the twenty-first century, Marvel Comics' Kamala Khan, a.k.a. Ms. Marvel, has plastic powers as well.[9] Khan is an "inhuman" in the Marvel Comics universe, a kind of superhero who receives power from fictional "Terrigen mists." After getting her powers, Kamala Khan fights socially resonant forms of crime and villainy in her native Jersey City. Ms. Marvel's first villain is the Inventor, a bird-headed figure who seeks to create "sustainable" energy by using disenfranchised millennials as batteries. Fighting against the Inventor, Ms. Marvel channels modernist aesthetics. After shrinking herself, she enters a large robot, and tries to reprogram it. In a page from *Ms. Marvel* #11 (2015) reminiscent of an iconic scene in Charlie Chaplin's 1936 film *Modern Times,* Khan works her way through the machine's gears, while thinking about how her approach to superheroism, "working small," requires "thinking smart, not hard" (Wilson et al.). This twenty-first-century comic pits an inhuman superhero against forces of exploitation and gentrification that masquerade as progressive, her stretchy journey through Chaplin's gears a symbol of the industrialization that undergirds the character's complex political position. As Sarah Gibbons has argued, Ms. Marvel's plastic powers thematize the "figurative flexibility to crises" expected of subjects in our moment of privatization and increasing climate instability (450). With Kamala Khan, the plastic hero's narrative both figures the human as inherently synthetic and

9. Ms. Marvel, a.k.a. Kamala Khan, first appeared in *Captain Marvel,* vol. 7, no. 14 (September 2013), and the *Ms. Marvel* series featuring her began in 2014. For a scholarly account of Ms. Marvel, see Baldanzi and Rashid.

posits villainy in the entrepreneurial rhetoric of economic and sustainable development. In this series, Ms. Marvel fights to protect Jersey City, a notably smaller scale than in other superhero narratives. New York City–adjacent, Ms. Marvel's Jersey City is represented as a close-knit community of modest citizens. Plastic powers do not remake the world here, and indeed, Ms. Marvel's plastic powers become a way of thinking about adapting to social change while preserving community. From the Terrigen Mists and their connotation of air pollution to the local activism encouraged by the series, G. Willow Wilson and Adrian Alphona's *Ms. Marvel* emphasizes how petrochemical fantasies are also everyday realities that exploit, displace, and poison people. Accordingly, the comics-fan-turned-superhero Kamala Khan uses her plastic powers to stall rather than expedite capitalist development, for the sake of the public good.

In these stories, plastic heroes thematize anxieties about technology, the environment, and the economy, yet the plastic heroes themselves present the inevitability and even zany heroism of a synthetic body, suffused with plastics. Both a celebration and a warning, the plastic hero stretches from heroic to monstrous and envisions both technological advancement and maintenance of the status quo. In the world of plastic superheroes, the environment is already toxic, so the stories imagine lives within that toxicity. As Amanda Boetzkes notes, the challenge today is not knowing that plastics are harmful—this is well documented—but instead understanding "how we know in and through plastic as a condition, as an aesthetic predisposition, and as a possible ethical disposition" (214). In plastic superhero comics, the imbrication of plastics in our bodies and our imaginaries is evident, and the "ethical disposition" of plastic superheroes directs us toward an unflinching acceptance of plastics as a part of our perpetual present.

There is one key example of a plastic superhero coming undone in a way that further gestures to a more complex relationship to plasticity. In DC Comics' 2004 *Identity Crisis* series, Elongated Man's wife, Sue Dibny, is murdered. In a now iconic illustration by artist Rags Morales, Elongated Man cradles his wife's body as he loses control of his own. In text boxes, Dibny realizes that he is too late to save her: "I stretch as fast as I can . . . But I'm still not fast enough" (Meltzer and Morales). If the stretchy powers of these superhero characters often figure into narratives of whimsically elastic crime prevention, *Identity Crisis* twists this absurd flexibility into uncontrollable grief. Dibny's body expresses his inner state, no longer a superpower but an exaggeration of suffering. *Identity Crisis* follows clearly in the path of DC's gritty reframing of superheroes, and its Elongated Man pietà revokes the superhero's zaniness.

In this moment in *Identity Crisis,* Elongated Man's powers operate in a different, unintended way, signaling grief rather than heroic action.[10] Similar to Kamala Khan's local heroics, this revision of the plastic superhero points to different uses of plastics, a framework around them that does not propagate illusions of plastic's ephemerality but instead asserts plastic's persistence, integration within our ecologies and bodies, and material resilience. As Heather Davis has argued, the age of plastics—what she refers to as a "plastisphere"—requires us to "learn to accept strange lifeforms, both human and nonhuman" ("Imperceptibility" 192). Looking at plastics in new ways—not as a transparent packaging or a means of engaging in a mundane action like toting groceries—means, in part, being mindful of how plastics have shaped us and our behaviors, from conscious choices to unconscious habits. Plastic superheroes articulate petrochemical fantasies of flexibility and action, of expansion beyond limits. Yet, in the case of Elongated Man's grief, they may also illustrate the ways that plastics have proliferated beyond the limits of human control. This realization could, perhaps, be the occasion for a humble approach to living with and among the petrochemicals that are already here with us.

Writing about plasmatic animation, Eisenstein posits that in Disney's cartoons "essence and form are dissected" (104). In "the contour of a neck elongating beyond the neck itself," he argues, "the unity of an object and the form of its representation" ruptures (105). This stretching and breaking of form and content has been normalized in superhero narratives. The ubiquity of the plastic imaginary and its attendant fantasies of freedom and power is both a key ideology of our consumer society and a reason to look for new ways of being in relation to the plastics that surround and embolden us. Eisenstein valued the estrangement of form and content in plasmatic cartoons because it reconnected viewers to an animistic nature. What for Eisenstein triggered animistic fantasies might, for us today, clarify how petrochemicals have fundamentally altered the concept and reality of "nature." In 2023 journalist Mark O'Connell wrote a *New York Times* opinion essay about microplastics, beginning with a description of plastic-infused bodies reminiscent of Plastic Man and his fellow stretchy superheroes:

> There is plastic in our bodies; it's in our lungs and in our bowels and in the blood that pulses through us. We can't see it, and we can't feel it, but it is there. It is there in the water we drink and the food we eat, and even in the air that we breathe. We don't know, yet, what it's doing to us, because we have only quite recently become aware of its presence; but since we have

10. For a reading of how death works in superhero comics, see Alaniz, *Death.*

> learned of it, it has become a source of profound and multifarious cultural anxiety.

Comics are one artistic medium where this "cultural anxiety" about plastics has been worked through for decades. Plastic Man's zany heroics, Mr. Fantastic's scientific innovations, Elongated Man's plasticized grief, and Ms. Marvel's community activism connect plastics to actions and personalities, thus representing the imbrication of petrochemicals in everyday life through genre conventions.

Superhero comics stage fossil fuel culture as an ever-unfolding fantasy narrative, and those narratives can emphasize the limits of fossil fuels as well as their possibilities. In the 1970s, for example, Marvel Comics developed the "Roxxon Corporation," a villainous organization whose name resembles that of the large oil company Exxon. The Humble Oil and Refining Company adopted the name "Exxon" in 1972, and as historian Paul H. Giddens explains, "EXXON was one of hundreds of names that came out of a computer and was then tested linguistically, psychologically, and for design potential. The company made a full-scale market test of the name at company retail outlets in six cities. The name EXXON was chosen because it was quickly recognized, easily remembered, and ranked high in consumer acceptance" (365). The corporate name-change took place from 1972 to 1973, and shortly after the Humble, Enco, and Esso brands were replaced by Exxon, the 1973 oil crisis made fossil fuels a pressing economic and political issue, one that Marvel consolidated into the evil, vast Roxxon Corporation. In *Captain America* #180 from 1974, the Serpent Squad kidnaps "the president of Roxxon, the monstrous oil conglomerate," and in the next issue, the villain Krang gains control of the Roxxon president's mind when he places a magical Serpent Crown on his head (Engelhart et al.). In 1973 an Exxon executive was kidnapped while working for Exxon's affiliate company Esso Argentina, perhaps providing the real-world background for this superhero narrative that portrayed the fossil fuel industry as compromised by villains ("Exxon").

In the late 1970s and early 1980s, the series *Marvel Two-in-One* featured a story arc involving Roxxon that invokes the scale, scope, and violence of fossil capitalism.[11] In *Marvel Two-in-One* #73, the superhero characters Quasar and the Thing are transported to a parallel dimension where the Roxxon

11. *Marvel Two-in-One* featured the Fantastic Four's Thing with other Marvel superheroes in many Roxxon-related stoylines, including "Project Pegasus" (*Marvel Two-in-One* nos. 42–43 and 53–58 from 1978–79), the "Serpent Crown Affair" (*Marvel Two-in-One* nos. 64–67 from 1980), and "Pipeline through Infinity" (*Marvel Two-in-One* no. 73 from 1981).

Oil Corporation has started drilling, extracting, and refining the plentiful petroleum under an alien planet's surface (Macchio et al.). Quasar and the Thing meet with the exploited natives of the parallel dimension, who have assembled an army of dinosaurs to fight the Roxxon employees. The superheroes lead the dinosaurs in attack. In this fanciful comic book moment, dinosaurs tear through the Roxxon extraction site, gnawing on oil derricks with their giant jaws and crushing Roxxon's security forces with their powerful claws (color plate 4.4). Oil companies often use dinosaur imagery, such as Sinclair's famous green dinosaur logo or Exxon's "Universe of Energy" exhibit at Disney's Epcot Center with its animatronic dinosaurs. The imaginary source and well-worn symbol of oil, dinosaurs exact their revenge on fossil fuel corporations in the pages of *Marvel Two-in-One*. The political message of this comic book adventure is clear from today's vantage point: leave fossil fuels in the ground, or they will wreak havoc on the world.

Recent superhero comics have proposed zombie takeovers, a return of the fascist Red Skull as a world-conquering God, and the invasion of Earth by a pop-culture menagerie of creatures, from sentient alien vegetation to Norse ice giants. Visualizing planetary catastrophe is also a major activity of climate science today, yet in many late twentieth- and early twenty-first-century superhero comics, planetary catastrophes are caused by nefarious, otherworldly villains, and not the slow violence of carbon emissions and toxic environments. Even as comics may obfuscate the realities that undergird the medium's petrochemical fantasies, comics also encourage ethical action in the real world, and they often make visible how our natural environment is bound to human action, even in fantastical registers. As in Plastic Man's reckoning with the "plague of plastic people" and Ms. Marvel's fight against Jersey City gentrification, comics visualize how humans and their environments shape one another, and superhero narratives ask readers to think of their actions as the products of moral and even political agency. In keeping with this glimmer of activist possibility, the next chapter traces how comics—from nonfiction reportage to science fiction graphic novels—have represented climate change and projected alternatives to the medium's longstanding petrochemical fantasies.

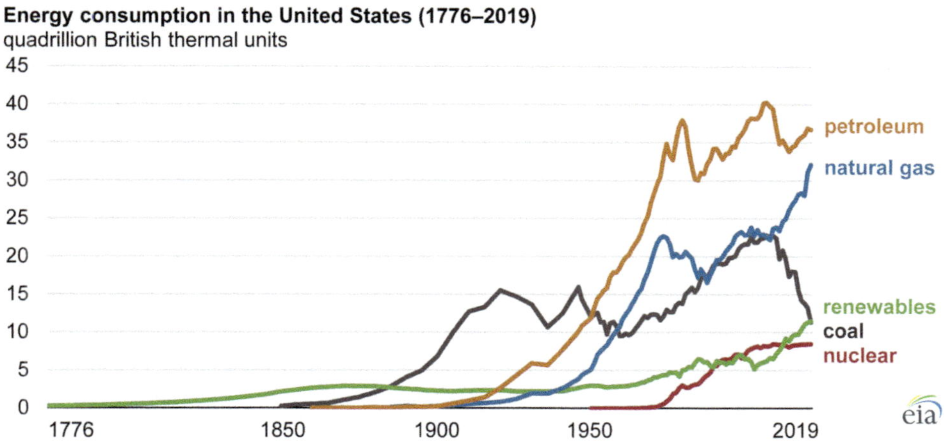

COLOR PLATE 0.1. Energy consumption in the United States (1776–2019). US Energy Information Administration, 2020.

COLOR PLATE 0.2. R. F. Outcault, "The Yellow Kid Treats the Crowd to a Horseless Carriage Ride." *New York Journal,* October 17, 1897. San Francisco Academy of Comic Art Collection, The Ohio State University, Billy Ireland Cartoon Library and Museum.

COLOR PLATE 0.3. R. F. Outcault, "Kelly's Kids Have a Shocking Time at the Electrical Show." *St. Louis Dispatch,* May 21, 1899. Courtesy of Peter Maresca / Sunday Press.

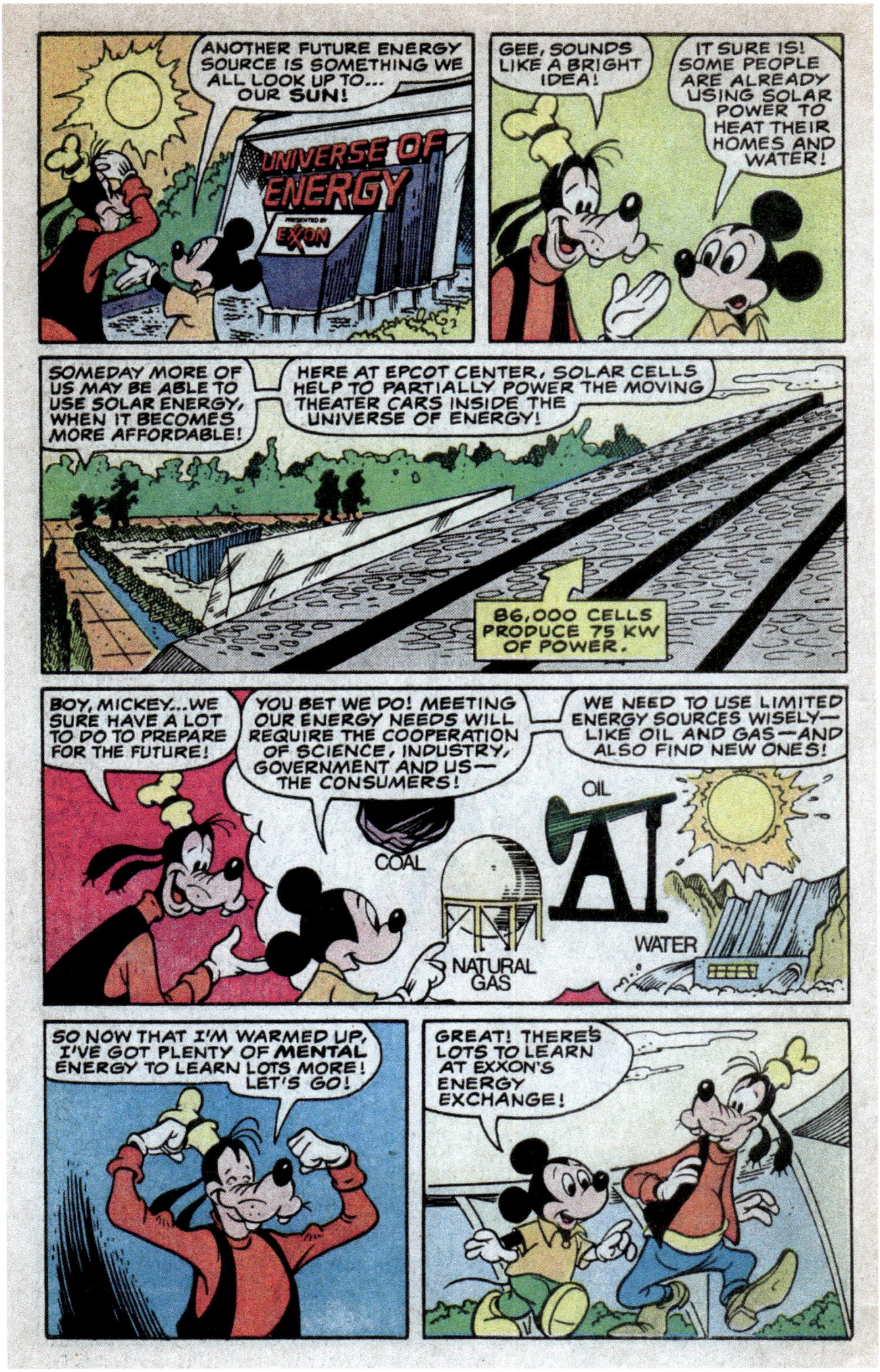

COLOR PLATE 0.4. Page from *Mickey and Goofy Explore the Universe of Energy.* Walt Disney Educational Media Company, 1985.

COLOR PLATE 1.1. Nathaniel Currier, lithographer, and William Keesey Hewitt, artist, *Awful Conflagration of the Steam Boat Lexington in Long Island Sound on Monday Eve, January 13th, 1840, by which melancholy occurrence, over 100 Persons Perished.* Published by the *New York Sun*, 1840. The Metropolitan Museum of Art.

COLOR PLATE 1.2. J. S. Pughe, "The Passing of the Horse." *Puck*, February 22, 1899. Library of Congress Prints and Photographs Division.

COLOR PLATE 2.1. R. F. Outcault, "The Constable." From *Buster Brown and His Bubble,* 1903. Library of Congress Prints and Photographs Division.

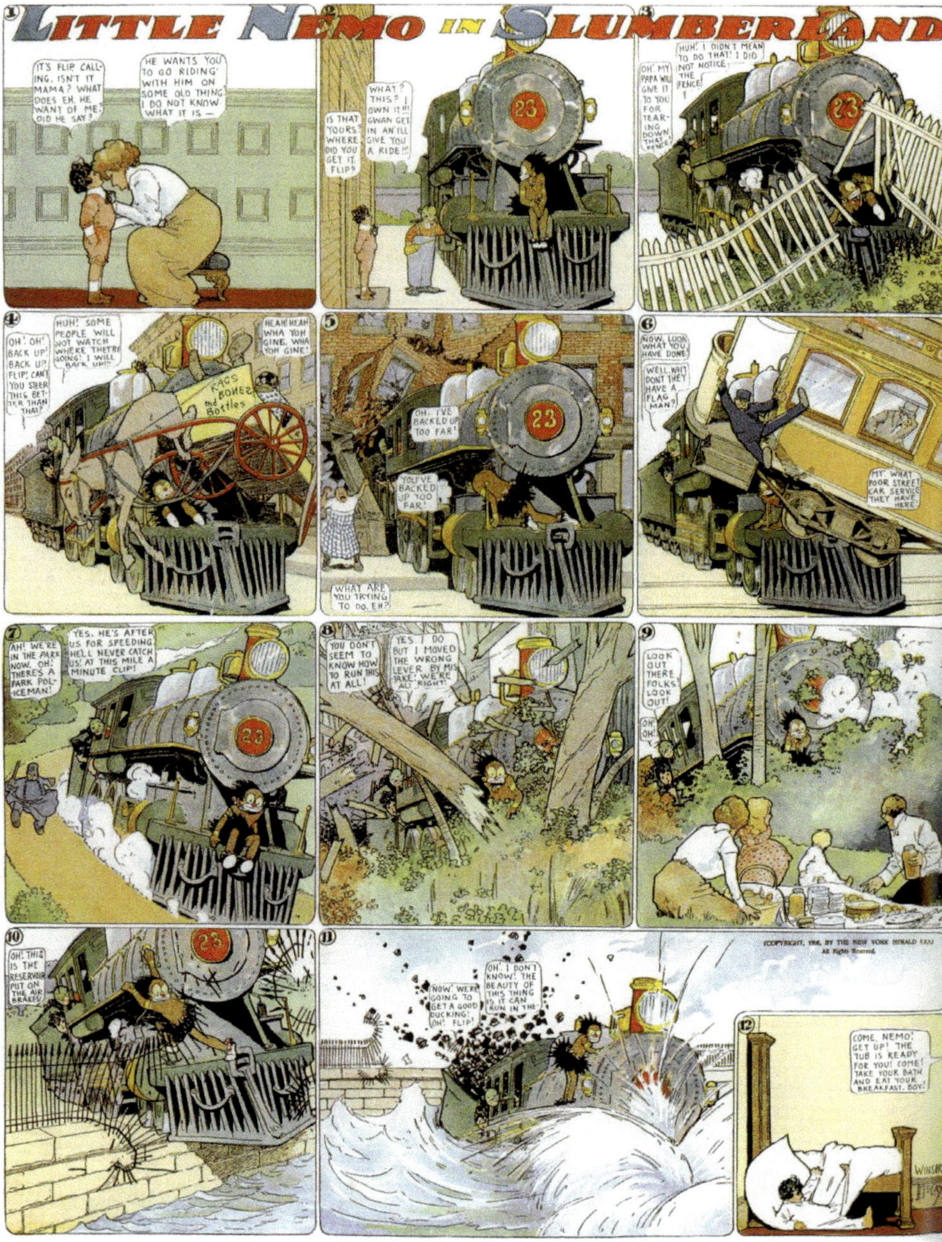

COLOR PLATE 2.2. Winsor McCay, *Little Nemo in Slumberland,* September 6, 1908. The Comic Strip Library.

COLOR PLATE 2.3. Rube Goldberg, "'And They Get Away with It!' III—The Automobile Mechanic." *Puck*, January 2, 1915. Library of Congress Prints and Photographs Division.

COLOR PLATE 3.1. Frederick Burr Opper, "Si and Mirandi." *Standard Oil Comics* no. 13A. Standard Oil Company, 1933.

COLOR PLATE 3.2. Vic Tor, "Curly and the Kids." *Gulf Funny Weekly* no. 403. Gulf Oil Corporation, January 10, 1941.

COLOR PLATE 3.3. Page from Jack Sparling, *History of Gas: Through the Ages with "Miss Flame."* American Gas Association, 1947. Courtesy of Hagley Museum and Library.

COLOR PLATE 3.4. F. O. Alexander, *Hairbreadth Harry. Famous Funnies* no. 1. Eastern Color Printing Company, July 1934. Library of Congress.

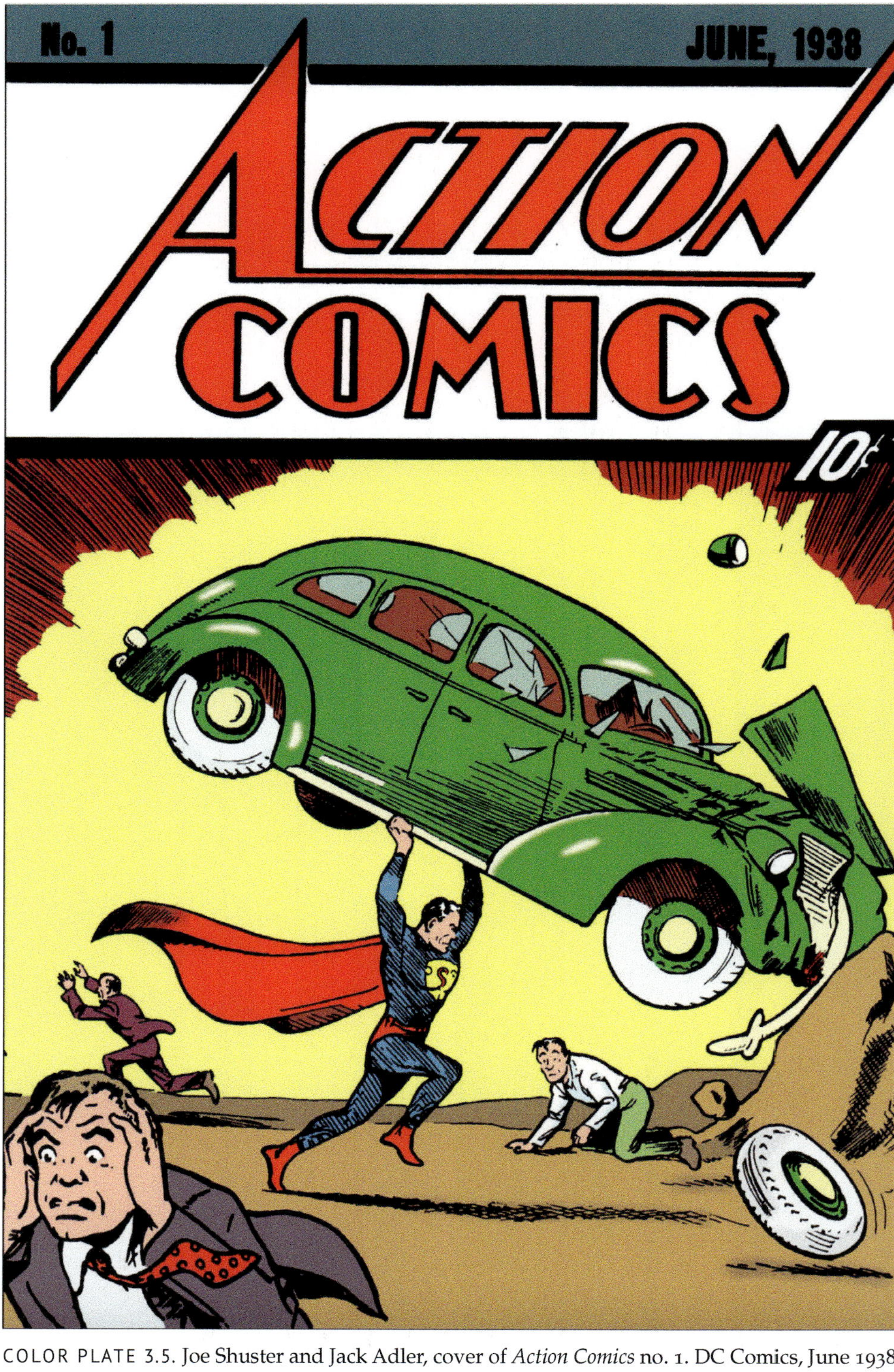

COLOR PLATE 3.5. Joe Shuster and Jack Adler, cover of *Action Comics* no. 1. DC Comics, June 1938.

COLOR PLATE 3.6. *RD-119: The Miracle in Your Gas Tank.* Sinclair Research Laboratories, 1950. Courtesy of Hagley Museum and Library.

COLOR PLATE 3.7. Panel from Gardner Fox and Cliff Young, "Hemisphere Defense." *All-Star Comics* no. 9. DC Comics, February/March 1942.

COLOR PLATE 3.8. Sid Greene, cover of *Strange Adventures* no. 120. DC Comics, September 1960.

COLOR PLATE 4.1. Jack Cole, cover of *Plastic Man* no. 7. Quality Comics, Spring 1947.

COLOR PLATE 4.2. Page from Robert Kanigher, Carmine Infantino, Joe Kubert, and Gaspar Saladino, "Mystery of the Human Thunderbolt!" *Showcase* no. 4. DC Comics, October 1956.

COLOR PLATE 4.3. Stan Lee, Jack Kirby, Sol Brodsky, Stan Goldberg, and Art Simek, "Fantastic Four Feature Page." *Fantastic Four* no. 16. Marvel Comics, July 1963.

COLOR PLATE 4.4. Panel from Ralph Macchio, Ron Wilson, Chic Stone, John Costanza, and George Roussos, "Pipeline through Infinity." *Marvel Two-in-One* no. 73. Marvel Comics, March 1981.

COLOR PLATE 5.1. Pablo Fajardo, Sophie Tardy-Joubert, and Damien Roudeau, *Crude: A Memoir,* translated by Hannah Chute. Graphic Mundi / Pennsylvania State University Press, 2021, p. 97.

COLOR PLATE 5.2. Rob Guillory, Taylor Wells, and Kody Chamberlain, *Farmhand* no. 1. Image Comics, July 2018, p. 14.

COLOR PLATE 5.3. Caitlin Cass, *Postal Constituent*, vol. 12, no. 2, 2022. Courtesy of Caitlin Cass.

COLOR PLATE 5.4. Michelle Gish, *We Are Here Forever.* Quirk Books, 2019, p. 38.

CHAPTER 5

The Climate of Comics

Published in 1976 by artist Leonard Rifas, *All-Atomic Comics* is an underground comics alternative to the corporate-sponsored comic books that told the story of American energy for decades. The first in a number of comic books from Rifas's Educomics publishing imprint, *All-Atomic Comics* features a talking mutated frog with three legs who gets into a losing argument with "Greedy Killerwatt," a mean light bulb who speaks for the interests of the energy industry. A parodic twist on the widely licensed electricity mascot Reddy Kilowatt (see chapter 3), Rifas's Greedy Killerwatt advocates for the use of nuclear power despite its dangers.[1] The comics' environmentalist frog realizes that Greedy Killerwatt is merely an industry spokesperson for the status quo, since "the oil companies are trying to monopolize all energy sources—coal, gas, oil, and uranium." *All-Atomic Comics* critiques American

1. Underground comics artist R. Crumb drew for the environmentalist periodicals *CoEvolution Quarterly*, *Whole Earth Review*, and *Winds of Change* from the late 1970s through the early 1990s. In a one-page "Mr. Appropriate" comic from *Winds of Change* in 1979, Crumb's environmentalist character "discovers power-plant politics in the Battle with Reddy Kilowatt." Crumb and Rifas both use the electricity mascot to personify the energy industry, and Crumb's "Mr. Appropriate" comic featuring Kilowatt was even reprinted in Rifas's *Energy Comics* (1980).

energy culture in a format long used to encourage and justify the outsized consumption of electricity, natural gas, and petroleum.

Rifas's *All-Atomic Comics* intentionally invokes and critiques the tradition of industry-sponsored comics about energy that accompanied the development and dominance of fossil fuels in twentieth-century America. Rifas notes that comic books promoting nuclear power alongside continued fossil fuel development proliferated after World War II:

> In 1948, at a time when comic books were a popular mass medium and frequently used for promotional purposes, General Electric sponsored *Adventures Inside the Atom.* General Electric was working, then and later, on both military and civilian applications of nuclear energy. That year, *Popular Science* magazine published a comics-format explanation of nuclear fission titled *Dagwood Splits the Atom,* which was expanded into a complete comic book in 1949. Utility companies and comics publishers continued to distribute comic books extolling nuclear power for the next several decades. ("Cartooning" 255)

Rifas goes on to explain that industry-sponsored comic books about nuclear power were complimented by "nuclear-themed *entertainment* comic books, including *Atomic Mouse* (1953–63), *Atomic Rabbit* (1955–58), and *Atom the Cat* (1957–59). The title character in the entertainment comic book series *Doctor Solar, Man of the Atom* (1962–69) was not a solar energy enthusiast, but a physicist working in a nuclear power plant who recharges his superpowers by exposing himself to radiation" (255). Nuclear power offered an even more ephemeral, immaterial, and futuristic reference point for superpowers and superheroics than fossil fuels, and it thus provided further imaginative power to the petrochemical fantasies that had eschewed energy's limits and materiality since the nineteenth century.

Underground comics represented the emerging environmentalist movement and oil crises of the 1970s, and not just through critiques of nuclear energy. Published by the Print Mint from 1972 to 1974, George Metzger's two-issue underground comics series *Truckin'* combines a paean to travel on the open road and living off the land with science fiction speculation about a new ice age brought on by human pollution. Published by Last Gasp, Trina Robbins's 1977 comic *Scarlett Pilgrim* is a spy story involving two women who are involved in a CIA plot to take over oil fields in the fictional Middle Eastern nation of Bahraq. Published since 1979, *World War 3 Illustrated* frequently publishes environmentalist comics. As comics scholar Margaret Galvan has noted, *World War 3 Illustrated*'s recent issues devoted to "Youth and Climate Change" (2015) and "Climate Chaos" (2016) include comics that, if printed as posters, could double as protest signs, thus "moving beyond simply representing a 'political' view by being created for the purpose of directly intervening in grassroots political action" (101). Rifas's *All-Atomic Comics* is, then, an early example of an explicitly environmentalist comic book, and following the general US retreat from nuclear power after the 1978 partial meltdown at the Three Mile Island Nuclear Power Plant, Rifas's *Energy Comics* in 1980 took on energy culture even more broadly and with more contributing artists. Mainstream and commercial comics had also begun to articulate environmentalist politics, such as in Walt Kelly's widely reproduced 1971 Earth Day poster featuring his comic strip character Pogo looking out upon a litter-strewn landscape with the quotation "We have met the enemy, and he is us."

Writing about his environmentalist comics in 2007, Rifas was heartened by the fact that "nonfiction comic books continue to appear" that further the comics tradition that he helped to establish ("Cartooning" 259). Yet he also found that "nevertheless, comic books explaining global climate change, peak oil, strategies for transitioning to hydrogen fuel, or household energy conservation advice apparently do not yet exist" (259). Since then, though, comics creators have become increasingly interested in and adept at representing climate change, energy cultures, and the need for energy transition. Nonfiction comics such as Kate Beaton's *Ducks: Two Years in the Oil Sands* (2022), Angela Boyle and Les McClaine's *Maker Comics: Live Sustainably!* (2022), Kate Evans's *Weird Weather: Everything You Didn't Want to Know about Climate Change but Probably Should Find Out* (2007), Grady Klein and Yoram Bauman's *The Cartoon Introduction to Climate Change* (2022), Simon Orpana's *Gasoline Dreams: Waking Up from Petroculture* (2021), and Philippe Squarzoni's *Climate Changed: A Personal Journey through the Science* (2014) dramatize and visualize climate change and the energy industry through a range of artistic and narrative techniques, from autobiography about labor in the oil industry to visual analysis of carbon emissions data.[2] Building on the work of artists and publishers like Rifas who created environmentalist comics in the 1970s and 1980s, contemporary comics artists have moved that tradition forward by drawing from contemporary climate change research with a political urgency that comes from the ongoing climate crises around the globe today.[3]

2. For more readings of contemporary comics that emphasize formal experimentation, climate change, and the Anthropocene, see Philip Smith; Squier.

3. For scholarship on comics history and environmentalism, see Alaniz "How Many Trees"; Dobrin. For an analysis of DC Comics' Aquaman and the Anthropocene, see Poll.

In the comics medium, the spatial and temporal scales of climate change have been represented in an increasing variety of works, including nonfiction comics like Josh Neufeld's *A.D.: New Orleans After the Deluge* (2009), journalistic exposés like the edited collection *Extraction! Comix Reportage* (2007), how-to manuals like *The Comic Book Guide to Growing Food* (2021) by Joseph Tychonievich and Liz Anna Kozik, comics poetry like Andrew White and Madeleine Witt's collection *Warmer* (2017), and educational texts like *Wild Weather: Storms, Meteorology, and Climate* (2019) by M. K. Reed and Jonathan Hill, published in First Second Books' *Science Comics* series. Monthly comic books also developed climate change as a theme, like Alan Moore's influential ecological allegory in DC Comics' *Swamp Thing* (1984–87), Nancy A. Collins's striking "environmentalist family romance" in DC's *Swamp Thing* from 1991 to 1993 (Costello), the oceanic garbage-patch adventure of the Image Comics series *Great Pacific* (2012–14), and the eco-activist thriller *The Massive* (2012–14). The widespread artistic interest in telling the story of climate change is, in part, due to the urgency and impasse of the situation. Climate change's massive scale yet technical explanations make the phenomenon difficult to characterize. As Dipesh Chakrabarty has argued, climate change and its concomitant reframing of our era as the Anthropocene complicates many long-held assumptions about time and history (namely, that humans are the center of both):

> Indeed, one way to think about the current crisis of anthropogenic climate change is to think of it as a problem of mismatched temporalities. Human institutions and practices are geared to a human sense of time and history. But we now have to use these institutions to address processes that unfold over much larger scales of time. (49)

The political impasse of climate legislation has similarly been characterized as a cultural problem, even more so than an economic or technical problem, for decades. The environmentalist politics evident in many alternative and underground comics from the 1960s onward have led today to a global array of contemporary comics about energy and the environment. These comics articulate a political imaginary that synthesizes the mundane and the speculative in the immediate context of global climate change, and they document how a transformed, unpredictable, even toxic environment has already become an intimate feature of everyday life. From history and autobiography to science fiction and how-to guides, comics document a time when the slow violence of climate change becomes unignorably visible.[4] In so doing,

4. On the concept of "slow violence," see Nixon.

comics visualize climate change and its jarring temporalities as a part of everyday life, an irreversibly toxic past that still determines the present but that may not completely decide the future. In this way, comics represent the contemporary climate, with a concomitant sense that time is out of joint.

Space and Time of Climate Change

Titled "Earth Temperature Timeline," the September 15, 2016, installment of Randall Munroe's webcomic *xkcd* is really long. If converted from screen to paper, it would measure 4.5 inches wide by 8 feet. The comic is a vertical timeline of the average temperature of the Earth since 20,000 BCE, when "Earth [was] 4° colder than during the late 20th century." The reader scrolls down, eventually, to the year 2100 CE, about seventy-five years into the future. The timeline concludes with three branching possibilities for Earth's warming: (1) a dramatically warmer "current path"; (2) a more moderate "optimistic scenario"; and (3) a less warm, but still warmer than any previous average, "best-case scenario assuming immediate massive action to limit emissions." The relatively steady global temperatures enjoyed by humans for the past four thousand years change radically toward the end of the timeline. Since the year 1900 CE, temperatures have risen more dramatically than at any other time on the chart. The warming spike in our present day interrupts the relatively steady global temperatures of millennia, ironically reinforcing the timeline's subtitle: "When people say 'the climate has changed before,' these are the kinds of changes they're talking about." The subtitle directs the reader to view the timeline as evidence of contemporary, human-caused climate change.

Munroe's "Earth Temperature Timeline" comic went viral in 2016, and it was even tweeted by the United Nations Framework Convention on Climate Change: "Tired of explaining #climate facts? Try this cartoon showing globe's sudden temperature rise" (UN Climate Change). Refuting the logic of climate skeptics, Munroe's timeline is a work of comics art that both expands on the formal conventions of the medium and, through that formal experimentation, becomes an example of the perspectival shift in thinking that the comic itself encourages in the reader. As Jordan Alexander Stein has argued about another long-running webcomic, Ryan North's *Dinosaur Comics* (2003–present), a serial webcomic can "cover a breathtaking range of theoretical propositions—from Marxism to Buddhism, computer science to queer theory—in order to show that any theory in the wrong (or, perhaps, the right) hands could become a conceptual mess. Theory, the comic shows us, is what we make of it. Thinking is an act of becoming, one of the more important ways in which we learn who we are." In particular, *xkcd*'s timeline is an example of how art about climate change finds what critic Heather Houser has identified as an "inventive dimension" in geological data, one that telegraphs a "coming-to-mind" narrative through which climate skeptics realize the errors in their thinking (34, 61). Munroe's *xkcd* facilitates this kind of thinking, as it positions comics readers as stick-figure participants in the Anthropocene.

xkcd's "Earth Temperature Timeline" is also a webcomic that calls attention to the virtual yet also material space produced by comics. It is impossible to read the *xkcd* timeline without scrolling down multiple times on laptop, tablet, or smartphone. As comics studies scholar Aaron Kashtan has noted, *xkcd* "demands physical effort and tactile contact from the reader" (102). This attention to the production of space, through the reader's navigation of a comic that requires participatory engagement, is emblematic of how comics facilitate shifts in perspective and thinking that can illuminate new ways for readers to understand climate change. As Art Spiegelman has famously said, "comics turn time into space" (Solomon), and *xkcd*'s comics about climate change routinely visualize the spatial and temporal concepts that make evident how activities like industrialization have changed the Earth.

Similarly juxtaposing the ice age with contemporary capitalism, Munroe's comic "4.5 Degrees" is a temperature chart with three comics panels dropped onto it, visualizing life at the temperatures of twenty thousand years ago, our present moment, and eighty-six years in the future. And in "Global Temperature over My Lifetime" from 2021, Munroe plots his own life on a line graph, coordinated by average global temperature and year. This chart includes both mundane bits about Munroe's childhood (the entry for "Fall 1996" is "I stand around awkwardly at my first middle school dance"), as well as moments of rising environmental awareness (the entry for "Summer 2006" is "I see *An Inconvenient Truth* in the theater and feel anxious"). The commingling of personal experience with climate data works in *xkcd* to ground abstract conceptions of the Anthropocene in everyday life, through both the ironic perspective of stick-figure drawings speaking complex truths and the casual intimacy of a humor webcomic. As *xkcd*'s climate change comics demonstrate, an understanding of geological time is fundamental to environmental awareness, and that awareness is only possible when climate change is understood as an effect of contemporary capitalism, a system through which Americans and Europeans have produced outsized carbon emissions. Like capitalist ideology, geological time is not immediately visible to us in everyday life, unless one knows how to look, and as a medium that "turns time into space," comics are uniquely suited to describe, document, and respond to climate change.

As a visual art that thrives on sequence and juxtaposition, comics can dramatize profound connections between everyday life and its entanglements with larger systems and structures. Donna Haraway uses Munroe's "Bee Orchid" comic from *xkcd* to demonstrate how art can posit new conceptions of life and nature that do not give priority to human experience and exertion. "Bee Orchid" is a multipanel comic about an orchid that mimics the appearance of an extinct bee. Now a self-pollinator, the *ophrys apifera* orchid is the only living evidence of its extinct pollinator bee's existence. In Haraway's reading of the comic, Munroe's elegiac final panels resonate with possibilities for "all terran creatures":

> In *xkcd*'s cartoon "Bee Orchid," we know a vanished insect once existed because a living flower still looks like the erotic organs of the avid female bee hungry for copulation. But the cartoon does something very special; it does not mistake lures for identity; it does not say the flower is exactly like the extinct insect's genitals. Instead, the flower collects up the presence of the bee aslant, in desire and mortality. The shape of the flower is "an idea of what the female bee looked like to the male bee . . . as interpreted by a plant . . . the only memory of the bee is a painting by a dying flower." Once embraced by living buzzing bees, the flower is a speaker for the dead. A stick figure promises to remember the bee flower when it comes time. The practice of the arts of memory enfold all terran critters. That must be part of any possibility for resurgence! (69)

Following Haraway's analysis, *xkcd*'s stick figure is a figural representation of how humans should be displaced and made more relational in works of art about the environment. In the webcomic's abstract caricature, humans lose their distinctiveness, and humans are outdone by both natural beauty (in "The Bee Orchid") and natural history (in "Earth Temperature Timeline"). While *xkcd* is not a political comic in any programmatic way, and while it does not recommend any lifestyle or policy changes to mitigate the problems it diagnoses, Munroe's webcomic nonetheless represents a way of thinking and art-making that accounts for climate change and its attendant reorientation of cultural and natural history. Although *xkcd* is just one example of how a comic has represented climate change, it acts as a useful lead into the ways in which other comics represent climate change through a range of genres, styles, and narratives. Taking up such a range, this chapter will further elaborate how comics stage climate change as a historical fact, a model for the future, and a personal reality.

Documentary Histories of Climate

The novelist Amitav Ghosh concludes his analysis of climate change narratives in *The Great Derangement* with "the rise of the graphic novel" (84). He characterizes the graphic novel as one of the "new, hybrid forms" capable of representing the Anthropocene and its revised narratives of space and time (84). While Ghosh does not go into detail about the graphic novel—nor does he use the more inclusive and less literary name for the medium, "comics"—it is certainly the case that contemporary nonfiction comics about climate change represent the space and time of fossil fuel culture and juxtapose it to alternative conceptions of everyday life. For example, comics journalist Joe Sacco's *Paying the Land* (2020) begins with a representation of cyclical time. The book's first section is titled "You Find Yourself in the Circle," and it begins with narration by Dene Nation broadcaster Paul Andrew, who describes growing up in Northern Canada's Mackenzie River Valley. For twenty pages, Sacco depicts Andrew's childhood, beginning with a full-page illustration of Andrew's birth and the following text: "My grandfather tells me that when they were traveling in a moose-skin boat, that's when I came into the world" (3). Throughout this first chapter, an adult Paul Andrew appears in black panels on most pages, but otherwise the illustrations of his childhood forgo panel borders. Scenes intermingle with one another, visually exemplifying the cyclical, ecological order of Andrew's account of the Dene past. In passages like this one, quotations are embedded across the two-page spread, juxtaposed with images of fishing, moose, and cooking by fire: "And I remember our lives being dictated by the environment, by the animals"; "There's a fish run at a certain place. It's time to go there"; "The moose skin is thick now"; "It's time to get moose"; "Basically [you] grew up having meat three times a day, a lot of times fish also, and berries" (26; brackets in original). Each sentence above is in a particular area on the page, overlaid on drawings of each distinct yet interconnected moment. This sense of intertwinement with nature and seasonal time is starkly interrupted when "a plane shows up" and Andrew is taken to a boarding school (22).

As in his earlier long-form works about the Bosnian War, the Israel-Palestine conflict, the Battle of the Somme, and Eritrean migrants, Joe Sacco uses first-person testimony as a structuring principle in the book. In most pages of *Paying the Land,* as in the sequence described above, a speaking subject's portrait appears in a black panel, serving as voice-over narration to the scene on the page. This invocation of past and present, through the juxtaposition of the present-day speaker and their recollections in panels, is distinctive of comics form. As Hillary Chute has argued, comics can juxtapose the present and the past, and Sacco's work in particular makes evident "that witnessing and memory can be treated as a creative interlocutionary process, rather than something anchored in the unfaceable" (254). Through this mediated, visual, and textual process, Sacco's *Paying the Land* produces a complicated connection to the past, bringing it into the present as a cluster of emotions, events, and fragments that disclose the rewriting of time, life, and purpose undertaken by the fossil fuel industry, as well as alternatives to those values.

Time is complicated by the Anthropocene, the popular geological and historical designation that signals the dramatically increased burning of fossil fuels by humans and the resulting changes to the planet's climate. The concept itself troubles many understandings of the human, from the Cartesian sense of the reflective self, able to grasp truth from within rather than without, to the Lockean notion of the Earth as passively awaiting the arrival of human labor to be activated. Yet as noted earlier in this book, the Anthropocene also universalizes climate change rather than identifying its particular historical context. For instance, Roy Scranton's book *Learning to Die in the Anthropocene* contends that the very concept of the Anthropocene demands that privileged humans of the high-consumption West embrace new limits that ultimately demand "learning to die" in a ruined world, an argument that romanticizes the gas-guzzling Westerner more than it undermines it as an ideal. Scranton argues "that we have failed to prevent unmanageable global warming and that global capitalist civilization as we know it is already over, but that humanity can survive and adapt to the new world of the Anthropocene if we accept human limits and transience as fundamental truths, and work to nurture the variety and richness of our collective culture heritage" (25–26). In this passage, Scranton's fatalism ultimately gives way to an optimistic sense of human resilience. Humans are not the center of Earth's story, and the timescales of climate change make this axiomatic. Yet Scranton's fixation on the Anthropocene as a category turns a historical problem into an existential one. Alternatively, Sacco juxtaposes different conceptions of time in *Paying the Land* to a more practical effect than critics like Scranton, who find in the Anthropocene a dark existentialism. In *Paying the Land,* time is a matter of culture, and different ways of inhabiting time are evident still in Sacco's representation of contemporary Canada.

Sustainable forms of time become something that communities can create and preserve, against the industrial time of fossil fuel companies.[5]

Paying the Land documents how time itself has different meanings to those in support of continued fossil fuel development and to those against it. Using a series of narrators, Sacco details the conflicting perspectives of those living in an extraction site. As he details in the book, some figures welcome the oil industry, seeing in it a chance at gainful employment and new social supports for long marginalized communities. Others see the oil industry as another form of extractive colonialism, a particularly toxic variation on the fur and logging operations that preceded fossil fuel interests. Yet, as Sacco notes in a section of the book that takes place in Yellowknife, "I rarely hear indigenous people reject mining out of hand no matter how differently they weigh its benefits and costs" (42). Denendeh Industries CEO Darrell Beaulieu explains his view of fossil fuel development next to drawings of a highway traffic jam, smartphone users, Iranian oil fields, and Chinese pipeline construction, and Beaulieu's real-world pragmatism casts these disparate global scenes as all supporting everyday life for Canadian fossil-fuel consumers: "If you don't like development of oil and gas, you don't like fracking, you don't like mining, then stop driving your car or stop using your iPhone" (Sacco 43; see figure 5.1). On this page, Sacco's illustrations of fossil fuel consumption (traffic, smartphones) and "dirty fuel" extraction juxtapose sites of production and transport, rendering Beaulieu's fatalist capitalism—"Humans 'are not going to stop' taking what they need, he says. 'It's just a matter of *how* we do that"—into an irrefutable reality, one that makes any negotiation of climate change much trickier than a simple issue of individual consumer choice (43).

Narratives of both progress and stasis are embedded within fossil fuel industry discourse. Fossil fuels and their byproducts provide the basis for modern civilization, the industry PR material consistently claims, and oil brings modernity to the world. Yet, once the fossil fuel industry is established, it must be maintained at all costs, to sustain the very ways of life that it facilitates with nonrenewable energy. The destructive and industrially powered machinery of the oil industry is a necessity only if one cannot imagine life outside of contemporary capitalism. In *Paying the Land,* Indigenous culture represents a different relation to the land, one that focuses not on extracting value but on leaving the land for others in the future. Leave no ruins behind, *Paying the Land* seems to encourage.

5. For more work on the Canadian oil industry, see Dembicki; Hern et al.; Szeman and Petrocultures Research Group.

FIGURE 5.1. Joe Sacco, *Paying the Land*. Metropolitan Books, 2020, p. 43.

While *Paying the Land* documents a resilient worldview that persists within a fossil fuel culture, *Crude: A Memoir* presents remediation and reparation as an ongoing process. With a story contributed by environmental activist Pablo Fajardo, scripted by journalist Sophie Tardy-Joubert, and drawn by graphic journalist Damien Roudeau, *Crude* (originally published in French as *Texaco*) opens with the gradual development of oil drilling in Ecuador, then shifts to the legal battle launched by Indigenous people seeking remediation for the pollution and destruction caused by the decades-long practices of the Texaco oil company, now a part of Chevron. Over five pages of landscape illustration, the book introduces its setting and context:

> Oriente, in eastern Ecuador. . . . A slice of the Amazon that stretches out over almost 90,000 square miles. . . . They say this region is the lungs of the planet. . . . This area is also one of the world's most polluted. Texaco, an American oil company, exploited its black gold for more than 20 years, from 1967 to 1993. . . . It's one of history's largest cases of oil pollution. 30 times the oil spilled by the Exxon Valdez shipwreck in Alaska in 1986. 3,000 times that of Erika in 1999. (Fajardo et al. 1–5)

Crude presents both the sublime industrial destruction of the fossil fuel industry and the slower, much more procedural and far less sublime processes of legal remediation and historical revision. Those five pages of setting are followed by more traditional memoir, as Pablo Fajardo introduces himself by grounding his personal identity in the land and the political struggle he has devoted decades to: "In 1993, 30,000 inhabitants—indigenous peoples and colonists together—filed suit against Texaco to have their land cleaned up. Their battle has lasted 25 years. I am their lawyer" (6). Fajardo's personal determination is intertwined with the much larger legal effort that he has helped to initiate, thus making this memoir less of a document of a personal journey than a commitment to environmentalism that recognizes the large-scale systems that have ruined ecosystems for profit.

Subtitled "a memoir," *Crude* synthesizes first-person narrative with an ongoing legal battle, presenting its protagonist as a dedicated activist. This personal narrative is juxtaposed and expanded with full- and double-page illustrations of the Ecuadorian environment, complementing Fajardo's memoir with a sense of the land and people that he represents. Rather than "learning how to die" in the Anthropocene, as Scranton encourages, Fajardo learns how to represent his community against the violence of the fossil fuel industry. The book's imagery places Fajardo in a global context, often making him visually subordinate to the environmental history that he is seeking to establish through law. On one page, three panels shift perspective from the planet to the law, then on to continued action, as they depict first a map, then a shelf of books documenting Texaco oil wells, and lastly Fajardo speaking as an activist (color plate 5.1). On this three-paneled page, the climate justice movement spans different spaces and institutions, linked by Fajardo's commitment that "Chevron can be brought to justice in any country where it's active" (97). The narration goes on to emphasize the long time span of climate justice, especially when it comes to legal action against a large fossil fuel company like Chevron. Noting at the bottom right that "each proceeding will take years to resolve" and emphasizing that "we must be patient," the creators of *Crude: A Memoir* present Fajardo's work as an ongoing process, unfolding through time and space, rather than a singular pursuit that can result in one clear victory (97). In this vein, *Crude* establishes a commitment to activism, a disciplined patience, and persistence in solidarity with others as appropriate responses to the world-altering effects of climate change. *Crude* also clarifies the effects of the American oil industry on other nations, people, and regions. Like in Sacco's *Paying the Land,* the comics memoir uses the temporal and spatial qualities of the comics medium to represent how fossil fuel extraction and consumption destroys lives and communities.

While *Crude: A Memoir* blends first-person narrative with legal proceedings and the history of fossil fuel extraction, *The Adventures of Alexander von Humboldt* details the history of ecology as a concept through Alexander von Humboldt's expedition to America from 1799 to 1804, during which the Romantic naturalist documented the plants, animals, geography, and meteorological conditions in South America and Mexico that would inform his writings. Written by historian Andrea Wulf and drawn by illustrator Lillian Melcher, the historical comic also juxtaposes the past with the present. Using images from Humboldt's own diaries, books, and drawings, the book blends a more traditional comics form with the illustrated memoir popularized in works like Phoebe Gloeckner's *Diary of a Teenage Girl* (2002) and Jeff Kinney's *Diary of a Wimpy Kid* (2007) that combine comics, illustration, and prose. As comics studies scholar Frederik Byrn Køhlert argues, autobiographical comics involve readers in complex negotiations with the text,

> because comics rely on both highly personal hand-drawn aesthetics and a serially networked approach to narrative, the form can challenge conventional representational schemes in a complex dance of appropriation and resignification that is always open to the creation of new meanings. Further, the multimodal hybridity of the comics form—consisting, as it does, of mul-

> tiple overlapping, interdependent, and often competing verbal and visual codes—creates a distinctively unstable and decentered reading experience that enables the drawn performance of the autobiographical self as a site of ideological struggle. (3–4)

A biography that adopts the conventions of the diary comic, *The Adventures of Alexander von Humboldt* displays the "multimodal hybridity" of comics, as the text brings together a number of different textual, visual, and even material artifacts. Following from her 2015 prose book *The Invention of Nature: Alexander von Humboldt's New World,* Andrea Wulf's collaboration with artist Lillian Melcher in *The Adventures of Alexander von Humboldt* develops a characterization of Humboldt as a thinker of the Anthropocene avant la lettre. As Colin Thubron noted in a review of *The Invention of Nature* in the *New York Times Book Review,* Humboldt has been represented in a variety of different ways, all pertaining to the sociopolitical conditions of their respective historical moments: "Especially in Germany, there have been many Humboldts. His works are so voluminous and wide-ranging that successive regimes have extracted from them the person they desire (even, during the Third Reich, an Aryan supremacist). Andrea Wulf's Humboldt is the ecological visionary and humanist." Wulf and Melcher's portrait of Humboldt is suited to the contemporary moment, emphasizing less his scientific rigor or imperialist perspective than his artistic craft and intimate friendships.

If Andrea Wulf's version of Humboldt emphasizes the prescient climatology of his thinking, writings, and drawings, then that clearly reflects the demands of our contemporary moment, wherein climate change is increasingly recognized as a reality that must reshape our connections to the environment. Illustrator Lillian Melcher's juxtaposition of comics panels with maps, historical drawings, and decorative objects connected to Humboldt's travels makes the process of ecological understanding a material and social activity. Humboldt's practice of drawing and observation is a model for Wulf and Melcher's own contemporary practice of historical narrative, and on one page, for example, Melcher draws herself into the narrative to make clear that some of the material in the book is from Humboldt's own notebooks and sketchbooks. On the page, Humboldt narrates from Callao, Lima's port: "We set up everything and all we can do now is wait . . . But the clouds worry me. To distract myself, I sketch some of the animals in the harbor" (Wulf and Melcher 197; ellipses in original). Two sketches are reproduced on the page, both signed by Humboldt and dated 1802. In the bottom right corner of the page, Humboldt stands next to Melcher's drawing table, and he says, "I just wanted to say that Lillian Melcher didn't draw the penguin . . . It looks very similar to her style, but I assure you that I sketched it in Callao" (ellipses in original). The spatial and temporal layering on this page is remarkable, as it connects Humboldt's own drawing style in 1802 to Melcher's in 2019, as well as noting how the species of penguin in Humboldt's sketch would later be named after Humboldt himself, thus demonstrating how his drawings not only represent but also create the world that Melcher inhabits. This connection of science to drawing emphasizes how ecology has long been understood though image and text, scientific analysis that looks like artistic creation as well as empirical description.

All three of these comics approach climate change through different nonfiction forms, and all three make the global connections necessary today for climate activism, global connections that are also increasingly important in twenty-first-century comics culture. In Sacco's *Paying the Land,* journalistic documentation and travelogue amount to a representation of fossil fuel extraction and the sense of connection that it displaces for profit and industry. In *Crude: A Memoir,* autobiography and legal drama reveal how climate change has already had a terrible effect on those who live in neocolonial extraction sites and how struggles that emanate from those sites create new modes of activism. *The Adventures of Alexander von Humboldt*'s diaristic and trompe l'oeil images represent a historical figure as an emblem for the present and future, finding in Humboldt's curiosity a model of interconnection and a willingness to pursue ecological thinking beyond conventional limits. Across their forms, settings, and themes, these three different works share an interest in how climate change revises human-centered, progress-oriented time into a complex tangle of slow violence, ongoing struggle, and cultural resilience.

Science Fiction Speculation

Like in documentary and nonfiction comics, science fiction comics have frequently used climate change as a theme and subject, yet science fiction's status as a popular genre has often excluded it from serious study as art or literature. As Ghosh has noted,

> fiction that deals with climate change is almost by definition not of the kind that is taken seriously by serious literary journals: the mere mention of the subject is often enough to relegate a novel or short story to the genre of science fiction. It is as though in the literary imagination climate change were somehow akin to extraterrestrials or interplanetary travel. (7)

Moreover, science fiction scholar Gerry Canavan has argued that both critical theory and science fiction share qualities with the documentary comics discussed above, insofar as they all engage in both apocalyptic and utopian speculation:

> the impulse toward the miserable, deflationary naming of all the various ongoing ecological catastrophes is always matched (if only in negative) by an inflationary, futurological impulse toward the better world that might yet be. Here utopia and apocalypse unexpectedly collapse into one another—they are each disguised versions of an imaginative leap into futurity. (16)

This insistence in climate change narratives that "things, after all, might yet be otherwise" is a core ideology in science fiction comics, just as in prose fiction and nonfiction science writing. Like in science fiction, comics often pair apocalyptic and utopian modes to imagine an Earth that is undergoing climate change but that can still, through collective social action, remain habitable for humans in a different register than before. In contemporary comics culture, science fiction continues to thrive, and accordingly, contemporary comics artists have visualized climate change as a narrative device. A background for dystopian stories and a framework for imagining the effects of profligate consumption, climate change in these comics emerges as a large-scale, world-shaping force and an emotional, all-too-personal reality to which characters must adapt.

Inés Estrada's *Alienation* takes place in Alaska in the year 2054. The graphic novel's main character, Elizabeth Smith, is a virtual reality (VR) sex worker who gives birth to "the first Human/AI hybrid," a child fittingly named the Singularity (180). In Estrada's dystopian Alaska, pollution blocks the stars from view, and Elizabeth spends most of her time online through a "Google-gland" biotechnological implant (205). *Alienation*'s twinned themes of biology and technology, or nature and culture, are mutually reinforcing ideas. In one scene, Elizabeth exclaims, "I'm bored!" and then demands VR marine life appear in her room (61; see figure 5.2). These virtual projections of extinct marine life creep into Elizabeth's lived reality, and even her "Human/AI" child flees her apartment and eventually decides to hibernate with a polar bear, thinking, "Fuck it! I just want to chill" (227). Humans and their technology conjure the natural world, yearning for proximity to it. *Alienation* begins as Elizabeth and her partner, Carlos, watch a total lunar eclipse on a "Starbucks Live Cam," necessary since the sky is so polluted. Carlos asks if the eclipse "is real? . . . Like, is this really happening, or is it

FIGURE 5.2. Inés Estrada, *Alienation.* Fantagraphics Books, 2019, p. 61.

CGI?" (6). Elizabeth eventually settles the issue when she responds, "Who gives a shit. This world is all a big lie anyway" (7). *Alienation* embraces hybridity, envisioning transhuman life as both exploitative and open, with possibilities for simply checking out of the daily grind of service work.

Reviewer Patrick Kyle remarked in *The Comics Journal* that Estrada's *Alienation* was "originally serialized in Xeroxed mini-comics throughout 2016 and 2017," and the work's hand-drawn aesthetic and experimental sci-fi narrative further invoke how the medium of comics in particular is "limited only by what you can personally imagine—your own perfect Internet, untouchable and free of exterior influence or capitalistic degradation." Estrada's pencil drawings create a complex future world, saturated with virtual technologies and gig economy labor. But the comic itself is not a big-budget science fiction production, so the world is less immersive than it is a thought experiment, a projection of a possible future that invokes possibility and community rather than passive spectacle. As an indie comic, *Alienation* provides an answer to the problem diagnosed in the book's title. Through artistic community and creation from within a growing technological dystopia, something different may emerge. Based in Mexico City, Estrada founded the Gatosaurio label and website in 2013, where she distributes her own work and the work of other artists in Mexico City and beyond. This kind of small-scale, artisanal distribution is one way of undoing alienation and making new social worlds possible.

While Estrada's *Alienation* invokes comics-making as a way of imagining a world beyond capitalist exploitation, Rob Guillory's *Farmhand* dwells on the commodification of natural resources. Published by Image Comics since 2018, *Farmhand* has, as of this writing, reached twenty issues of a projected twenty-six. Guillory's work of agricultural science fiction takes place in Freetown, Louisiana. In *Farmhand*'s alternate reality, a Black farmer named Jedidiah Elias Jenkins develops the "Jedidiah Seed," described in the first issue as "a new type of human stem cell. An intelligent cell that not only adapted to surrounding tissue, but seemed to instinctually know how tissue ought to be repaired" (11). This miracle stem cell grows like a plant, and Jenkins's farm becomes a biotech company that provides "safe, transplant-ready farm-grown organs, without the expensive limitations that hampered past bioengineering techniques" (14). In the first issue of *Farmhand,* the illustrations of "factory farming" emphasize the body horror element in the comic's premise. A gardener prunes bloody fingers from trees, and kidneys grow in a hydroponic reservoir (color plate 5.2). Evident in its organ farm and plant-human hybrids, *Farmhand* employs zombie imagery familiar to readers of twenty-first-century American comic books. In issue 7,

Guillory even references Image Comics' bestselling zombie series, *The Walking Dead* (2003–19), when the protagonist, in a flashback, mentions his copy of "*The Walking Dead* #500 with the chromium cover," a comic that was never published but that exists in *Farmhand*'s sci-fi future (2).

More than just a play on the zombie genre, *Farmhand* interweaves the zombie's troubling of the human/nonhuman divide with the history and future of environmental exploitation. Inspired by the Freetown neighborhood in Guillory's hometown of Lafayette, Louisiana, *Farmhand*'s Freetown was founded by Isaiah Jenkins to be "an oasis of peace springin' forth in the middle of the blood-soaked South" (*Farmhand* no. 11, 13). It is revealed in the series that Isaiah was lynched, and "a bitter root had been planted in the Jenkins bloodline," symbolized in *Farmhand* by a demonic tree and likely connected to the organ-growing "Jedidiah seed." A speculative account of human body parts grown from "blood-soaked" soil, *Farmhand* weaves agriculture, race, toxicity, and biotechnology into a representation of the Gulf Coast fossil fuel industry as well. In contemporary Freetown, the Lafayette Oil and Gas company underwrites the Jenkins Farm, a fictionalized demonstration of how agriculture and "green technology" are part of, and not necessarily alternatives to, fossil fuel culture. In the comic, Jedidiah's son Ezekiel struggles to make sense of his family's past, and eventually becomes a part of the fight against the human-plant hybrids that take over Freetown. Building upon this complex allegory of agriculture, bodies, oil, pollution, and race, the main villain in *Farmhand* is Monica Thorne, who is transformed into a plant-human hybrid by the Jedidiah Seed. She seeks out the experimental treatment because she suffers from "rhinocerebral mucormycosis," described by her doctor as "a fungal infection. There was an uptick in reported cases after Katrina II" (*Farmhand* no. 13, 22–23). In Guillory's speculative future, "an unprecedented superstorm dubbed Katrina II destroyed the city of New Orleans, killing thousands. As the bodies of the dead littered the floodwaters, a deadly plague added to the body count" (*Farmhand* no. 14, 1). Monica Thorne's origin is bound to climate disaster, just as she is also representative of "green" gentrification. She develops her villainous plot to take over Freetown by promising a beautification program during her mayoral campaign, and gains support in the local community by growing organic produce in raised garden beds. The fantastical premise of the comic book series is a stage from which Guillory can explore the limits and possibilities of environmentalism in an ecosystem thoroughly intertwined with fossil fuels.

Farmhand's adoption of "green" imagery into a science fiction horror narrative makes visual the coextension of human bodies into the ecosystem.

As in Estrada's *Alienation, Farmhand* posits a near future of further climate disaster that is still structured around familiar corporate interests and capitalist traditions. Neither utopia nor dystopia, these genre stories visualize realities that are proximate in the Anthropocene. As David Wallace-Wells argues, climate change presents humans not only in a much longer temporal context—that of deep time and geology—but also in the much shorter time span of rapid, recent climate change: "Global warming has improbably compressed into two generations the entire story of human civilization" (29). This collapse of climate change into two brief human generations is figured by both Estrada and Guillory, both of whom feature protagonists torn between the accumulated human past and an emergent transhuman future.

Everyday Change

The speculative technologies and toxic environments of science fiction comics visualize a world beyond our own, but often only in increments. Other comics dwell on the present day and seek a sense of connection and possibility through first-person or diaristic narratives. Climate change often resonates as a large-scale, structural condition, and this can feel overpowering and defeating. Yet as formally inventive comics can emphasize, there remain ways to be ecological, reflective, and responsible.

In contemporary comics culture, a growing number of climate change–themed comics seek to understand and visualize ways to inhabit space given the ecological conditions of everyday life. Published in her long-running *Postal Constituent* series (2009–present) distributed through subscription by mail, Caitlin Cass's broadsheet comic about hope in the Anthropocene dwells on what an individual life might mean in this broader geological and historical context. Folding out into four pages, Cass's comic is a meditation on finding beauty in nature while simultaneously recognizing the smallness and insignificance of that beauty. On the work's first page, the first-person text asks, "Hope? Is it worth something? In the face of such dire environmental destruction it feels naïve to hope. Still, last week I planted wildflowers" (color plate 5.3). This hand-lettered, cursive text is among residential garden images, and then at the bottom of the page, the word "wildflowers" is complemented by an image of a turkey that anchors the page. In cursive text, Cass describes that she "watched a wild turkey and remembered: It's not about me." This disinvestment in personhood is hopeful and uplifting. Cass associates a less individualistic and less human perspective with viewing the world in images, a visual and experiential mode in which even words are visibly drawn. The work concludes with an affirmation: "Something will survive / It just might not be human / And I think about how symbols and images hold hope more willingly / Words are too razor sharp." Cass's embrace of "symbols and images" resounds with the Anthropocene and the species humility that necessarily accompanies the fact of climate change. Comics offer a different perspective, an escape from the language and reason that led to the Anthropocene.

Like Cass's lyrical work about climate change, Michelle Gish's *We Are Here Forever* imagines a future where humans are not important. Originally published as a webcomic and subsequently collected in book form, *We Are Here Forever* tells the stories of a group of purple blob creatures who have populated the Earth after the extinction of humans. The purple blob creatures repurpose human tools, develop social rituals, and explore their environment. Often cute and whimsical, the comic also ironizes its own cuteness in moments that invoke desperation. In one scene, three purple blob creatures are frightened by televisions showing static in a store window, declaring, "That ruined our good time" (Gish 28). They eventually throw a boulder into the glowing bank of televisions and learn that they must "protect themselves" from "rude things" like these electricity-consuming devices (color plate 5.4). Smashing things with rocks in a posthuman environment, the purple blob creatures face no human opposition and are free to remake the city. The life-affirming title of the webcomic and collection, *We Are Here Forever,* further emphasizes how the work takes joy in the possibility of an altered world, since the "we" in the comics' title does *not* include the reader or any other humans. Like Caitlin Cass's meditation on beauty beyond the individual, Gish's purple creatures reflect an awareness that the fundamental assumptions about human progress must be rethought to foster a different relation to the world. Gish's purple creatures reappropriate human artifacts and have no respect for their previous uses. Their willingness to smash old structures and improvise new ones is a model for the kinds of immediate activism needed today to stop carbon emissions.

Whether set in the past, present, or future, these comics about climate change posit a changed way of life as a given. Comics can move forward from that premise to piece together a vision of sustainable life. For example, Richard Monastersky and Nick Sousanis's short comic "The Fragile Framework" was published in a special issue of the science journal *Nature* devoted to the 2015 Paris climate talks, and it concludes with a tempered optimism that fuses the reality of climate change with a commitment to ongoing activism: "The framework to fix the planet is coming together, but it is fragile and far too small. The job of finishing the task will fall to future generations"

(435). The comic envisions continued rather than explosive action, an ongoing struggle for current and future generations of humans. Similarly looking to the future through climate change, works like Ezra Clayton Daniels and Ben Passmore's *BTTM FDRS* (2019), Hugh Goldring and Nicole Burton's *The Beast: Making a Living on a Dying Planet* (2018), Dan Nott's *Hidden Systems: Water, Electricity, and the Secrets behind the Systems We Use Every Day* (2023), Sophie Yanow's *The Contradictions* (2021), and the graphic adaptations of Yuval Noah Harari's popular bestseller *Sapiens* (2020–21) all depict new ways of thinking about and inhabiting the environment, modes of imagining life that are informed by the well-established reality of climate change.

Comics are an artisanal medium as well as a major part of global popular culture, and comics have a lot to do with climate change, both as a medium historically tied to fossil fuel culture and as a medium that can make climate change visible to potential environmentalists. As climate activist Greta Thunberg has said, "almost everything is black and white" when it comes to climate change:

> Today we use 100 million barrels of oil every day. There are no politics to change that. There are no rules to keep that oil in the ground. So we can't save the world by playing by the rules. Because the rules have to be changed. Everything needs to change. And it has to start today. (11)

What better medium to articulate this message than comics? Long the booster of fossil fuels, comics can instead participate in the energy transition that we need now. The transition from fossil fuels to renewable energy requires a shift in culture. Making, reading, and sharing comics with others is one way to cultivate a sustainable culture. Instead of driving in a car for hours on end, wouldn't you rather stay home, read a comic, and draw your own?

CONCLUSION

"This Is NOT Fine!!"

Artist K. C. Green's 2013 webcomic "On Fire" has become iconic over the past ten years, circulating widely on the internet and available as a signed art print, a plastic model, a plush toy, and even a video game. Originally posted on his website *Gunshow,* Green's "On Fire" features his recurring character Question Dog, an anthropomorphic brown dog with black ears, large cartoon eyes, and a brown bowler hat.[1] In the comic, Question Dog sits on a chair next to a table. A coffee mug sits on the table, and the surrounding room is in flames. Question Dog smiles in the second panel and says, "This is fine." He takes a drink from the coffee mug, and in the final panel, his face melts off. A comics motif that invokes both Robert Crumb's "Stoned Agin!" (1971), a single-page comic also printed as a wall poster, and the melting face of Nazi henchman Toht in the film *Raiders of the Lost Ark* (1981), Green's "On Fire" became a popular internet meme. The comic's fire motif can be interpreted to signify a broad range of problems, and it has been used in a variety of contexts over the past decade. Green commented in an interview on the tenth anniversary of "On Fire" that he "made it vague on purpose," so that "like any good piece of art, people interpret it how they want to"

1. Green's "On Fire" (2013) is available online at https://gunshowcomic.com/648.

(Emma Bowman). "On Fire" is not explicitly about climate change, but like many artworks today, it is also not *not* about climate change.[2]

Question Dog expresses a slacker resignation familiar to alternative comics culture, yet the character's "this is fine" remark also doubles as an ironic critique and recognition of the flames that surround him. It is notable that the general metaphor of something being "on fire" was increasingly associated not with metaphor but with reality in the 2010s. As the US Environmental Protection Agency notes, wildfires have been on the rise in the late twentieth and early twenty-first centuries: "the extent of area burned by wildfires each year appears to have increased since the 1980s. According to National Interagency Fire Center data, of the 10 years with the largest acreage burned, all have occurred since 2004, including the peak year in 2015" ("Climate Change"). When Green returned to "On Fire" in 2016 with a new comic for the website *The Nib,* Question Dog sits again in a fiery room, but this time he screams "This is NOT Fine!!," grabs a fire extinguisher, and puts out the flames. The comic ends with a frazzled Question Dog, head in hands, seated in a sooty, ruined room.[3]

Green's "This Is Not Fine" offers an alternate ending, in which Question Dog's resignation transforms into too-late action. Question Dog exclaims, "There was no reason to let it last this long and get this bad!" as he extinguishes the flames, invoking the neoliberal workplace slogan of "putting out fires" to describe spontaneous problem-solving. Vague by design, Question Dog's situation can allegorize countless social problems, personal struggles, and environmental crises. It aims to motivate action on the part of the reader, to find some humor and even hope from within compromised and deteriorating social conditions.[4] When asked about the myriad circumstances that readers could project onto Question Dog's fire, Green responded, "we're not just accepting it, but working past it, trying to grow from it" (Emma Bowman). As Question Dog's resignation gave way to resilience, so have many comics creators, editors, fans, publishers, readers, and scholars sought to envision new ways of acting and living today. Comics narratives document everyday life and catastrophe within the ongoing climate crisis, in a work like Brian Fies's *A Fire Story* (2019) about Northern California wildfires, as

2. Green's "On Fire" is a prime example of what Mark Bould has described as the "Anthropocene Unconscious," since climate change is obviously a subject of the comic and yet not exclusively *the* subject of the comic. See Bould 1–17.

3. Green's "This Is Not Fine" is available online at https://thenib.com/this-is-not-fine/.

4. Like print comics, webcomics often engage readers in dialogue and offer points of identification for fans. On webcomics, see Kashtan; Kleefeld. On comics publics, see Woo and Stoll.

well as in genre stories that directly allegorize resistance to extractive capitalism, such as Cole Pauls's *Dakwäkãda Warriors* (2019). Just as comics once documented the transition to fossil fuels, so too are comics today documenting the ongoing yet catastrophically slow transition away from fossil fuels and to renewable energy. Just as the transition to fossil fuels changed cultural norms, practices, and stories, so too will the current transition require changes to the fossil fuel–intensive practices of Americans today. Question Dog's attitude change from 2013's "This is fine" to 2016's "This is NOT fine!!" signals the broader cultural urgency of climate activism and energy transition today. Following Question Dog's lead, I have written this book because comics can play a vital role in the transition to renewable energy. Because of the medium's educational and imaginative capacities, comics holds much promise for a sustainable future if it isn't yet too late.

Energy is a preeminent motif in some of the major comics adaptations of the twenty-first century. It is even the central object of struggle in many big-budget transmedia productions. In director Ryan Coogler's *Black Panther* (2018) and *World of Wakanda* (2022) films, for example, villains and governments seek access to vibranium, a metal that can absorb, generate, and transfer massive amounts of energy. The centrality of energy to Marvel's *Black Panther* films extends back to the character's origins in comics. As Qiana Whitted notes, Jack Kirby and Stan Lee developed the Black Panther in the mid-1960s "as part of a larger effort to connect with Black readers and bring more diversity to Marvel's stories," and Kirby made "concept sketches of a Black hero that he and Lee called the Coal Tiger" ("Introduction" xxii). The fictional material vibranium began with the real-world energy of coal. As the "Coal Tiger" was revised into the "Black Panther," so too have fossil fuels given way to petrochemical fantasies of limitless, renewable power that demands no radical changes to capitalism's social structures. Yet as *World of Wakanda* makes clear through its introduction of an anti-capitalist Namor the Sub-Mariner, superhero narratives have long imagined heroism as a form of resistance too. As Ramzi Fawaz and Anna F. Peppard have both demonstrated, post-1960s superhero narratives are often about queer identities and nonnormative communities, and climate change activism has long been a part of comics' countercultural politics in America as well. As reported by the *New York Times*, a 1971 course on comics at Brown University even recognized environmentalism as a unifying political issue: "Captain America openly sympathizes with campus radicals, the Black Widow fights side by side with the Young Lords, Lois Lane apes John Howard Griffin and turns herself black to study racism, and everybody battles to save the environment" (Saul Braun, "Shazam!"). Comics have long encouraged environmental awareness and even activism, despite the medium's historical ties to the fossil fuel industry.

In the *Avengers Infinity War* (2018) and *Endgame* (2019) films, the cosmic villain Thanos enacts a genocidal plan to kill half of the universe's living creatures so that life can flourish without exhausting natural resources. As articulated in the films, Thanos's plan and its justification recycles well-worn ideas from Paul R. Ehrlich and Anne Howland Ehrlich's 1968 book *The Population Bomb* and the Club of Rome's 1972 report *Limits to Growth*, both of which projected an impending crisis due to rising populations and limited resources. In the *Infinity Gauntlet* comics series (1991), the Silver Surfer explains the premise to Doctor Strange: "the fact that there are more people alive today than have ever died was a type of cosmic imbalance" (Starlin et al.). In works like the *Infinity Gauntlet* and its film adaptations, American comics have worked through the conditions of climate change, ventriloquizing real-world problems in supervillains that imperil the planet and superheroes that seek solutions.

Comics do not just tell stories about climate change. Comics is a medium that can reorient space and time in ways that foster sustainable practices and discourage capitalism-as-usual. Small press and independent comics have long articulated and envisioned lives outside of fossil capitalism, and many cities and towns around the world have independent comics scenes. For example, I live in Rochester, New York, where I belong to a volunteer group that puts on RICE, the Rochester Indie Comics Expo.[5] An annual event in downtown Rochester, RICE brings together dozens of regional comics creators, many of whom make their comics locally. Last year, RICE hosted its first comics-making workshop with Rochester's own Rathaus Press, a local risograph printer where artists can make affordable print runs using sustainable materials.[6] Making comics takes time, and taking the time to make a mini-comic demands that you take time away from other activities that probably burn more fossil fuels than the act of putting pencil to paper. Getting more people to make local comics can help to build the communities and networks necessary for sustainable practices.

A more sustainable society through comics is one that localizes its arts production, decouples from global logistics, shutters fossil fuel infrastructure, and uses sustainable materials. I also believe that more social support

5. More information about the Rochester Indie Comics Expo is at http://wnycomicarts.com/. There are many other indie comics events like it. Try to find one near you, or start one where you live!

6. More information about Rathaus Press is at https://rathaus.press/. There are local printers in lots of cities and towns, so try to find one near you!

for comics-making in America could help to propel the cultural changes necessary to stop carbon emissions. Imagine a society where local governments fund comics-making projects about regional history, gardening, public transportation, local foodways, bike paths, and the process of converting to solar panels or an electric vehicle. Running comics workshops at community centers, libraries, schools, and universities does not cost a lot, but it does create a community that can revalue space and time. Comics-making initiatives cannot provide the infrastructural changeover necessary to decouple from fossil fuel power plants and pumps. Yet comics communities can establish stories and visions of what the future could look like. The future does not have to be a catastrophe. Comics are one medium through which we can imagine the necessary transition away from fossil fuels.

WORKS CITED

Adcock, John. "Wings Winfair and *Gulf Funny Weekly*." *Yesterday's Papers,* 16 June 2014, http://john-adcock.blogspot.com/2014/06/wings-winfair-and-gulf-funny-weekly.html.

Ahern, Gene. "Otto Auto." *Evening Journal* [Wilmington, DE], 4 Sept. 1919, p. 14.

Alaniz, José. *Death, Disability, and the Superhero: The Silver Age and Beyond.* UP of Mississippi, 2014.

———. "How Many Trees Had to Be *Cut Down* for This Essay?: Crumb as Ironic Eco-Elegist." *The Comics of R. Crumb: Underground in the Art Museum,* edited by Daniel Worden, UP of Mississippi, 2021, pp. 79–107.

Alexander, F. O. "Hairbreadth Harry," 8 Apr. 1934. Rpt. in *Famous Funnies,* no. 1, Eastern Color Printing, July 1934.

Anderson, Benedict. *Imagined Communities: Reflections on the Origin and Spread of Nationalism.* Revised ed., Verso, 2006.

Anderson, Brianna. "Reimagining Plastic Pollution and Climate Activism: Contradictions of Eco-Education in Rachel Hope Allison's *I'm Not a Plastic Bag.*" *Lion and the Unicorn,* vol. 45, no. 2, Apr. 2021, pp. 172–91.

Baker, Kyle. *Plastic Man: On the Lam!* DC Comics, 2005.

Baker, Nicholson, and Margaret Brentano. *The World on Sunday: Graphic Art in Pulitzer's Newspaper (1891–1911).* Bullfinch Press, 2005.

Baldanzi, Jessica, and Hussein Rashid, editors. *Ms. Marvel's America: No Normal.* UP of Mississippi, 2020.

Banta, Martha. *Barbaric Intercourse: Caricature and the Culture of Conduct, 1841–1936.* U of Chicago P, 2003.

Barrett, Ross. "Picturing a Crude Past: Primitivism, Public Art, and Corporate Oil Promotion in the United States." *Oil Culture,* edited by Ross Barrett and Daniel Worden, U of Minnesota P, 2014, pp. 43–68.

Barrett, Ross, and Daniel Worden, editors. *Oil Culture.* U of Minnesota P, 2014.

Beaty, Bart. "Superhero Comics." *Fueling Culture: 101 Words for Energy and Environment,* edited by Imre Szeman, Jennifer Wenzel, and Patricia Yaeger, Fordham UP, 2017, pp. 333–37.

Beerbohm, Robert L., and Richard D. Olson. "Expanded Concise Origins of the Modern Comic Book." *Official Overstreet Comic Book Price Guide,* 33rd ed., edited by Robert M. Overstreet, House of Collectibles / Gemstone, 2003, pp. 297–307.

Bell, Blake, and Michael J. Vassallo. *The Secret History of Marvel Comics: Jack Kirby and the Moonlighting Artists at Martin Goodman's Empire.* Fantagraphics, 2013.

Benjamin, Walter. "The Formula in which the Dialectical Expression of Film Finds Expression," translated by Edmund Jephcott. *Selected Writings, Vol. 3: 1935–1938,* edited by Howard Eiland and Michael W. Jennings, Harvard UP, 2002, pp. 94–95.

Beringer, Alex. "Transatlantic Picture Stories: Experiments in the Antebellum Comic Strip." *American Literature,* vol. 87, no. 3, Sept. 2015, pp. 455–88.

Black, Brian. *Petrolia: The Landscape of America's First Oil Boom.* Johns Hopkins UP, 2003.

Blackbeard, Bill, editor. *The Smithsonian Collection of Newspaper Comics.* Abrams/Smithsonian, 1977.

B.L.T. "Romance." *Puck's Monthly Magazine,* May 1910, p. 1.

Boccioni, Umberto, Carlo Carrà, Luigi Russolo, Giacomo Balla, and Gino Severini. "Futurist Painting: Technical Manifesto 1910," translated by Robert Brain. *Futurist Manifestos,* edited by Umbro Apollonio, MFA Publications, 2001, pp. 27–31.

Boetzkes, Amanda. *Plastic Capitalism: Contemporary Art and the Drive to Waste.* MIT Press, 2019.

Boetzkes, Amanda, and Andrew Pendakis. "Visions of Eternity: Plastics and the Ontology of Oil." *e-flux,* no. 47, Sept. 2013, https://www.e-flux.com/journal.

Bould, Mark. *The Anthropocene Unconscious: Climate Catastrophe Culture.* Verso, 2021.

Bowman, Daniel. "Horsepower: Animals, Automobiles, and an Ethic of (Car) Care in Early US Road Narratives." *Journal of American Studies,* vol. 56, no. 4, 2022, pp. 613–34.

Bowman, Emma. "A Decade on, the 'This Is Fine' Creator Wants to Put the Famous Dog to Rest." *NPR,* 26 Jan. 2023, https://www.npr.org/2023/01/26/1151624434.

Boyer, Dominic, and Imre Szeman, editors. *Energy Humanities: An Anthology.* Johns Hopkins UP, 2017.

Braun, Emily. "Futurist Fashion: Three Manifestoes." *Art Journal,* vol. 54, no. 1, Spring 1995, pp. 34–41.

Braun, Saul. "Shazam! Here Comes Captain Relevant." *New York Times,* 2 May 1971, p. 32.

"A Brief Summary of Next Week's Anniversary Number of Puck." *Puck,* 26 Dec. 1914, p. 3.

Brinker, Felix, Alex Beringer, Jonathan Najarian, Rebecca Wanzo, Margaret Galvan, and Leah Misemer. "Forum: New Approaches to Comics in Periodical Media." *American Periodicals,* vol. 32, no. 2, 2022, pp. 91–132.

Brinkley, Nell. "The Adventures of Cupid." *Buffalo Enquirer,* 10 May 1912, p. 5.

Broome, John, Carmine Infantino, Murphy Anderson, and Gaspar Saladino. "The Elongated Man's Secret Weapon!" *The Flash,* no. 115, DC Comics, Sept. 1960.

Broome, John, Carmine Infantino, Joe Giella, and Gaspar Saladino. "The Mystery of the Elongated Man!" *Flash,* no. 112, DC Comics, May 1960.

Buell, Frederick. "A Short History of Oil Cultures; or, the Marriage of Catastrophe and Exuberance." *Oil Culture,* edited by Ross Barrett and Daniel Worden, U of Minnesota P, 2014, pp. 69–88.

Bukatman, Scott. *Matters of Gravity: Special Effects and Supermen in the Twentieth Century.* Duke UP, 2003.

———. *The Poetics of Slumberland: Animated Spirits and the Animating Spirit.* U of California P, 2012.

"Buster Brown and His Bubble." *Burr McIntosh Monthly,* Mar. 1904, p. 384.

"Buster Brown and His Bubble." *Burr McIntosh Monthly,* Aug. 1903, p. 77.

Canavan, Gerry. "Introduction: If This Goes On." *Green Planets: Ecology and Science Fiction,* edited by Gerry Canavan and Kim Stanley Robinson, Wesleyan UP, 2014, pp. 1–21.

Carey, John. "Oil in Good Time." *Donald Duck,* no. 170, Gold Key, Apr. 1976.

Cass, Caitlin. *Postal Constituent,* vol. 12, no. 2, 2022.

Chakrabarty, Dipesh. *The Climate of History in a Planetary Age.* U of Chicago P, 2021.

Chute, Hillary. *Disaster Drawn: Visual Witness, Comics, and Documentary Form.* Harvard UP, 2016.

Chute, Hillary, and Marianne DeKoven. "Comics and Graphic Novels." *Cambridge Companion to Popular Fiction,* edited by David Glover and Scott McCracken, Cambridge UP, 2012. 174–95.

The Clean-Up: A Moving Picture of Science, Industry, and Taxation Featuring Petroleum Pete. American Petroleum Industries Committee, 1933.

"Climate Change Indicators: Wildfires." *Climate Change Indicators in the United States,* United States Environmental Protection Agency, 2023, https://www.epa.gov/climate-indicators/climate-change-indicators-wildfires.

Cole, Jack. "Plague of Plastic People." *Plastic Man,* no. 22, Quality Comics, Mar. 1950.

———. "Plastic Man," *Police Comics,* no. 1, Quality Comics, Aug. 1941.

Cole, Jean Lee. *How the Other Half Laughs: The Comic Sensibility in American Culture, 1895–1920.* UP of Mississippi, 2020.

Coll, Steven. *Private Empire: ExxonMobil and American Power.* Penguin, 2012.

Costello, Brannon. "Strange Daddy: Uprooting the Environmentalist Family Romance in Nancy A. Collins' *Swamp Thing.*" *Inks,* vol. 6, no. 1, 2022, pp. 1–25.

Crawford, Neta C. *The Pentagon, Climate Change, and War: Charting the Rise and Fall of U.S. Military Emissions.* MIT Press, 2022.

"Creator of Gumps Signs a Million Dollar Contract and Rides Off in This Car." *The Times* [Montgomery, AL], 31 Mar. 1923, p. 3.

Crucifix, Benoît. "Speed Machines in Early Comics." *Graphixia,* 2 July 2015, https://www.graphixia.ca/2015/07/210-speed-machines-in-early-comic-strips/.

Crumb, R. "Mr. Appropriate." *The Complete Crumb Comics,* vol. 12, edited by Ilse Thompson and Gary Groth, Fantagraphics, 1997, p. 93.

Crutzen, Paul J. "Geology of Mankind." *Nature,* no. 415, 3 Jan. 2002, p. 23.

Crutzen Paul J., and Eugene F. Stoermer. "The 'Anthropocene.'" *Global Change Newsletter,* no. 41, May 2000, pp. 17–18.

"Cubism and Abstract Art," 1936. Museum of Modern Art, https://www.moma.org/calendar/exhibitions/2748.

Currier, Nathaniel, lithographer. *Awful Conflagration of the Steam Boat Lexington in Long Island Sound on Monday Eve, January 13th, 1840, by Which Melancholy Occurrence, over 100 Persons Perished.* Drawing by William Keesey Hewitt. Published by the *New York Sun,* 1840.

———, lithographer and publisher. *Blower, The King of the Road.* 1846. New York Historical Society Collection of Caricatures and Cartoons.

Currier and Ives. *Across the Continent: "Westward the Course of Empire Takes Its Way."* Drawing by Frances Palmer. 1868.

———. *Off His Nut: "Gracious Massy, I'se Struck de Comet!"* Ca. 1886.

———. *The Progress of the Century—The Lighting Steam Press. The Electric Telegraph. The Locomotive. The Steamboat.* 1876.

Daggett, Cara New. *The Birth of Energy: Fossil Fuels, Thermodynamics, and the Politics of Work.* Duke UP, 2019.

———. "Energy and Domination: Contesting the Fossil Myth of Fuel Expansion." *Environmental Politics,* vol. 20, no. 4, 2021, pp. 644–62.

Dahlquist, Marina, and Patrick Vonderau, editors. *Petrocinema: Sponsored Film and the Oil Industry.* Bloomsbury, 2021.

Dauber, Jeremy. *American Comics: A History.* Norton, 2022.

Davis, Heather. "Imperceptibility and Accumulation: Political Strategies of Plastic." *Camera Obscura,* no. 92, 2016, pp. 187–93.

———. *Plastic Matter.* Duke UP, 2022.

Dembicki, Geoff. *The Petroleum Papers: Inside the Far-Right Conspiracy to Cover Up Climate Change.* Greystone, 2022.

Denning, Michael. *Mechanic Accents: Dime Novels and Working-Class Culture in America.* Revised ed., Verso, 1998.

Dobrin, Sidney I., editor, *Eco-Comix: Essays on the Environment in Comics and Graphic Novels.* McFarland, 2020.

Dorfman, Ariel, and Armand Mattelart. *How to Read Donald Duck: Imperialist Ideology in the Disney Comic.* OR Books, 2018.

"The Edison Electric Lighting Station." *Scientific American,* 26 Aug. 1882, pp. 127–30.

Eisenstein, Sergei. *On Disney.* Edited by Jay Leyda, translated by Alan Upchurch, Seagull, 1986.

"Energy Consumption in the United States (1776–2019)." *Today in Energy,* US Energy Information Administration, July 2020. https://www.eia.gov/todayinenergy/detail.php?id=44277.

Engelhart, Steve, Sal Buscema, Vince Colletta, Linda Lessmann, and Tom Orzechowski. *Captain America,* no. 180, Marvel Comics, Dec. 1974.

Estrada, Inés. *Alienation.* Fantagraphics, 2019.

Evans, Mel. *Artwash: Big Oil and the Arts.* Pluto Press, 2015.

"Exxon Is Said to Agree to Pay $10-Million Argentine Ransom." *New York Times,* 13 Dec. 1973, p. 2.

Fajardo, Pablo, Sophie Tardy-Joubert, and Damien Roudeau. *Crude: A Memoir.* Translated by Hannah Chute. Pennsylvania State UP / Graphic Mundi, 2021.

Fawaz, Ramzi. *The New Mutants: Superheroes and the Radical Imagination of American Comics.* New York UP, 2016.

Fawaz, Ramzi, Shelley Streeby, and Deborah Elizabeth Whaley, editors. *Keywords for Comics Studies.* New York UP, 2021.

Finger, Bill, and Mart Dellon. "The Green Lantern." *All-American Comics,* no. 16, July 1940, pp. 1–8.

Finger, Bill, Bob Kane, Jerry Robinson, and George Roussos. "Secret of the Iron Jungle." *Batman,* no. 6, DC Comics, Sept. 1941. Rpt. in *Batman: The Golden Age,* vol. 2, DC Comics, 2017, pp. 293–305.

Fisher, Bud. "Mutt and Jeff," Aug. 1910. History of Comic Strips Scrapbooks, vol. 27, The Ohio State University, Billy Ireland Cartoon Library and Museum.

Fox, Fontaine. *Toonerville Trolley and Other Cartoons.* Cupples and Leon, 1921.

Fox, Gardner, and Sid Greene. "The Attack of the Oil Demons!" *Strange Adventures,* no. 120, DC Comics, Sept. 1960.

Fox, Gardner, E. E. Hibbard, Sheldon Moldoff, Bernard Baily, Ben Flinton, and Cliff Young. "Hemisphere Defense." *All-Star Comics,* no. 9, DC Comics, Feb./Mar. 1941.

Freese, Barbara. *Coal: A Human History.* Perseus, 2003.

Frost, A. B. *A Book of Drawings.* P. F. Collier and Son, 1904.

———. *Stuff and Nonsense.* Charles Scribner's Sons, 1888.

Gabilliet, Jean-Paul. *Of Comics and Men: A Cultural History of American Comics Books.* Translated by Bart Beaty and Nick Nguyen. UP of Mississippi, 2010.

Galvan, Margaret. "Adjacent Genealogies, Alternate Geographies: The Outliers of Underground Comix and *World War 3 Illustrated.*" *Inks,* vol. 3, no. 1, 2019, pp. 92–113.

Gardner, Jared. "The American King." *The Cartoon Monarch: Otto Soglow and the Little King,* edited by Dean Mullaney, Library of American Comics / IDW, 2012, pp. 9–31.

———. *Projections: Comics and the History of Twenty-First Century Storytelling.* Stanford UP, 2012.

———. "Sidney Smith's Open Road." *The Gumps: The Saga of Mary Gold,* edited by Jared Gardner, Library of American Comics / IDW, 2013, pp. 7–25.

Ghosh, Amitav. *The Great Derangement: Climate Change and the Unthinkable.* U of Chicago P, 2016.

Gibbons, Sarah. "'I Don't Exactly Have Quiet, Pretty Powers': Flexibility and Alterity in *Ms. Marvel.*" *Journal of Graphic Novels and Comics,* vol. 8, no. 5, 2017, pp. 450–63.

Giddens, Paul H. "Historical Origins of the Adoption of the EXXON Name and Trademark." *Business History Review,* vol. 47, no. 3, Autumn 1973, pp. 353–66.

Gish, Michelle. *We Are Here Forever.* Quirk, 2019.

Goldberg, Rube. "'And They Get Away with It!' III—The Automobile Mechanic." *Puck,* 2 Jan. 1915.

Gordon, Ian. "Comic Strips." *Comics Studies: A Guidebook,* edited by Charles Hatfield and Bart Beaty, Rutgers UP, 2020, pp. 13–24.

———. *Comic Strips and Consumer Culture, 1890–1945.* Smithsonian Institution Press, 1998.

———. *Superman: The Persistence of an American Icon.* Rutgers UP, 2017.

Graham, Richard L. *Government Issue: Comics for the People, 1940s–2000s.* Abrams, 2011.

Green, K. C. "On Fire." *Gunshow,* 2013, https://gunshowcomic.com/648.

———. "This Is Not Fine." *The Nib,* 3 Aug. 2016, https://thenib.com/this-is-not-fine/.

Guillory, Rob. *Farmhand,* no. 1, Image Comics, July 2018.

———. *Farmhand,* no. 7, Image Comics, Apr. 2019.

———. *Farmhand,* no. 11, Image Comics, Nov. 2019.

———. *Farmhand,* no. 13, Image Comics, Jan. 2020.

———. *Farmhand,* no. 14, Image Comics, Mar. 2020.

Gunning, Tom. "The Art of Succession: Reading, Writing, and Watching Comics." *Critical Inquiry,* vol. 40, no. 3, Spring 2014, pp. 36–51.

Hanieh, Adam. "Petrochemical Empire." *New Left Review,* no. 130, July/Aug. 2021, pp. 25–51.

Hansen, Gwen, and Jack Cole. "A Whale of a Tale." *Plastic Man,* no. 3, Quality Comics, Spring 1946.

Haraway, Donna J. *Staying with the Trouble: Making Kin in the Cthulucene.* Duke UP, 2019.

Harp, Stephen L. *A World History of Rubber: Empire, Industry, and the Everyday.* Wiley and Sons, 2016.

Harvey, Robert C. "Outcault, Goddard, the Comics, and the Yellow Kid." *The Comics Journal,* no. 9, June 2016, https://www.tcj.com/outcault-goddard-the-comics-and-the-yellow-kid/.

Hatfield, Charles. "Comic Books." *Comics Studies: A Guidebook,* edited by Charles Hatfield and Bart Beaty, Rutgers UP, 2020, pp. 25–39.

———. *Hand of Fire: The Comics Art of Jack Kirby.* UP of Mississippi, 2012.

Hatfield, Charles, and Bart Beaty, eds. *Comics Studies: A Guidebook.* Rutgers UP, 2020.

Heise, Ursula K. "Plastic Nature: Environmentalism and Animated Film." *Public Culture,* vol. 26, no. 2, 2014, pp. 301–18.

"Here Are the First Pictures Ever Telegraphed." *New York Journal,* 25 Oct. 1896, p. 31.

Hern, Matt, Am Johal, and Joe Sacco. *Global Warming and the Sweetness of Life: A Tar Sands Tale.* MIT Press, 2018.

Herriman, George. "Krazy Kat," 3 Nov. 1918. Rpt. in Gilbert Seldes, *The Seven Lively Arts* Harper & Brothers, 1924.

———. "Major Ozone's Fresh Air Crusade." *Washington Times,* 13 Mar. 1904, Comic Section.

Hirsch, Paul S. *Pulp Empire: The Secret History of Comic Book Imperialism.* U of Chicago P, 2021.

Hix, Sid. "Smiling Slim: Standard Oil Agent Helps Jimmy Brown Get Started." *Standard Oil Comics,* no. 13A, Standard Oil Company, 1933.

Houser, Heather. *Infowhelm: Environmental Art and Literature in an Age of Data.* Columbia UP, 2020.

Housnell, David A. *From the American System to Mass Production, 1880–1932: The Development of Manufacturing Technology in the United States.* Johns Hopkins UP, 1984.

Huber, Matthew. *Lifeblood: Oil, Freedom, and the Forces of Capital.* U of Minnesota P, 2014.

Humphreys, Richard. "Futurism: May the Force Be with You." *Futurist Manifestos,* edited by Umbro Apollonio, MFA Publications, 2001, pp. 221–27.

Inge, M. Thomas. *Comics as Culture.* UP of Mississippi, 1990.

IPCC. *Climate Change 2023: Synthesis Report.* IPCC, 2023. https://www.ipcc.ch/report/ar6/syr/.

Irr, Caren, editor. *Life in Plastic: Artistic Responses to Petromodernity.* U of Minnesota P, 2021.

Johnson, Bob. *Carbon Nation: Fossil Fuels and the Making of Modern American Culture.* U of Kansas P, 2014.

———. *Mineral Rites: An Archaeology of the Fossil Economy.* Johns Hopkins UP, 2019.

Jones, Amelia. *Irrational Modernism: A Neurasthenic History of New York Dada.* MIT Press, 2004.

Jones, Christopher F. *Routes of Power: Energy and Modern America.* Harvard UP, 2014.

Jones, Clint. *Apocalyptic Ecology in the Graphic Novel: Life and the Environment after Societal Collapse.* McFarland, 2020.

Juergens, George. *Joseph Pulitzer and the New York World.* Princeton UP, 1966.

Kaneko, Mina. "Framing Dreams and the Technological Uncanny," *Pop Junctions,* 20 Apr. 2017, http://henryjenkins.org/blog/2017/04/framing-dreams-and-the-technological-uncanny-part-one.html.

Kanigher, Robert, Carmine Infantino, Joe Kubert, and Gaspar Saladino. "Mystery of the Human Thunderbolt!" *Showcase,* no. 4, DC Comics, Oct. 1956.

Kashtan, Aaron. *Between Pen and Pixel: Comics, Materiality, and the Book of the Future.* The Ohio State UP, 2018.

Kelly, Walt. "We Have Met the Enemy and He Is Us." Poster, 1971. Toni Mendez Collection, The Ohio State University, Billy Ireland Cartoon Library and Museum.

Kelp-Stebbins, Katherine. *How Comics Travel: Publication, Translation, Radical Literacies.* The Ohio State UP, 2022.

Keppler, Udo. "Next!" *Puck,* 7 Sept. 1904.

Kern, Stephen. *The Culture of Time and Space, 1880–1918.* Harvard UP, 2003.

Kidd, Kenneth B. *Making American Boys: Boyology and the Feral Tale.* U of Minnesota P, 2004.

Kidman, Shawna. *Comic Books Incorporated: How the Business of Comics Became the Business of Hollywood.* U of California P, 2019.

King, Frank. "Gasoline Alley," 18 June 1923. Rpt. in *Walt and Skeezix: 1923 and 1924,* edited by Jeet Heer, Kent Worcester, and Chris Ware, Drawn and Quarterly, 2006.

———. *Walt and Skeezix: 1921 and 1922.* Edited by Jeet Heer, Chris Oliveros, and Chris Ware, Drawn and Quarterly, 2005.

King Motor Car Company advertisement. *Washington Times,* 16 May 1917, p. 3.

Kleefeld, Sean. *Webcomics.* Bloomsbury Academic, 2020.

Køhlert, Frederik Byrn. *Serial Selves: Identity and Representation in Autobiographical Comics.* Rutgers UP, 2019.

Kunzle, David. *Father of the Comics Strip: Rodolphe Töpffer.* Jackson: UP of Mississippi, 2007.

———, editor. *Rodolphe Töpffer: The Complete Comics Strips.* UP of Mississippi, 2007.

Kupperberg, Paul, Dick Giordano, Adrienne Roy, and Ben Oda. "Oil, Oil . . . Nowhere!" *The Brave and the Bold*, no. 163, DC Comics, June 1980.

Kyle, Patrick. Review of *Alienation*. *The Comics Journal*, 12 Sept. 2019, https://www.tcj.com/reviews/alienation/.

Land of the Pioneers: A Story of Ohio. Standard Oil Company, 1952.

Lears, Jackson. *Fables of Abundance: A Cultural History of Advertising in America*. Basic, 1994.

LeBeau, Bryan F. *Currier and Ives: America Imagined*. Smithsonian Institute Press, 2011.

LeCain, Timothy J. *Mass Destruction: The Men and Giant Mines that Wired America and Scarred the Planet*. Rutgers UP, 2009.

Lee, Stan, and Jack Kirby. *The Fantastic Four Omnibus*. Vol. 1, Marvel Comics, 2013.

LeMenager, Stephanie. "The Aesthetics of Petroleum, after *Oil!*." *American Literary History*, vol. 24, no. 1, 2012, pp. 59–86.

———. *Living Oil: Petroleum Culture in the American Century*. Oxford UP, 2014.

Lessing, Gotthold Ephraim. *Laocoön: An Essay upon the Limits of Painting and Poetry*. Translated by Ellen Frothingham, Roberts Brothers, 1887.

Macchio, Ralph, Ron Wilson, Chic Stone, John Costanza, and George Roussos. *Marvel Two-in-One*, no. 73, Marvel Comics, Mar. 1981.

Mager, Gus. "'Oily John,' the Detective." *New York Evening Journal*, 26 Sept. 1905. San Francisco Academy of Comic Art Collection, The Ohio State University, Billy Ireland Cartoon Library and Museum.

Magnolia Oil News. Magnolia Oil Company, Mar. 1918–Feb. 1928.

Malm, Andreas. *Fossil Capital: The Rise of Steam Power and the Roots of Global Warming*. Verso, 2016.

———. *How to Blow Up a Pipeline*. Verso, 2021.

Marinetti, F. T. "Extended Man and the Kingdom of the Machine." *Critical Writings*, edited by Günter Berghaus, translated by Doug Thompson, Farrar, Strauss and Giroux, 2006, pp. 85–88.

———. "The Foundation and Manifesto of Futurism," *Critical Writings*, edited by Günter Berghaus, translated by Doug Thompson, Farrar, Strauss and Giroux, 2006, pp. 11–17.

Masur, Louis P. "'Pictures Have Now Become a Necessity': The Use of Images in American History Textbooks." *Journal of American History*, vol. 84, no. 4, Mar. 1998, pp. 1409–24.

McCay, Winsor. *Dream of the Rarebit Fiend: Bucking Automobile*. 1907. National Gallery of Art.

———. "Little Nemo in Slumberland," 6 Sept. 1908. *The Comic Strip Library*, https://www.comicstriplibrary.org/display/501.

McLuhan, Marshall. *Understanding Media: The Extensions of Man*. MIT Press, 1994.

McNeill, J. R. and Peter Engelke. *The Great Acceleration: An Environmental History of the Anthropocene Since 1945*. Harvard UP, 2014.

McShane, Clay, and Joel Tarr. *The Horse in the City: Living Machines in the Nineteenth Century*. Johns Hopkins UP, 2007.

Meikle, Jeffrey L. *American Plastic: A Cultural History*. Rutgers UP, 1997.

Meltzer, Brad, and Rags Morales. *Identity Crisis*. DC Comics, 2016.

Meyer, Christina. *Producing Mass Entertainment: The Serial Life of the Yellow Kid*. The Ohio State UP, 2019.

Mickey Mouse: The Mail Pilot. Amoco ed., Whitman Publishing, 1933.

Mickey and Goofy Explore the Universe of Energy. Walt Disney Educational Media Company, 1985.

Mickey Mouse and Goofy Explore Energy. Walt Disney Educational Media Company, 1976.

Mickey Mouse and Goofy Explore Energy Conservation. Walt Disney Educational Media Company, 1978.

Millard, Joe, and John Spranger. "The Evil Dr. Volt." *Plastic Man*, no. 7, Quality Comics, Spring 1947.

Mitchell, Timothy. *Carbon Democracy: Political Power in the Age of Oil*. Verso, 2011.

Mitchell, W. J. T. *Iconology: Image, Text, Ideology*. U of Chicago P, 1986.

Monastersky, Richard, and Nick Sousanis. "The Fragile Framework: Can Nations Unite to Save Earth's Climate?" *Nature*, no. 527, 2015, pp. 427–35.

Moore, Jason W. *Capitalism in the Web of Life: Ecology and the Accumulation of Capital*. Verso, 2015.

———, editor. *Anthropocene or Capitolocene? Nature, History, and the Crisis of Capitalism*. PM Press, 2016.

Morris and Goscinny. *A Lucky Luke Adventure, Vol. 5: In the Shadow of the Derricks*. Translated by Luke Spear, Cinebook, 2007.

Munroe, Randall. "4.5 Degrees." *xkcd*, 9 June 2014, https://xkcd.com/1379/.

———. "Bee Orchid." *xkcd*, 2 Sept. 2013, https://xkcd.com/1259/.

———. "Earth Temperature Timeline." *xkcd*, 15 Sept. 2016, https://xkcd.com/1732/.

———. "Global Temperature over My Lifetime." *xkcd*, 9 Aug. 2021, https://xkcd.com/2500/.

Nadel, Alan. *Containment Culture: American Narratives, Postmodernism, and the Atomic Age*. Duke UP, 1995.

Nadis, Fred. *Wonder Shows: Performing Science, Magic, and Religion in America*. Rutgers UP, 2005.

Najarian, Jonathan. "Comics and Modernism: An Introduction." *Comics and Modernism: History, Form, Culture*, edited by Jonathan Najarian, UP of Mississippi, pp. 3–12.

———, editor. *Comics and Modernism: History, Form, Culture*. UP of Mississippi, 2024.

Nasaw, David. *The Chief: The Life of William Randolph Hearst*. Mariner, 2000.

Nast, Thomas. "Our Standard (Gauge) Adopted All Over the Union." *Harper's Weekly*, 5 June 1886, p. 364.

———. "Senatorial Roundhouse." *Harper's Weekly*, 10 July 1886, p. 436.

Newman, Barnett. "The Plasmic Image." *Barnett Newman: Selected Writings and Interviews*, edited by John P. O'Neill, U of California P, 1990, pp. 138–55.

Ngai, Sianne. *Our Aesthetic Categories: Zany, Cute, Interesting*. Harvard UP, 2012.

Nixon, Rob. *Slow Violence and the Environmentalism of the Poor*. Harvard UP, 2011.

North, Michael. *Machine-Age Comedy*. Oxford UP, 2009.

Nyberg, Amy Kiste. *Seal of Approval: The History of the Comics Code*. UP of Mississippi, 1998.

Nye, David. *Consuming Power: A Social History of American Energies*. MIT Press, 1998.

O'Connell, Mark. "Our Way of Life Is Poisoning Us." *New York Times*, 20 Apr. 2023, https://www.nytimes.com/2023/04/20/opinion/microplastics-health-environment.html.

Opper, Frederick Burr. "Diogenes Gets a Free Ride on Railroad!" *The Commercial Appeal* [Memphis, TN], 23 Nov. 1912, p. 6.

———. "Si and Mirandi." *Standard Oil Comics*, no. 13A, Standard Oil Company, 1931.

Oreskes, Naomi, and Erik M. Conway. *Merchants of Doubt: How a Handful of Scientists Obscured the Truth on Issues from Tobacco to Global Warming*. Bloomsbury, 2010.

Ott, John. "Iron Horses: Leland Stanford, Eadweard Muybridge, and the Industrialised Eye." *Oxford Art Journal*, vol. 28, no. 3, 2005, pp. 407–28.

Otto, Eric C. "Killing Oliver Queen: Environmentalist Meaning and Demeaning in *Green Arrow*." *Eco-Comix: Essays on the Environment in Comics and Graphic Novels*, edited by Sidney I. Dobrin, McFarland, 2020, pp. 161–74.

"Our Reproductions." *Burr McIntosh Monthly*, Dec. 1903, p. 109.

Outcault, R. F. "Buster Brown and His Bubble." *Burr McIntosh Monthly*, Aug. 1903, p. 76.

———. "Buster Brown and His Bubble." *Burr McIntosh Monthly*, Sept. 1903, p. 164.

———. "The Electrical Inventor and the Capitalist." *Electrical World*, 3 Mar. 1894, p. 271.

———. "How the Yellow Kid Was Born." Rpt. in *R. F. Outcault's* The Yellow Kid, edited by Bill Blackbeard, Kitchen Sink Press, 1995, p. 146.

———. "Kelly's Kids Have a Shocking Time at the Electrical Show." *St. Louis Dispatch*, 21 May 1899. Rpt. in *Society Is Nix: Gleeful Anarchy of the Dawn of the American Comic Strip, 1895–1915*, edited by Peter Maresca, Sunday Press, 2013.

———. "The Yellow Kid Treats the Crowd to a Horseless Carriage Ride." *New York Journal*, 17 Oct. 1897. San Francisco Academy of Comic Art Collection, The Ohio State University, Billy Ireland Cartoon Library and Museum.

Patton, Jack, and John Rosenfeld Jr. *Texas History Movies*. PJM, 1970.

Peppard, Anna F., editor. *Supersex: Sexuality, Fantasy, and the Superhero*. U of Texas P, 2020.

Peppis, Paul. "Popular Modernism in the Late *Krazy Kat* Comics: Industry and Innovation in the Color Sundays." *Journal of Modern Periodical Studies*, vol. 9, no. 2, 2019, pp. 157–76.

Poll, Ryan. *Aquaman and the War against Oceans*. U of Nebraska P, 2022.

Pughe, J. S. "The Passing of the Horse." *Puck*, 22 Feb. 1899.

———. "Roped In: How Lariat Lem Got It Good in the Bad Lands." *Puck*, 13 Apr. 1904.

RD-119: The Miracle in Your Gas Tank. Sinclair Research Laboratories, 1950.

Regalado, Aldo J. *Bending Steel: Modernity and the American Superhero*. UP of Mississippi, 2015.

Rich, Nathaniel. *Losing Earth: A Recent History*. Farrar, Straus and Giroux, 2019.

Ridlington, Elizabeth, and John Rumpler. *Fracking by the Numbers: Key Impact of Dirty Drilling at the State and National Level*. Environment American Research and Policy Center, 2013, https://environmentamerica.org/.

Rifas, Leonard, editor. *All-Atomic Comics*. Educomics, 1976.

———. "Cartooning and Nuclear Power: From Industry Advertising to Activist Uprising and Beyond." *PS: Political Science and Politics*, vol. 40, no. 2, 2007, pp. 255–60.

Robertson, Benek. "ExxonMobil Moves to Resume Offshore Drilling in Santa Barbara County." *And the West*, 17 May 2022, https://andthewest.stanford.edu/2021/exxonmobil-moves-to-resume-offshore-oil-drilling-in-santa-barbara-county/.

Robbins, Trina. *Nell Brinkley and the New Woman in the Early 20th Century*. McFarland, 2001.

Roeder, Katherine. *Wide Awake in Slumberland: Fantasy, Mass Culture, and Modernism in the Art of Winsor McCay*. UP of Mississippi, 2014.

Sacco, Joe. *Paying the Land*. Metropolitan, 2020.

Saguisag, Lara. *Incorrigibles and Innocents: Constructing Childhood and Citizenship in Progressive Era Comics*. Rutgers UP, 2019.

Sattler, Peter R. "Ballet Méchanique: The Art of George Herriman." *Word and Image*, vol. 8, no. 2, 1992, pp. 133–53.

Schivelbusch, Wolfgang. *The Railway Journey: Trains and Travel in the Nineteenth Century*. Urizen, 1979.

Scott, Heidi C. M. *Fuel: An Ecocritical History*. Bloomsbury Academic, 2018.

Scranton, Roy. *Learning to Die in the Anthropocene: Reflections on the End of a Civilization*. City Lights, 2015.

Seiler, Cotton. *Republic of Drivers: A Cultural History of Automobility in America*. U of Chicago P, 2009.

Seldes, Gilbert. *The Seven Lively Arts*. Harper and Brothers, 1924.

Shinick, Kevin, Gerardo Sandoval, Victor Nava, Israel Silva, and Clayton Cowles. *Guardians of the Galaxy: Cosmic Rewind*, no. 1, Marvel Comics, 2022.

Siegel, Jerome, and Joe Shuster. "Superman, Champion of the Oppressed!" *Action Comics*, no. 1, DC Comics, 1938. Rpt. in *Superman: The Golden Age Omnibus*, vol. 1, DC Comics, 2019, pp. 7–20.

———. "Superman's Phony Manager." *Action Comics*, no. 6, DC Comics, 1938. Rpt. in *Superman: The Golden Age Omnibus*, vol. 1, DC Comics, 2019, pp. 73–86.

Smith, Philip. "Rhyming Events: Contested Narratives and 'Cli-Fi' in Richard McGuire's *Here*." *Inks*, vol. 2, no. 1, 2018, pp. 38–48.

Smith, Sidney. "Old Doc Yak." *Chicago Sunday Tribune*, 5 May 1912, p. 13.

Smolderen, Thierry. *The Origins of Comics: From William Hogarth to Winsor McCay*. Translated by Bart Beaty and Nick Nguyen. UP of Mississippi, 2014.

Solomon, Alisa. "The Haus of Maus." *The Nation*, 27 Aug. 2014, https://www.thenation.com/article/archive/haus-maus/.

Sparling, Jack. *History of Gas: Through the Ages with 'Miss Flame.'* American Gas Association, 1947.

Special Agent: A Picture Story about the Railroad Police. Association of American Railroads, 1958.

Spiegelman, Art, and Chip Kidd. *Jack Cole and Plastic Man: Forms Stretched to Their Limits*. Chronicle, 2001.

Squier, Susan M. "The Narrative and Aesthetic Strategies of Climate Change Comics." *Life Re-Scaled: The Biological Imagination in Twenty-First-Century Literature and Performance*, edited by Liliane Campos and Pierre-Louis Patione, Open Book, 2022, pp. 299–322.

Starlin, Jim, George Pérez, and Ron Lim. *The Infinity Gauntlet*. Marvel Comics, 2011.

"State Motor Vehicle Registrations by Years, 1900–1995." *Highway Statistics Summary to 1995*, Federal Highway Administration, 2018, https://www.fhwa.dot.gov/ohim/summary95/mv200.pdf.

Statistical Abstract of the United States, no. 50. US Department of Commerce, 1928. https://www.census.gov/history/pdf/carproduction.pdf.

Stein, Daniel. "The Comic Modernism of George Herriman." *Crossing Boundaries in Graphic Narrative: Essays on Forms, Series and Genres*, edited by Jake Jakaitis and James F. Wurtz, McFarland, 2012, pp. 40–70.

Stein, Jordan Alexander. "How to Be a Theory Dinosaur." *Postmodern Culture*, vol. 21, no. 2, Jan. 2011, https://www.pomoculture.org/2013/09/03/how-to-be-a-theory-dinosaur/.

Stella, Joseph. "The Brooklyn Bridge (A Page of My Life)." *Transition*, nos. 16–17, June 1929, pp. 87–88.

Sterrett, Cliff. *Polly and Her Pals*. Library of American Comics, 2013.

The Story of Colonel Drake. American Petroleum Institute, 1954.

Szeman, Imre, and Dominic Boyer. "Introduction: On the Energy Humanities." *Energy Humanities: An Anthology*, edited by Imre Szeman and Dominic Boyer, Johns Hopkins UP, 2017, pp. 1–13.

Szeman, Imre, and Petrocultures Research Group. *After Oil*. West Virginia UP, 2016.

Szeman, Imre, Jennifer Wenzel, and Patricia Yaeger, editors. *Fueling Culture: 101 Words for Energy and the Environment*. Fordham UP, 2017.

Taunton, Matthew. "Print Culture." *Discovering Literature*, British Library, 15 May 2014. https://www.bl.uk/romantics-and-victorians/articles/print-culture.

T. B. Angel in "Take a Little Tip from Me!" B. F. Goodrich Tire Company, 1959.

Thomas, Roy. "A New Phenomenon." *Golden Age Marvel Comics Omnibus*, vol. 1, Marvel Comics, 2019, pp. 24–26.

Thompson, Kirsten Moana. "Living Electrically with Reddy Kilowatt, Your Electrical Servant." *Animation and Advertising*, edited by Malcolm Cook and Kirsten Moana Thompson, Palgrave Macmillan, 2019, pp. 127–44.

Thubron, Colin. "'The Invention of Nature' by Andrea Wulf." *New York Times*, 25 Sept. 2015, https://www.nytimes.com/2015/09/27/books/review/the-invention-of-nature-by-andrea-wulf.html.

Thunberg, Greta. "Almost Everything Is Black and White." *No One Is Too Small to Make a Difference*, Penguin, 2019, pp. 5–11.

Tilley, Carol L. "Seducing the Innocent: Fredric Wertham and the Falsifications that Helped Condemn Comics." *Information and Culture*, vol. 47, no. 4, 2012, pp. 383–413.

Tisdall, Caroline, and Angelo Bozzolla, *Futurism*. Oxford UP, 1978.

Töpffer, Rodolphe. *The Adventures of Mr. Obadiah Oldbuck. Brother Jonathan Extra*, no. 9, Wilson and Company, 1842.

———. "Essay on Physiognomy." *Enter: The Comics, Rodolphe Töpffer's Essay on Physiognomy and Monsieur Crépin*, edited and translated by E. Wiese, U of Nebraska P, 1965, pp. 1–36.

Tor, Vic. "Curly and the Kids." *Gulf Funny Weekly*, no. 403, Gulf Oil Company, 10 Jan. 1941.

Tsing, Anna Lowenhaupt. *The Mushroom at the End of the World: On the Possibility of Life in Capitalist Ruins.* Princeton UP, 2015.

UN Climate Change (@UNFCCC). "Tired of explaining #climate facts? Try this cartoon showing globe's sudden temperature rise http://xkcd.com/1732/." Twitter, 14 Sept. 2016, 2:45 p.m., https://twitter.com/unfccc/status/776129715799224320.

United States Rubber Company. "Take a Tip from a Navy Torpedo" advertisement. *Police Comics,* no. 1, Quality Comics, Aug. 1941.

Vasari, Giorgio. *Vasari on Technique.* Edited by G. Baldwin Brown, translated by Louisa S. Maclehose, J. M. Dent and Company, 1907.

Verlaine, Paul. "The Scene behind the Carriage Window-Panes." *Poems of Paul Verlaine,* translated by Gertrude Hall, Duffield and Company, 1906, p. 22.

Vischer, Friedrich Theodor. "Töpffer's Comic Picture Novels." Rpt. in David Kunzle, *Father of the Comic Strip: Rodolphe Töpffer,* UP of Mississippi, 2007, pp. 187–89.

Wallace-Wells, David. *The Uninhabitable Earth: Life after Warming.* Tim Duggan, 2019.

Wanzo, Rebecca. *The Content of Our Caricature: African American Comic Art and Political Belonging.* New York UP, 2020.

"Welcoming a New Feature in Puck." *Puck,* 24 Oct. 1914, p. 3.

White, Richard. *Railroaded: The Transcontinentals and the Making of Modern America.* Norton, 2011.

Whitted, Qiana, editor. *Desegregating Comics: Debating Blackness in the Golden Age of American Comics.* Rutgers UP, 2023.

———. "Introduction." *Black Panther,* Penguin Classics Marvel Collection, Penguin/Marvel, 2022, pp. xxi–xxxvi.

Wiggin, Bethany, Carolyn Fornoff, and Eunji Kim, editors. *Timescales: Thinking across Ecological Temporalities.* U of Minnesota P, 2020.

Williams, Jack P. "Shale Gas: An American Success Story." *ExxonMobil,* 20 Sept. 2012. https://web.archive.org/web/20230329155911/https://corporate.exxonmobil.com/news/newsroom/speeches-and-blog-posts/2012/0920_shale-gas-an-american-success-story.

Williams, Orville P. "Gasoline Gus." *Los Angeles Times,* 11 Apr. 1915, p. 104.

Wilson, G. Willow, Adrian Alphona, Ian Herring, and Joe Caramagna. *Ms. Marvel,* no. 11, Marvel Comics, Apr. 2015.

Wilson, Sheena, Adam Carlson, and Imre Szeman, editors. *Petrocultures: Oil, Politics, Culture.* McGill-Queen's UP, 2017.

"With the Retailers." *Coal Trade Journal,* 9 Dec. 1896, p. 710.

Wolfman, Marv, John Byrne, Joe Sinnott, Joe Rosen, and Carl Gafford. *Fantastic Four,* no. 215, Marvel Comics, Feb. 1980.

Wolfman, Marv, Bill Mantlo, John Byrne, Pablo Marcos, Irv Watanabe, Michael Higgins, and Carl Gafford. *Fantastic Four,* no. 216, Marvel Comics, Mar. 1980.

Woo, Benjamin, and Jeremy Stoll, editors. *The Comics World: Comic Books, Graphic Novels, and Their Publics.* UP of Mississippi, 2021.

Worden, Daniel. "The Legacy of Conquest in Comics: *Texas History Movies,* Jack Jackson, and Revision." *The Divided States: Unraveling National Identity in the 21st Century,* edited by Laura J. Beard and Ricia Anne Chansky, U of Wisconsin P, 2023, pp. 90–115.

Wright, Bradford. *Comic Book Nation: The Transformation of Youth Culture in America.* Johns Hopkins UP, 2001.

Wulf, Andrea, and Lillian Melcher. *The Adventures of Alexander von Humboldt*. Pantheon, 2019.

Yaeger, Patricia. "Editor's Column: Literature in the Ages of Wood, Tallow, Coal, Whale Oil, Gasoline, Atomic Power, and Other Energy Sources." *PMLA*, vol. 126, no. 2, Mar. 2011, pp. 305–10.

Yusoff, Kathryn. *A Billion Black Anthropocenes or None.* U of Minnesota P, 2018.

Zorbaugh, Harvey, and Mildred Gilman. "What Can YOU Do about Comic Books?" *Family Circle*, Feb. 1949, pp. 60–63.

INDEX

STUDIES IN COMICS AND CARTOONS

Charles Hatfield and Rebecca Wanzo, Series Editors
Lucy Shelton Caswell and Jared Gardner, Founding Editors Emeriti

Books published in Studies in Comics and Cartoons focus exclusively on comics and graphic literature, highlighting their relation to literary studies. The series includes monographs and edited collections that cover the history of comics and cartoons from the editorial cartoon and early sequential comics of the nineteenth century through webcomics of the twenty-first. Studies that focus on international comics are also considered.

Petrochemical Fantasies: The Art and Energy of American Comics
DANIEL WORDEN

Drawing (in) the Feminine: Bande Dessinée *and Women*
EDITED BY MARGARET C. FLINN

Lost Literacies: Experiments in the Nineteenth-Century US Comic Strip
ALEX BERINGER

Growing Up Graphic: The Comics of Children in Crisis
ALISON HALSALL

Muslim Comics and Warscape Witnessing
ESRA MIRZE SANTESSO

Beyond the Icon: Asian American Graphic Narratives
EDITED BY ELEANOR TY

Comics and Nation: Power, Pop Culture, and Political Transformation in Poland
EWA STAŃCZYK

How Comics Travel: Publication, Translation, Radical Literacies
KATHERINE KELP-STEBBINS

Resurrection: Comics in Post-Soviet Russia
JOSÉ ALANIZ

Authorizing Superhero Comics: On the Evolution of a Popular Serial Genre
DANIEL STEIN

Typical Girls: The Rhetoric of Womanhood in Comic Strips
SUSAN E. KIRTLEY

Comics and the Body: Drawing, Reading, and Vulnerability
ESZTER SZÉP

Producing Mass Entertainment: The Serial Life of the Yellow Kid
CHRISTINA MEYER

The Goat-Getters: Jack Johnson, the Fight of the Century, and How a Bunch of Raucous Cartoonists Reinvented Comics
EDDIE CAMPBELL

Between Pen and Pixel: Comics, Materiality, and the Book of the Future
AARON KASHTAN

Ethics in the Gutter: Empathy and Historical Fiction in Comics
KATE POLAK

Drawing the Line: Comics Studies and INKS, *1994–1997*
EDITED BY LUCY SHELTON CASWELL AND JARED GARDNER

The Humours of Parliament: Harry Furniss's View of Late-Victorian Political Culture
EDITED AND WITH AN INTRODUCTION BY GARETH CORDERY AND JOSEPH S. MEISEL

Redrawing French Empire in Comics
MARK MCKINNEY